D1527797

Nature-Oriented Activities

THIRD EDITION

Betty van der Smissen

Oswald H. Goering

UNIVERSITY PRESS, AMES, IOWA, U.S.A.

THE AUTHORS:

BETTY VAN DER SMISSEN is Professor
of Recreation, The Pennsylvania State
University.

OSWALD H. GOERING is Professor of Outdoor
Education, Northern Illinois University

© 1965, 1968, 1977 The Iowa State University Press
All rights reserved. Printed in the U.S.A.

First edition, 1965
Second printing, 1965

Second edition, 1968
Second printing, 1969
Third printing, 1972
Fourth printing, 1974

Third edition, 1977

Library of Congress Cataloging in Publication Data

Van der Smissen, Margaret Elisabeth, 1927-
    A leader's guide to nature-oriented activities.

    Bibliography: p.
    1. Outdoor recreation. 2 Outdoor life.
3. Handicraft. I. Goering, Oswald H., 1923-
joint author. II. Title.
GV191.6.V36 1977   796   77-1513
ISBN 0-8138-1125-2

FOREWORD

A LEADER'S GUIDE TO NATURE-ORIENTED ACTIV-ITIES is a timely book that describes many purposeful activities out-of-doors. The authors suggest a wide variety of approaches in getting acquainted and working with the natural world. The book is an outgrowth of the extensive experiences of the authors as leaders of youth and adults, as teachers, and as observers of nature programs in many communities.

We in America are living in an increasingly urbanized culture. In spite of this situation (and also because of it), interest in the out-of-doors and in all forms of outdoor recreation has been intensified. Public and private agencies serving youth and adults are becoming more aware of their opportunities to educate people to enjoy and appreciate their natural environment. Schools, by stepping up certain science courses and other outdoor-related programs, are contributing in an important way to the knowledge and understanding of the out-of-doors. The land-holding and recreation-related agencies of the government, which have a special responsibility for helping people learn how to use and enjoy their natural environment, are expanding their educational programs in this area.

Lack of trained leadership for good outdoor programs has been a major roadblock for public and private agencies. This book is an outstanding source of information for both professional and volunteer leaders. Directions for carrying out many projects are given in detail, making the book a practical aid even to users who may not have technical backgrounds.

The authors realize that it is not enough merely to suggest outdoor activities. Our natural lands today receive such heavy usage that they will be destroyed unless American citizens become concerned about the underlying principles of conservation and pattern their behavior accordingly. The suggestions in this book should lead to usage that will contribute greatly toward the conservation of outdoor America.

REYNOLD E. CARLSON
Emeritus Professor of Recreation and
    Park Administration
Indiana University

CONTENTS

Foreword — *Reynold E. Carlson*   v

Part One.   Developing a Program   1

CHAPTER I.   HOW TO BEGIN   2

Section 1.   Basic Organization   3

    Who Will Enjoy Nature-oriented Activities?   3
    Why Nature-oriented Programs?   4
    Who Should Sponsor Programs?   5
    What Leadership Is Required?   7
        The Organizing Leader   7
        The Knowledge Leader   8
        Professional Staff   9

Section 2.   Program Development   10

    Scope of Nature-oriented Program Services   11
        Interpretive Services   12
        Clubs   12
        Instructional Programs   13
        Training Programs   14
        Special Events   14
        Outdoor Living Programs   15
        Adventure Activities — Outing Sports   15
    Developing the Overall Program   16
    Structural Organization of Programs   17
        Integrated into Ongoing Programs   17

Nature-oriented Activities for Special Groups   18
The Nature Center   18
Selection of Specific Program Content   20
Organizations To Help You Plan   21

Section 3.   Interpretive Programs   22

Nature Trails   23
Construction of Trails—Some Basic Principles   25
Tips for Labels and Displays on Self-guiding Trials 26
The Printed Guide   31
Trailside Museums   32
Field Trips   33
Techniques   33
Mobile Facilities and Loan Services   35
Museumobiles or Traveling Naturemobiles   35
Starwagons   35
Animal Loan Service   35
Audio-visual Loan Service   35
Audio-visual Presentations   36
Principles of Technique   36

Section 4.   Community Resources   39

Bird Sanctuaries and Wildlife Preserves   40
Farms   40
Forests and Woodlands   41
Gardens and Greenhouses   42
Historical Resources   43
Museums   43
Observatories and Planetariums   44
Parks   44
Rock Quarries   45
Water Areas   45
Zoos   45
References   46

Part Two. Activities   51

CHAPTER II.   NATURE CRAFTS   52

Materials From Trees   54
How To Carve Wood   55
Driftwood   56

Roots and Burls   56
Twigs and Branches   56
    How To Make a Willow Whistle   57
    How To Make a Whisk Broom   58
Bark   59
    The Making of Cordage   59
Nuts   59
Pine Needles (long)   59
    Basketry   60
Pine Cones   60
    Nature Pixies   60
Materials From Plants Other Than Trees   61
Berries   61
Cattails   61
Corn   61
Fungi and Lichens   61
Gourds   61
Grasses   62
    How To Make a Navajo Loom   62
Mosses   64
Pods   64
Seeds Other Than Nuts   64
Nonplant Materials   64
Bones   64
Clay   64
Feathers   64
Horns   65
Rocks   65
Sand   65
    Sand Painting   65
Shells   65
Reproductions   66
Nature Prints of Leaves, Flowers, Grasses   66
    Blueprinting   66
    Oil Printing   66
    Ozalid Printing   67
    Smoke Printing   68
    Spatter Printing   68
    Spore Printing   69
Casting   69
    Plaster Casting   69
    Sand Casting   70
    Plastic Casting   71
Sketching   71

Preservation   71
    Drying Flowers   71
    Pressing Flowers   72
    Sunbaked Flowers   72
    Parchment   72
Dyeing   73
References   73

CHAPTER III.   NATURE GAMES   78

Map and Compass Games   79
    Area Identification   79
    Compass Relay   80
    Compass Treasure Hunt   80
    Competitive Compass Game   80
    Map Search   80
    Map Symbol Quiz   80
    Square Play   80
Campcraft Games   81
    Bucking Contest   81
    Campcraft Tournament   81
    Endless Rope   81
    Fire-building Contest   82
    Fuzz Stick Contest   82
    Hand Axe Accuracy   82
    Knot-tying One Step Forward   82
    Knot-tying Relay   82
    Lashing Contest   83
    One-hand Tie   83
    Overhand Knot   83
    Pole-chopping Contest   83
    Skudding   83
    Square Knot Gamble   83
    String-burning Contest   84
    Tent Peg and Sliver   84
    Tent Pitching   84
    Water-boiling Contest   84
Hiking Games   84
    Beeline Hike   84
    Heads and Tails Hike   85
    Hold the Front, or Number-One Spot   85
    I Spy   85
    Nature Far and Near   86
    Nature Scouting   86

Trailing Games   87
    Hare and Hounds   87
    Tree Trailing   87
Hunting Games   87
    Find the Trees   87
    Photography Treasure Hunt   88
    Scavenger Hunts   88
Quiet Games: Observation   90
    Animal Tracks   90
    Bird Silhouettes   90
    Kim's Game   90
    Mystery Bag   91
    Observation Lotto   91
    Sounds   92
    What Is Wrong With This Picture?   92
    Woodcraft Hike   92
Quiet Games: Action   93
    Bird Description   93
    Flower Authors   93
    Nature Charades   93
    Nature Crows and Cranes   95
    Star Groups   95
    What Am I?   96
Quiet Games: Pencil and Paper   97
    An Astronomy Test   97
    Building Birds   97
    Buried Birds (Flowers, Trees)   98
    Categories, Guggenheim, Nature Squares, Versatility   100
    Find the Trees in the Forest   101
    A Hiking Romance   101
    Name These Trees   102
    Nature Riddles   104
    Nature Symbolism Race   105
    Scrambles   106
References   107

CHAPTER IV.   OUTDOOR LIVING SKILLS   108

Gear and Shelter   110
Firecraft   111
Ropecraft   112
Toolcraft   113
Outdoor Cookery   114
    Basic Equipment   115

Sanitation and Food Preservation 116
Methods of Cooking 117
    Coffee Making 117
    Dehydrated and Quick-frozen Foods 118
    Direct Coals Cookery 118
    Dutch Oven Cookery 120
    Foil Cookery 123
    Hole Cookery 126
    Hunter-Trapper Fire 128
    One-Pot Meal 130
    Reflector Baking 133
    Stick Cookery 135
    Tin Can Cookery 138
Picnics 142
References 143

CHAPTER V. PROJECTS AND HOBBIES 146

Conservation/Environmental Quality 149
Animals 149
Astronomy 151
Birds 153
Creative Expression 155
Historical-cultural Activities 156
    Homesteading 156
    Income-producing Activities 157
    Archeological "Digs" 157
Plants, Including Gardening 158
    Preserving Herbarium Specimens 160
    Children's Gardening 162
        Junior Gardeners' Pledge 162
Insects 165
    Ant House 168
Nature Photography 169
Rocks and Minerals 170
Water—Streams and Ponds 172
    Water Ecology 172
    Water Qualities 175
Weather 176
References 184

CHAPTER VI. ADVENTURE-OUTING SPORTS 192

Adventure Activities 194

Initiative Tasks   196
Bicycling and Hosteling   197
   Cycling   197
   Hosteling   198
Canoeing and River Running   198
Casting and Fishing   200
   Instructional Program   200
   Competitive Casting Activities   201
   Special Activities   201
Field Archery   202
Firearms Safety and Hunting   203
   Instructional Program   204
   Knowledge Useful in Hunting   204
   Clubs and Competitive Activities   204
   Special Activities Related to Hunting   205
Hiking and Backpacking   205
Orienteering   209
   Maps   210
   Compass   210
   Map and Compass Combined   211
Rock Climbing   213
Skiing — Cross-country   214
Spelunking (Cave Exploring)   214
References   215

CHAPTER VII.   PROGRAM VARIETIES   222

Campfire Programs   223
   Campfires in Parks   223
   Campfires on the Playground   224
   The Small Group Campfire   224
   Campfires in the Camp Setting   225
   Planning the Campfire   225
   Structure of the Fire   226
   Lighting the Fire   228
   Planning   231
   Content   232
Outings and Day Camping   232
   Outings   232
   Day Camping   233
Family Camping   234
   Organized Family Camping   234
   Individual Family Camping   234
Indian Life   236

Games 237
Crafts 237
Living Skills 238
Ceremonials and Dances 238
Stories and Legends 238
Nighttime Activities 239
Creatures of the Night 239
Lights in the Night 239
Fellowship Around the Campfire 240
Winter Activities 240
Snow Sculpture and Painting 240
Hobbies 241
Social Activities 241
Camping 241
Carnivals 242
Snow Games 242
Reading for Pleasure 243
References 243

PART ONE

Developing a Program

Every child should have mud pies, grasshoppers, waterbugs, tadpoles, frogs, mud turtles, elderberries, wild strawberries, acorns, chestnuts, trees to climb, brooks to wade in, water lilies, woodchucks, bats, bees, butterflies, various animals to pet, hay fields, pine cones, rocks to roll, sand, snakes, huckleberries, and hornets, and any child who has been deprived of these has been deprived of the best part of his education.

—Luther Burbank

CHAPTER 1

How To Begin

1. BASIC ORGANIZATION

WHAT ARE NATURE-ORIENTED ACTIVITIES? Nature-oriented activities include all outdoor experiences related to the use, understanding, or appreciation of the natural environment and all indoor activities that use natural materials or are concerned with the understanding and appreciation of the out-of-doors.

The three primary areas of activity are interrelated:

Knowledge. This area includes an understanding of the materials, processes, and relationships among the various science fields dealing with rocks and soils, plants, animals, and water. Understanding may be gained through study groups, hobby clubs, special projects, interpretive programs, and other activities.

Appreciation. This area concerns aesthetics and discernment. It includes beauty of form, design, and color and an appreciation of literature, our cultural heritage, and the importance of our natural environment.

Action skills. This area involves the use of hands and body in crafts, games, sports, and hobbies.

WHO WILL ENJOY NATURE-ORIENTED ACTIVITIES?

The out-of-doors has a lure for everyone, although the way in which each person responds may be different. The community program of nature-oriented activities is for:

3

the traveler and observer who enjoys museums, zoos, formal gardens, historical sites

The daring adventurer who engages in tripping, spelunking, and mountaineering

the armchair nature lover who relaxes with literature and travelogue films

the beautiful-day person who loves a drive through the park, a band concert on the green, and a walk in the woods

the hobbyist who intensely pursues bird watching, photography, or gardening

the generalist who just likes the out-of-doors and all its activities

the person who seeks rugged outdoor living, fishing, and hunting

the inquisitive person who finds the wonders of nature fascinating

the creative person who excels in the arts of painting, sketching, crafts, poetry, and music

the sportsman who enjoys skiing, skating, boating, and horseback riding.

WHY NATURE-ORIENTED PROGRAMS?

People are a strange paradox! Three centuries ago our American forefathers' very existence depended upon their mastery of the outdoors. The heritage of the pioneers was rooted in the soil and there was abundance for all. But as the explorers and the early settlers pushed westward, they also exploited the wide-open spaces and the natural resources until today, with an ever-increasing population, the need for conservation of these spaces and resources is critical.

In the decade of the seventies, participation in outdoor recreation—boating, family camping, fishing, pleasure driving, outdoor sports, and picnicking—is extensive and has an impact on the environment. Strangely, people do not seem to realize that the very continuation of outdoor-recreation activities depends upon their attitudes and conduct while they are in the natural environment.

Furthermore, there appears to be inadequate understanding of the problems as well as appreciation of the world in which we live. Environmental concerns apply not only to the United States and personal use of the environment but also to the world, with its ever increasing population and resultant world hunger, and the threatened depletion of natural resources worldwide.

Nature-oriented activities play a vital role in today's world because a program of such activities:

increases understanding and appreciation of natural history and of the heritage of the American people

develops skill and interest in activities which use the natural environment for personal recreational pursuits and pleasure

promotes perception resulting in appreciation of the beauty and serenity of the natural world and an awareness of the infinite variety in the world

stimulates a desire to gain greater knowledge and understanding of the processes of growth and development of the natural world and its interrelatedness and interdependence

makes people cognizant of their dependence upon natural resources and responsibility for conserving them

recognizes the worldwide communal need for quality environment to enhance the lives of all people.

WHO SHOULD SPONSOR PROGRAMS?

All organizations and agencies with an interest in and concern for the natural environment and people's relationship to it should actively sponsor nature-oriented activities and programs.

Voluntary youth agencies (Boy Scouts, Girl Scouts, Camp Fire Girls, and 4-H) have excellent opportunities to provide their participants with some exposure to nature-oriented activities through their structured programs of merit badges, proficiency badges, summer camps, and informal outdoor activities.

Schools, both through curriculum experiences and through extracurricular activities, are increasingly utilizing the natural environment as an integral aspect of the education process as well as taking advantage of the interpretive services provided by public agencies.

Private organizations (sportsmen's clubs, Garden clubs, Audubon Society clubs, and special interest clubs) actively promote nature-oriented activities not only for their own members but also for the youth of the community.

Museums are of many types — scientific, industrial, historical, and the like. In the nature field, museums have generally been dedicated to the preservation and display of nonliving materials interpretive of natural and human history. However, today the museum curator is not merely a custodian of treasures of civilization, but a creative educator. Rather than a collection of specimens, artifacts, and curios in an austere and formal display, the modern museum makes history come alive by telling a story in an attractive manner, frequently with action displays and objects which viewers can touch.

Junior museums, sometimes also referred to as children's or youth museums, usually touch on a variety of fields of interest to young people rather than natural science only. Their displays are presentations which tell a story about life processes and natural history. The emphasis in the past usually has been on the preservation of nonliving materials.

Today, however, the junior museum has taken on many of the functions of the nature-center program, having activity centered in one building, for example, hobby clubs, classes, workshop space, library, lectures, and demonstrations. The emphasis is upon activity for youth. Although a nature center may have a "museum" area, most frequently a junior museum is a separate structure located in a population center without an adjacent natural area. This limits the capacity for outdoor area programs of the kind a true nature center has.

Public recreation and park systems, in response to the public's interest in outdoor recreation and the vital concern necessary for the conservation of the natural environment, are developing extensive nature-oriented programs. While emphasis has been primarily upon interpretive services, other types such as clubs, instructional and training programs, special events, outdoor living skills and outing sports are increasingly offered. These services may provide with or without a nature center; however, the trend is for the services to focus in and extend from such a center.

WHAT LEADERSHIP IS REQUIRED?

Ideally the nature-oriented program is under the direction and supervision of competent and well-trained professional staff. Very few organizations, however, employ full-time naturalists or environmental interpreters to conduct their programs unless they maintain a full-scale nature center complete with interpretive services. In carrying out their programs they rely heavily upon part-time and volunteer leadership.

Two types of leadership are of great importance to the success of any nature-oriented program, regardless of whether the leadership is volunteer or professional. Both the organizing leader and the knowledge leader, each serving special functions, are essential in the operation of a successful program.

The Organizing Leader

Contrary to popular belief, one need not be an expert on nature to spearhead the development of a nature-oriented program or to organize nature-oriented activities. The organizing nature leader should have these characteristics:

Genuine enthusiasm for the outdoors that will inspire others to enjoy it also.

General knowledge of the outdoors with the ability to use resources for increasing this knowledge. The nature leader who is organizing the program or who conducts general activities on an elementary basis does *not* need to be an expert, nor even to know all the answers to questions raised by participants. He must not be afraid to say "I do not know," but must be willing to work with the group in finding answers to their questions. There should be no hesitancy in calling upon experts to assist in the program.

Curiosity and awareness. The leader need not be creative, but must try to be discerning and perceptive in the study of nature.

Ability to converse easily with people and to have a genuine liking for them.

Concern for quality environment.

Usually this organizing leader is a professional person responsible for developing programs—the recreation leader of the municipal recreation department, a Y youth worker, a Boys' Club leader. Or this leader may be serving in a volunteer capacity with a responsibility for nature-oriented programs, for instance, a Scout troop leader. The primary task of the organizing leader is to determine interests, assess resources, stimulate participation, and develop organizational structure. This person may conduct some general nature-oriented activities; but, for the most effective program, this leader must make use of the knowledge leader. *Too frequently this is where many nature programs fail.* The activities are too shallow in basic natural science knowledge; many activities are without substance.

The Knowledge Leader

It is not necessary that a person knowledgeable about nature serve on a full-time basis. Many of these people in the community, though not available for full-time service, are willing to serve on a part-time basis, for example:

•hobbyists, members of specialized clubs or individuals

•some camp leaders and individuals who have grown up enjoying the outdoors

•teachers in the natural science fields

•professional people in fields related to natural science— taxidermists, horticulturalists, gardeners, geologists

•government service employees—conservation officers, and extension service and soil conservation service personnel

•housewives (and others) who majored in the sciences in college

These experts, working cooperatively with the organizing leader, will enable the development of an effective and dynamic nature-oriented program in the community. They can be asked to "go along" and serve as resource leader on a special hike, conduct a field trip, present a special program in their area of interest, lead an interested group of adults or youngsters, assist in laying out a nature trail, instruct a class for interested people, or train others to lead elementary nature activities.

Most people are willing to give their time generously for single activities and short-term projects; however, a person asked to assume leadership of a class which means special preparation over a six- to eight-week period should be offered remuneration.

The primary function of the knowledgeable leader is to bring to the nature-oriented program authenticity and accuracy in the basic understanding of nature. Only in this way will a program really stimulate a deeper inquiry into the natural sciences and give the greatest satisfaction.

Professional Staff

The program stemming from a nature center and the interpretive services provided are made effective through staff. There are usually three levels of professional personnel found in public recreation and park systems: the environmental interpreter, the nature center director, and the supervisor of nature-oriented activities. In addition there are technical staff.

The *environmental interpreter,* frequently also called interpretive naturalist, may serve as a park naturalist who leads nature trips and conducts evening campfire programs, as a liaison person who gives lectures and demonstrations in the schools or as an interpreter with the naturemobile at schools, fairs, special events, and playgrounds. The interpreter may serve as advisor-leader of a club, instruct in special interest classes, or give training sessions for adult and junior leaders. The preparation of audio-visual materials, such as exhibits, displays, bulletins, and slides, may be a part of his responsibilities.

Every nature center should have at least one professionally trained *director* to supervise and conduct the program. The director is in charge of the entire nature center, including the natural area, the building, and the staff. The director plans for and supervises the educational, scientific, and aesthetic program. He prepares the annual budget and makes reports to the authority responsible for setting policy and approving major administrative decisions. The director usually supervises a small staff—the interpretive naturalists, technical personnel to assist in the preparation of exhibits and displays, and maintenance and clerical help. The director is also responsible for the training of this staff and frequently assists with teaching and programming as well as preparation of exhibits, displays, and printed literature. He is also responsible for the care and maintenance of the buildings, facilities, equipment, and natural area. At a small center, or in the early stages of the development of a program, the director may assume any of the foregoing tasks including some physical work such as clean-up and maintenance.

In a recreation and park system of some size, there should be a *supervisor of nature-oriented activities.* Sometimes the title is supervisor of outdoor recreation or supervisor of camping and outdoor activities. In a small department, the duties of nature center director and supervisor of nature-oriented activities will be vested in the same person. The supervisor is responsible for the development of a community-wide program of nature-oriented activities of the scope presented in the various chapters of this book.

The Association of Interpretive Naturalists (AIN) is the professional organization for environmental interpreters. It encompasses both the interpretive naturalist and the historical/cultural interpreter. National conferences, as well as regional workshops, are held annually. Interpreters from private and public (local, state, federal) agencies participate.

2. PROGRAM DEVELOPMENT

As a program area (whether sponsored by public recreation, the schools, youth agencies, or private organizations) nature-oriented activities offer many advantages:

Low in cost. Nature's treasures are free to all. The nature-oriented program is one of the least expensive program areas.

Year-round. Interests aroused in the summertime can be carried throughout the year, for nature is ever-changing with the seasons. "Every season has a reason."

Pleasurable. Nature experiences are pleasurable in themselves for they provide exercise, relaxation, or escape from the city environment.

Ever-changing. Nature is life itself, and therefore ever-unfolding. One never learns everything about nature; interest may endure for a lifetime.

Adaptable; varied. The tremendous variety of activity available makes nature adaptable to various age groups and special interests. Furthermore, whatever community resources are available can be used.

Easily integrated. Because of their variety and adaptability, nature activities can be integrated easily with such program areas as drama, music, arts, and crafts.

In addition, they:

Promote environmental quality. Quality of life is entwined with the quality of environment in which one lives. Nature activities not only can develop citizen concern for environmental quality but also stimulate action to enhance the quality of the environment.

Teach conservation. Conservation of natural resources is of prime importance today. Nature activities can teach the importance of conservation and how best to conserve resources.

Stimulate learning. Projects help people acquire knowledge without their realizing they are learning. Such projects and activities may also stimulate them to learn more about the world in which they live, to appreciate how nature influences design, and to find new interest in primitive people and the history of crafts.

Encourage appreciation. People acquire love of the out-of-doors, respect for growing things, and appreciation for the way the beautiful things of nature enrich life.

Offer satisfactions. Being in close contact with nature, individuals may learn to appreciate the basic things of life, which are beautiful in their simplicity. Nature crafts particularly offer opportunity for creativity, ingenuity, and originality—an unexcelled field for self-expression.

Provide for adventure. People, children in particular, have a basic need and craving for adventure that is both physically challenging and intellectually stimulating.

SCOPE OF NATURE-ORIENTED PROGRAM SERVICES

Nature-oriented program services encompass seven major categories. A well-rounded community program will provide a balance of all types. Each, as a whole or in component parts, is discussed in subsequent chapters of this manual.

Interpretive Services

A vital aspect of a nature-oriented program is the interpretive program. The primary functions of interpretive services are to stimulate interest through providing opportunities for gaining knowledge and understanding of the natural world and to make available natural areas for individual participation in nature recreation. The major types of services include:

Nature centers and museums, facilities serving as focal points of activity and presenting information about nature-oriented activities through exhibits, displays, and literature.

Nature trails and trailside displays in natural areas, such as parks and preserves. Most frequently these are self-guiding.

Feature presentations by a naturalist through illustrated lectures, talks, demonstrations, and guided field trips.

Audio-visual materials available to clubs, organizations, and schools either for display or for presentation. Such materials would include films, slides, recordings, exhibits, and displays.

Interpretive services are discussed in the next section of this manual—3. Interpretive Programs.

Clubs

Special interest clubs ("rock hounds," family camping, or archery) are familiar ways of offering a nature program. Anyone interested, regardless of age, may attend and participate. Very frequently these are hobby groups and may affiliate with a national organization if there is one. For example, a field archery club may affiliate with the National Field Archery Association; a hosteling club with the American Youth Hostels; and a family camping club with the National Campers and Hikers Association.

Another type of special interest club is limited to a certain age group, usually youth. These clubs may be interested in nature in general—Junior Naturalists—or in a specific aspect of nature or outing activities—Junior Bird Watchers. They may also be associated with such national programs as the Junior Audubon Club, the Junior Air Rifle Club, the NRA Junior Rifle Club, and 4-H Club. Most national groups give organizational help; however, affiliation with a national organization certainly is not necessary. Many club groups are sponsored by public recreation departments, voluntary agencies, churches, civic groups, libraries, and museums.

Instructional Programs

Untold possibilities exist for extending our knowledge and understanding of the natural environment and for the teaching of skills through instructional programs. Essentially, there are three types:

Study Groups

These are very similar to hobby and special interest clubs but focus upon study of a nature area rather than projects or activities. Most frequently this group will "instruct itself" through shared leadership and will use an expert consultant only occasionally. This type of organization sustains unity over a considerable period.

Classes

Many individuals like to have some instruction and formal study in a particular subject but are not sufficiently interested to join a study group which meets regularly over the entire season or year and in which one must participate in leadership. For these people a real service can be rendered through short courses. Frequently, class sessions are held weekly over a six- or eight-week period. The instructor is a specialist in the area and course content is formalized, although there is seldom much, if any, "homework." Examples of such instruction are: techniques for family campers, mountaineering techniques, lapidary, firearms safety, nature photography, and nature crafts.

Special instruction resulting in certification by national or state organizations may also be offered: campcrafter and advanced campcrafter ratings by the American Camping Association; instructor training programs of the National Rifle Association, National Association of Casting and Angling Clubs, and National Field Archery Association; and hunter safety and home firearms safety courses sponsored by the National Rifle Association, frequently in cooperation with the State Conservation Commission.

Workshops

These are single training sessions covering a single evening, one day, or a weekend. The same kind of materials that might be presented through classes can be used here; however, the amount needs to be limited to either a general overview or a depth study of one small facet of the topic.

Training Programs

Training programs for adult and junior leaders are becoming increasingly important as a nature-oriented program service. The preceding section on instructional programs focuses upon instruction for individuals. Training programs are directed toward various groups — schoolteachers who want to include some outdoor education in their curriculum, Scout leaders who seek some ideas for nature-oriented activities for the girls or boys of their troops, camp staff who desire basic campcraft and counseling skills along with some understanding of the natural environment.

These leadership training programs may take the form of a one-day clinic, an institute, a workshop, or even an extended formal course with methods and materials as the content.

Special Events

Special events are a single-occurrence activity, although they may become traditional and be held each year. They serve three purposes: to give the members of clubs an opportunity to demonstrate their hobbies and activities to the public; to stimulate interest among people who are not presently participating; and to provide an opportunity for persons who are interested in occasional participation but feel they do not have the time or interest to participate regularly in a club. Examples of some special events are science fairs, trips, illustrated lectures, hobby shows, outings, tournaments (casting, skeet shooting).

Outdoor Living Programs

The aspect of outdoor recreation often thought of first is camping. Camping takes many forms, and fundamental outdoor living program services should be an integral part of any nature-oriented program. These cover five areas:

Outdoor living skills, as individual program elements rather than combined into a camping experience, are basic to living outdoors comfortably and enjoyably. Such skills include firecraft, ropecraft, gear, shelters, toolcraft, outdoor cookery, etc.

Outings may encompass a whole or part of a day and may be conducted as part of another program or as a special event complete within itself. An outing usually is composed of several activities but with one central feature.

Day camping has traditionally been conducted by youth agencies and private enterprises; however, it is being included more and more as a public recreation function.

Resident camping has been the primary aspect of outdoor living programs for more than one hundred years, yet today, with increasing urbanization, its importance to the development of children and special groups has increased considerably.

Family camping, as considered in the context of nature-oriented services, refers to individual families and the services which can be provided for them.

Each of these types of outdoor living services is discussed in Chapters IV and VII.

Adventure Activities—Outing Sports

A variety of adventure activities and outing sports is essential to a balanced nature-oriented program. Of the many possibilities, selected adventure activities and ten sports (bicycling, boating, casting and fishing, field archery, hunting, hiking and backpacking, orienteering, rock climbing, cross country skiing, and spelunking) are presented in Chapter VI.

DEVELOPING THE OVERALL PROGRAM

Before an overall program of nature-oriented activities for the community can be developed, a community survey must be taken which asks three basic questions.

1. What nature-oriented activities are currently being conducted in the community for various age groups and population classifications?

> What are the schools doing in their science classes and in extracurricular activities? Do they have an environmental education program?

> What programs are the voluntary agencies engaged in?

> Who is serviced by special interest clubs and hobby groups?

> What are the libraries, museums, and greenhouses doing in the way of programs in the community?

> Which community clubs and organizations are active in nature-oriented programs?

> What park programs are in operation?

2. What is needed in the community to have a well-balanced and complete nature-oriented program?

> Determine which population groups are not receiving an opportunity to participate.

> Determine which facets of the nature-oriented program areas are not being provided.

3. What are the resources for meeting recognized needs?

> What natural and human resources in the community are available for developing nature-oriented program areas to meet specific needs?

> Is the agency which I represent the best one for carrying out this phase of the program?

What are the possibilities for developing cooperative agreements?

STRUCTURAL ORGANIZATION OF PROGRAMS

Nature-oriented activities may be organized in a multitude of ways. The discussion on scope has suggested some of these, that is, clubs; instructional classes, study groups, and workshops; training programs; and special events. No one structure will meet all needs; there must be a variety which will provide for the individual who wants to participate just now and then as well as the one who desires intensive study of nature.

Integrated into Ongoing Programs

Many aspects of nature-oriented activities fit very well into an ongoing program of a Scout troop, playground, etc. In such a program, the nature aspects may be planned as a special project or special event or as concentrated study for a short time. Or nature activities may be integrated into other phases of the program. For example, members might take a collecting field trip and return with materials to use in nature crafts.

An Example: Nature on the Playgrounds

In giving this example, may it be said first that there are no specific so-called "playground nature activities." Most of the nature-oriented activities presented in this guide may be used in the playground program — adaptations come from the environment, the playground participants, and the other community offerings. The activities selected as examples are just a few of the many that can be used.

First, nature-oriented activities should be a part of the program throughout the total summer, and year-round if playgrounds are open all year. To have a "nature week" is definitely limiting to the program; if such a week is to be designated, it should be for the purpose of highlighting, as a climax to the total nature-oriented program.

A few simple ideas that any inexperienced playground leader can manage with an in-service training program are:

nature corner where things are brought in for display and study

excursions to quarries, observatories, etc. (see Community
   Resources section)

hikes — many, many types

nature trails — have the group help lay a trail or take a trip over one

day camping — take the playground gang day camping once a week or
   every two weeks

evening campfire and star study

trip to collect materials — use them in nature crafts

storytelling — nature-oriented stories

nature games

grassroots jungle safari — see what you can find in one square yard
   of sod!

All these ideas are elaborated in special sections of this guide.

Nature-oriented Activities for Special Groups

What about nature-oriented activities for such special groups as
senior citizens and the handicapped? Throughout this guide you will
find no reference to activities specifically for any one age group or
special group because *all types of activities can be used with all kinds
of people and age levels*. These programs are cut from the *same*
cloth — it's the pattern that's different; and this pattern is determined by understanding the needs, interests, and abilities of the
group — whatever they may be and differentiated as they may be by
age or other special characteristics.

Many written materials are available to help you learn about the
characteristics of various groups, so no specifics are given here.
Many organizations will be willing to guide you also, if you need help
for a particular group.

The Nature Center

The nature center is the focal point of a complete interpretive
program and is usually a total community project, frequently

spearheaded by the public recreation and park department or a semipublic organization. It is *not* a competitor of other groups and institutions in the community, but serves them in addition to engaging in its own program.

While the word "center" connotes a building, a nature center is actually composed of a natural area, a building, and a staff, each making a unique contribution to the total interpretive program.

The Natural Area

This area, at least fifty acres and preferably much larger, should be as near a population center as possible. It serves not only as an open-space buffer strip in an urban area but it makes the program more accessible to the people.

The natural area is *not* a city park characterized by its artificial recreational facilities and often exotic plants and animals introduced into the park environment. The natural area is a representative sample of terrain and ecology with flora and fauna typical of the immediate locale.

In this area may be nature trails, trailside museums, live exhibits of animals in their natural habitat, or an outdoor meeting place for talks and campfires.

The Building

The building erected on the natural area is *not* a zoo with caged animals from other geographic regions or a museum with preserved dead specimens, although techniques of both the zoo and museum may be used in the displays and exhibits as they focus upon the flora and fauna native to the immediate locale.

Service facilities of the area are housed in the building: office, storage, toilet, etc.

A library, workshop area, meeting space for special meetings and training groups, saleable literature, exhibits, and displays are all located within the building.

Desirable as a nature center may be, it is recognized that all communities are not fortunate enough to have one; nevertheless, a fine and very effective interpretive program can be carried on without a center. A very useful alternative can be a "nature headquarters," which can be used as work area for preparing and displaying exhibits and collections, and for housing a small library. It may also serve as a place to meet for discussions or for departure and return of field trips. A room might be set aside in school or in another public building, or a temporary or permanent shelter in camp or park might be used, particularly if there is some storage space.

Interpretive program activities which can be an important aspect of the total community nature-oriented program with or without a center are described in the next section.

In the development of a nature center, it is recommended that you contact the National Audubon Society or the Natural Science for Youth Foundation. Excellent assistance can also be obtained from professional personnel in nature centers. Such personnel can be located through the Association of Interpretive Naturalists.

SELECTION OF SPECIFIC PROGRAM CONTENT

The Common

"We are surrounded, but we know not."

Because people have not really trained all of their senses to function effectively, particularly the powers of detailed observation, there are many so-called "commonplace" nature objects which are in reality storehouses of fascinating program materials. A person need not seek out the strange or import the exotic. Gaining new insight into everyday surroundings is one of the primary functions of nature programs. They should focus upon activities which reveal such basic principles of the natural environment as balance of nature, growth, and development.

Real Objects

"One frog in the pond is worth five in formaldehyde."

Natural objects in their natural setting are the best approaches to program content—nothing can ever take the place of firsthand experiences with a real nature object. Here focus in the beginning must be on the specific, not the general. A person does not learn about all animals at once, but should learn about a particular type of animal or an aspect of animal life.

Action

"Only I can discover."

The program must be based on doing things rather than hearing about them. People's interest is sustained only when they make discoveries themselves; their curiosity and initiative are whetted only when they may explore new vistas.

Timeliness

"Here today, gone tomorrow."

Ever-changing, ever-changing, ever-changing . . . that's the prime characteristic of the natural environment; therefore, it behooves every program planner to take advantage of the season at hand, shifts in weather, and "the teachable moment" when something outside the aim of the specific activity arises.

Stimulants

"Ignorance is *not* bliss."

What a person has not experienced and does not know, he will not try without encouragement. A prime function of a nature-oriented program is to introduce the various activities and inform the potential participant of those in his special interest areas. Certain program content must be selected for its contribution to this informative and interpretive role. Without exposure to opportunities, an individual may be oblivious to the joys of the outdoors.

ORGANIZATIONS TO HELP YOU PLAN

Throughout this guide are many resources specific to the activities being discussed, including both literature and organizations. However, some organizations encompass many areas of nature-oriented activities and can be of considerable help to you not only in overall planning but also in keeping you in-

formed of happenings in the outdoor recreation field. An organization you may wish to join is the National Audubon Society, 1130 Fifth Avenue, New York, N.Y. 10028. Its annual membership is reasonable and includes a subscription to its monthly magazine, *Audubon.* Other services and interests include: Audubon camps in summer, usually for two weeks, as training sessions for teachers, youth leaders, and other interested adults; Audubon junior clubs; publications, such as nature bulletins and charts; Audubon junior clubs; publications, such as nature bulletins and charts; photo and film services; Audubon centers, sanctuaries, wildlife research, and nature centers; wildlife tours; and consultative services.

Many other organizations (most of which are cited in this manual under the appropriate activity) are excellent resources.

3. INTERPRETIVE PROGRAMS

Through interpretation, understanding.
Through understanding, appreciation.
Through appreciation, protection.

Thomas Huxley has said that for many people a walk through the woods is like a tour through an art gallery with all of the pictures turned toward the wall. People look, but do not see; hear, but do not perceive; move in the outdoors, but are oblivious to it.

Interpretive programs reveal meanings and relationships of the natural world through the use of original objects, through firsthand experiences, and by illustrative materials which entice and stimulate people to want to learn more about the natural environment. Through such programs, we are able to enjoy the natural world more fully and appreciate it more keenly.

In developing interpretive programs, one must keep in mind that the purpose is to stimulate curiosity, not satisfy it; to put people into a receptive frame of mind for further interpretation and information. Information, as such, is not interpretation. Interpretation is revelation based upon information. Interpretation of what is being displayed or described must be related to something within the personality or experience of the participant.

NATURE TRAILS

Walking and hiking on nature trails are the most popular outdoor activities.

All trails are nature trails; however, they may be roughly classified into three groups: the nonguided trail, the guided walk over a trail, and the self-guiding trail.

A *nonguided trail* has an established route that is marked, particularly at turns. It has a known destination. Frequently these are paths to places of special interest located at a distance easily covered on foot. Or they may be longer trails over terrain noted for its beauty and ecological patterns. Two nationally known nonguided trails extending over many miles are the Appalachian Trail in the East and the Pacific Crest Trail in the West. Both are marked and have shelters en route for overnight stops; however, most trails are not of this length. One-half mile to two miles is a more common length for trails the average person enjoys.

The *guided walk,* as distinguished from the field trip which is considered later, is the second type of trail activity conducted by a naturalist or informed guide. The trail taken may be short and require only one-half hour for walking, or it may take a whole day. The guide stops at appropriate places to explain features of interest, seeking to stimulate the participants to further activity in the out-of-doors.  Guided walks are most effective when a seasonal approach is used with a series of walks related to the season, for instance, walks in the spring to look for birds or wild flowers. Optimum group size is 10-12 persons, although more often have to be accommodated.

A leader is not always available, yet it may be advisable to have some type of explanation regarding the natural area through which the trail is laid; in such situations a *self-guiding trail* is established. The self-guiding trails have signs, trailside displays, or printed leaflets with information about specific locations on the trail. These trails are most frequently ½ to ¾ mile in length, almost never longer, and take about 45 minutes.

Most trails, regardless of type, usually are located where people naturally congregate for outdoor activity — parks, picnic areas, nature centers, playgrounds, and camps. When trails begin off the roadside, there must be a parking area and well-marked notices that the trail begins there. Wherever the trail begins, the entrance must be easily accessible and obvious. Few people will hunt for a trail, but they are often curious enough to follow one they happen to come across. Frequently at the entrance there may a trailside museum, luring people onto the trail by describing its features. Also, a bulletin board may be used which displays a map of the area, information about the surroundings, or notices of other activities offered in the vicinity.

Trails should be established only when there is a worthy natural feature. Features will vary; a trail may be constructed to show things of generalized or specialized interest. General trails might include various types of vegetation, while a specialized trail might include a glacial deposit. People like to call a trail by name — names create a feeling of familiarity, and to make use of the special or general feature of the trail in the name helps to identify it.

The purposes, though, vary with the type of trail. The nonguided trail caters to the hiker, to the person who enjoys vigorous activity on foot, bicycle, or horseback. The person who likes the outdoors needs little stimulation to "take to the trails," although he does need information about available trails that have been constructed for public use, particularly in areas where he is not accustomed to hiking. As indicated, the guided walk is an effort to interpret the outdoors to the general public, with the hope of stimulating interest in more outdoor activities. It is often used also for educational information, especially with youth organizations and schools. The self-guiding trail, which is short, seeks to induce persons only mildly interested or even disinterested in nature to "try" a little bit of nature and perhaps thereby become more involved. The self-guiding trail may also be used for self-testing. Particularly where there is no naturalist or guide on duty or nearby, the labels provide information about the trail. Inspiration may also result from the manner of the labeling and the scenic beauty of a self-guiding trail.

The foregoing purposes of trails relate primarily to the trail user. Other values of trails, particularly important as they become an activity in camp, on the playground, or at the nature center, lie in their construction. Persons who participate in the construction of trails gain direct contact with the outdoors. They learn what information must be acquired in order to lay a trail. Construction itself incorporates principles of pioneering, handicraft, elementary engineering, and an awareness of the natural environment (essential to selecting the specific path of the trail). Responsibility for maintenance of the trail, both physical maintenance and keeping information current, is essential.

Construction of Trails—Some Basic Principles

1. Make trail narrow, necessitating single-file walking; otherwise, the wilderness quality of the surroundings may be destroyed.

2. The trail should be natural and winding, but the turns and twists should be for a purpose—taking the user past a special feature. Sharp corners invite shortcutting; avoid them. Do not tear up, destroy, or fake—use what is there! Trails should go through several types of areas, unless it is a special-feature trail.

3. Avoid steep grades and extremely low areas which may lead to erosion and seasonal wet spots. To go up a hill, use zigzag paths. Steps of logs may be used if necessary.

4. To mark a trail for construction, walk through area with a ball of twine, unwinding as you go. The path of twine should indicate where footpath is to be kept. Walk over area several times to be sure you have spotted the most interesting features. Do not have long distances in open sunlight.

5. Once a trail is established, keep it up-to-date! Periodically go over the signs changing them, if necessary, as the seasons and developments in the area change. Also, keep the trail maintained and beautiful. Remove any evidences of vandalism *immediately* as well as any other damage from natural elements, or litter and mutilation resulting from human inconsideration.

6. Short trails definitely should not connect two main points so that they become heavily traveled thoroughfares.

7. Self-guiding trails, particularly, and trails used for guided walks normally should be constructed as a loop with exit and entrance at the same point—but be sure the entrance is well-marked and the exit obscure so people do not start wrong. Sometimes a figure-eight trail is constructed so that people may take either the shorter or longer trail, depending on the time they have

available and their interest. Although the entrance should be obvious, the rest of the trail should be secluded from other activity.

8. Minimize natural hazards; eradicate poison ivy, remove stinging nettle, etc. However, you may keep small patches of poison ivy under control so persons can learn to identify it.

9. Benches and other rest spots and facilities might be appropriately placed along the trail or in the immediate vicinity.

10. When necessary to build bridges and railings, they should be sturdy, permanent, and of native material.

Tips for Labels and Displays on Self-guiding Trails

1. Markers should be attached to stakes in a manner to suggest permanency and in keeping with the woods. They should not be attached to trees.

2. Markers should be placed near enough to each other so that the next one can be seen clearly. About 20 ft. is a good distance. The first label generally explains the purpose of the trail. It may actually not be a label at all, but a trailside museum at the entrance.

3. Repetition of common names several times along the trail may reinforce learning.

4. Markers should be of a variety of types to add interest to the trail. Color, too, may be used, e.g., green for botanical markings, brown for geological, red for zoological, etc.

5. Wording should be short and catchy with no attempt at the scientific approach of Latin identification, but the *labels must be scientifically accurate.* Wording must also be simple.

Here are some more pointers on wording:

a. Give something more than just the name:

Staghorn sumach: the red top of sumach was used by the Indians to make "lemonade."

b. Include something to help the reader remember the information:

> Happy are cicadas' lives
> For they all have voiceless wives

c. If applicable, use informality or humor for emphasis:

> Just touch me to learn
> Why I'm called "touch-me-not"

d. Labels may indicate evidence of ecology:

> In 1945, cultivation of this open field was stopped. Seeds dropped by birds or blown in by wind have changed it into a thicket. Now, different kinds of wildlife have come to use the new food, cover, and nesting sites.

e. Labels may mention economic values:

> Red Cedar is often known as the lead-pencil tree for it is the favorite wood for making the common pencil. Cedar chests are made from this tree also.

f. Labels may include inspirational material:

> I am the heart of your hearth on the cold winter nights, the friendly shade screening you from the summer sun, and my fruits are refreshing draughts quenching your thirst as you journey on.

> I am the beam that holds your house, the board of your table, the bed on which you lie, and the timber that builds your boat.

> I am the handle of your hoe, the door of your homestead, the wood of your cradle, and the shell of your coffin.

> I am the bread of kindness and the flower of beauty.

> Ye who pass by, listen to my prayer; harm me not.
> —Portuguese Prayer of the Woods

Linen tag markers may be used but sparingly and for temporary, seasonal labels only. India-ink lettering or typing sprayed with clear plastic will withstand many rains.

A sheltered label is protected from rain.

A turnover label gives a question and an answer.

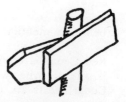

An object, such as a glacial boulder, flower bed, etc., may be pointed out by "aiming" such a sign at the object.

A string attached to a sign, like this, makes it possible to single out a specific thing such as an individual flower among many in a large bed.

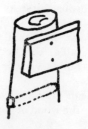

An interesting variation to the pointer type sign is a 1-in. hole drilled in a post to focus on a more distant object, such as a high nest. Or mount a 1-ft. length of ¾-in. pipe and similarly focus it on an object.

28

This sign, made by rolling the top and bottom edges of sheet metal (aluminum or galvanized iron) is very handy for frequently changed messages, such as sequential information about the rapid development of a flower bed.

An insect cage, made of a roll of cellulose acetate with sewed-on muslin ends, makes it possible to observe insects at work in the natural surroundings of their food plant. A temporary sign above can be changed often to follow the rapid development of the insects' life cycle.

A triangular block, made of three pieces of plywood fitted to triangular boards and rotated on a dowel, provides another action marker and permits three-part messages for more important natural phenomena. When messages need to be long, it is best to break them up into two or three parts.

This type of wooden sign, painted first, can be lettered with India ink by preparing the surface with Fuller's earth to prevent the ink from running.

g. Labels may correct superstitions and misinformation:

> A snake feels like dry linoleum — is not slimy.
> A snake's forked tongue is a feeler — is not a stinger.
> A snake has no eyelids, but over 100 pairs of ribs.

h. Timeliness is important — labels should reflect the current season:

> This is jack-in-the-pulpit.   (spring when plant
> Can you find jack?   is in flower)

> Here is the red-robed congre-   (fall when plant
> gation that jack-in-the-pulpit   is in fruit)
> preached to last spring.

Remember that the coming of winter does not necessitate closing the nature trail. Winter plants and animal tracks in the snow are two of many attractions of this season.

i. Labels may mention conservation values, calling attention to fire prevention, erosion, etc.:

> Nature provides a soft, lush carpet in the forest. But it is more flammable than your living room rug. Don't set it on fire!

> You wouldn't build a fire on your living room carpet.
> Outdoors you also need to use the proper fireplace.
> Save the rug!

j. Labels may play upon an association:

> American hornbeam is as tough as the muscular branches suggest.

k. Labels may suggest an activity:

> Silence! You may hear a red-eyed vireo singing nearby.

l. Words may be supplemented or supplanted with pictures; e.g., hand-drawn or cutout pictures pasted on the label

and spar varnished or sprayed with clear plastic to withstand the weather.

m. Question-and-answer labels.

Q. Is this tree named for a dog?

A. Early pioneers cut dogs, or skewers, from this tree; hence, the name DOGWOOD.

n. Adage to remember by:

Five needles to the cluster;
Five letters to the name—W-H-I-T-E pine.

The Printed Guide

Another form of self-guiding trail information is the printed leaflet which describes the natural features of the trail. Usually locations along the way are numbered to correspond to the descriptions in the booklet. The booklets are found at the beginning of the trail in a sheltered box and another box for returning the booklets is located at the end of the trail. A person who would like to keep the booklet, deposits a nominal amount, frequently 10¢ or 25¢.

Some of the advantages of a self-guiding trail having booklets and numbered locations are:

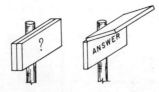

Along the nature trail people like to do things. Therefore markers which require some activity are very good. In this type, a question is shown on the outside panel and the hiker lifts the hinged panel to learn the answer. The message may be changed by tacking on paraffin-dipped or plastic-sprayed cards for questions and answers.

no signs and displays to protect from normal weather damage or damage from vandalism

the trail has a neater appearance when no signs or displays are in disrepair

for a nominal fee the user has a booklet to take along

the booklet can provide information in greater detail than a trail sign and may give supplemental information about activities and the area.

But some disadvantages are:

some people who wander on the trail do not bother to pick up a booklet

many people do not want to stop to read at given locations, much preferring the brief, visual, obvious signs en route

a few people forget to return the booklets or deposit their fee at the end of the trail

The booklet is not as flexible in keeping the materials on the trail up-to-date. Once printed, that's it until they're all used up; although it is possible to have seasonal booklets available.

TRAILSIDE MUSEUMS

Trailside museums or kiosks are self-explanatory exhibits that tell a story of the natural history of the immediate environment. They are distinguished primarily from junior museums and naturemobiles in that they deal with a single object or specific region. Persons may read or view the exhibit and relate its information directly by observing the natural phenomena which it describes. Frequently a trailside museum is alongside the entrance to a nature trail or at a wide rest point along the way; such museums, however, should not be restricted to trail use but also should be placed on picnic sites and campgrounds, roadside lookouts, and scenic observation points.

FIELD TRIPS

The term "field trip" has various meanings. To some it means taking a group out under leadership to a definite location for the specific purpose of obtaining information about that natural area, of observing a specific natural phenomenon, or of gathering natural specimens. However, to others the term "field trip" is used in place of a nature walk or nature hike as related to the guided-trail experiences because they feel the term is more acceptable to the public. The discussion in this section is focused upon the first meaning; however, many of the same procedures are indeed applicable to the latter since both involve leadership of a group seeking interpretation of the natural environment.

Techniques

1. Every field trip should have a purpose and a plan. The group should not only know the purpose at the time of departure but should have taken part in the planning for the field trip.

2. The length of the field trip depends upon the purpose and the nature of the group. A rock-collecting field trip with the "Rock Hounds Club" might be an all-day adventure, while a field trip to collect native materials with the youngsters on a playground might involve only an hour. Some experienced leaders feel that a 45-minute trip is a desirable length for children.

3. Practice of outdoor good manners is of extreme importance. The example of the leader is undoubtedly the best teacher. The leader should also insist upon good manners by the entire group—using disposal receptacles for litter, leaving flowers for others to enjoy rather than picking them, using fire prevention procedures when smoking, etc.

4. A field trip is *not* a lecture. The leader talks *with* the group, not *at* them. There should be a feeling within the group that they are free to ask questions and the leader must have no qualms about saying "I do not know, perhaps we can look that up together."

5. Stops on a field trip should be meaningful—stops should be made to observe something. Rest stops on field trips are unnecessary as each person rests when stopping to observe. On extended field trips, provision should be made for the physical comfort of the individuals.

6. The group should be kept together and be small enough for all to hear what the leader is disucssing and to participate in the observations and gathering of information and materials. This means that it is desirable for groups to be no larger than 15-20 persons.

7. The leader should have planned for the field trip not only by knowing the specific purposes but also by having made an advance trip to the area to know what to expect and how to make maximum use of the time available.

8. An effort should be made to have a "buildup" (anticipation for the field trip through group planning and other motivating devices). There also should be followup with the information obtained or the specimens collected. Why go if you are not going to use what you acquired? It may be desirable to plan a series of field trips in order to accomplish the group's goal.

9. While a field trip is taken for a specific purpose, the leader and group should be flexible enough to take advantage of unusual natural situations which present themselves.

10. Prepare the group adequately for the field trip by supplying plans for starting time and return time; suitable footwear, raincoats, and other garments; lunch; etc. Also, prepare the group through the use of background materials so that they may have the proper foundation to gain maximum benefit from the experience.

11. Evaluate the field trip so that future trips may be improved.

MOBILE FACILITIES AND LOAN SERVICES

An interpretive program must go to the people as well as have the people come to the nature center. For this reason, mobile facilities are of particular value.

Museumobiles or Traveling Naturemobiles

A naturemobile is usually a large, enclosed trailer equipped with exhibits and displays interpreting local natural history. It is designed primarily for educational use in the schools and youth groups, but it serves also as an important factor in stimulating interest in other community nature-oriented activities, particularly those of the nature center, if there is one. The naturemobile, as the name implies, travels to the people in schools, in camps, on playgrounds, and at other locations. Each location may have the naturemobile for a given length of time and then it moves on.

Starwagons

A starwagon may be an "observatory-on-wheels" with a telescope and charts, or may also include a planetarium projector. An interpreter, of course, accompanies the starwagon. For further description of the Milwaukee Starwagon, see section on Astronomy in Chapter 5, Projects and Hobbies.

Animal Loan Service

Many children are not able to obtain and care for an animal permanently — they may not have adequate space or the parents may not permit it; yet a child can gain valuable experience in caring for a live pet for a short period of time. Some zoos, nature centers, and children's museums have animals which may be loaned for a week or so at a time. Care instructions, of course, are important.

Audio-visual Loan Service

Portable exhibits and displays should be available for loan on a short-term basis to schools, clubs, camps, special events. They can stimulate considerable interest, as well as serve an important interpretive role.

Motion pictures, filmstrips, and 35mm slides should also be made available to groups interested in nature interpretive programs. See next section for further details.

AUDIO-VISUAL PRESENTATIONS

To promote enjoyment of the outdoors, as well as to develop a wholesome attitude toward the natural environment, adequate communication between the interpreter and the public is essential; therefore, audio-visual presentations are integral to an effective interpretive program.

An interpretive program should use the mass media for communication (television, radio, newspapers, and magazines), exhibits and displays, literature (e.g., nature-trail guides, newsletters), and personal appearance programs (lectures, campfires, slide presentations).

Although as interpretive devices, audio-visual materials are important, it must be emphasized that they are interpretive — interpretive of the "real thing," the natural environment to which they relate. They should not be so pretentious that they, in themselves, become the showpiece. Their purpose should be to stimulate curiosity about the outdoors and to lead the viewer to firsthand experiences with the real thing. Factual information is communicated, but the primary purpose and focus of these audio-visual materials should be to reveal meanings and relationships. Original objects are often a part of the displayed materials.

There are many types of audio-visual materials; already mentioned in the preceding sections are trail labels, naturemobiles, trailside displays. Additional important materials are both indoor and outdoor exhibits and displays, including dioramas, relief maps, models, automatic and action displays, live exhibits. Bulletin boards, posters, brochures and pamphlets, films, slides, cassettes, and recordings are also a part of audio-visual materials used for interpretive purposes.

While each of these has its own particular techniques to use for effectiveness, some general principles can be applied to all types of audio-visual interpretive materials.

Principles of Technique

Subject Matter

Significance. There are so many interesting things to tell, it is important that stories most worthy of presentation are selected, ones particularly significant to the immediate area.

Unity. Because there are so many choices worthy of presentation, one may tend to select too many. Each display, exhibit, and bulletin board should center around *one* theme, one single idea to get across and focus upon.

Content

Simplicity. The manner of presenting content must be influenced by the audience for whom the audio-visual material is being made. The viewer must be able to understand what is being presented. For the most part, viewers are nonprofessionals and the concepts must be presented so that they relate to something within the personality or experience of such a person.

Accuracy. In an effort to simplify presentation and to attract interest, one must not sacrifice accuracy. All materials presented must be scientifically accurate.

Up-to-dateness. While some displays may tend to be semipermanent, most audio-visual materials should change with the seasons and be kept up-to-date, both with the changing outdoor environment and with any new scientific materials. The viewer who returns from time to time should find new and stimulating presentations to further encourage him in firsthand experiences.

Appearance

Neatness. A presentation which is not neat leads not only to disrespect and vandalism but also to the loss of whatever appeal it might have had to stimulate the viewer toward firsthand experiences with the natural environment. The quality of neatness extends not only to the initial preparation but to regular maintenance also.

Placement. In viewing a sequence, it is most normal to go from left to right as this is the way we read in our American culture, so the sequence of exhibits, posters, etc., should be from left to right. Another factor important in placement is that the presentation must have its focus at *eye level.* People just do not tend to look upward unless their attention is attracted by the presentation. Similarly, audience participation presentations should have their action mechanisms appropriate for various ages which might be viewing.

Layout. There are seven elements of layout:

1. Balance. Informal balance is usually more attractive than formal. The main point of emphasis may be more effective slightly off center.

2. Mass. Too often the amateur designer of a display tends to want to get too many things in the display or on the board. Solid blocks of

material should be broken up with blank space for effect. Long
sentences and captions will not be read and remembered. Keep
captions brief, specific, and interesting. Pictures with captions
tend to be much more appealing than writing only. Symbolic
diagrams can be used effectively to get an idea across.

3. Texture. Having variety of texture for surfaces and lines adds
immeasurably to the appeal of the presentation. For surfaces, use
such materials as cloth, corrugated cardboard, screening, foil,
newsprint, etc. For lines, use yarn, ribbon, rubber bands, wire,
pipe cleaners, etc.

4. Color. The greater the contrast between lettering and
background, the more easily and quickly the lettering can be read.
Contrasting intensities should be used. Children usually notice
colors more than adults and prefer brighter colors and combinations of intense colors. Older children and adults prefer more
sophisticated color combinations.
    Unless you are deliberately emphasizing one thing, never
have a color appear only once. Repeat it somewhere in the design
or lettering. This directs the eye to different parts and relationships.

5. Lettering. Lettering is a most essential element of the presentation, for it points up the meaning. Keep lettering simple. Let
one style dominate. Not more than three sizes of letters should be
used in any one presentation.
    Uppercase letters are forceful and attract attention easily but
can be difficult to read because all letters are the same height;
therefore, use them for short words and simple phrases which
need special emphasis.
    In formation of letters, heavy, even strokes are easier to read
than light strokes. Also, spacing is extremely important. There
should be sufficient space between letters. If condensing is
necessary, use a narrower letter rather than make an important
word smaller, and condense space between letters, not between
words.

6. Mechanical devices. There is a trend toward audience participation, the use of action in displays and exhibits. Mechanical
devices must be carefully set up where they can be serviced
regularly and conveniently. There is nothing more annoying to a
viewer than an ''out-of-order'' sign.

7. Lighting. Even lighting is generally desirable on a display or other presentation; however, spotlights or shadow effects may point up something special that is being portrayed.

4.   COMMUNITY RESOURCES

The out-of-doors and its vast storehourse of native materials is not far away. You need only to step outside the door to find yourself in nature and at a place where you can begin outdoor activities. There is no need to travel to highly publicized distant lands to begin your explorations in nature, nor does your outdoor activity need to be expensive. Most of the materials with which you will want to work are free, and usually no admission prices are asked for areas where they are to be found.

Take time to look around in your community for areas which can be used for nature activities. Make a few inquiries. You will be amazed at the many opportunities waiting for you and others who are interested in nature. What community does not have a park, forest area, or stream nearby? Vacant lots, gardens, and other natural areas are just around the corner waiting to be explored.

Don't forget to include local personnel in your survey of resources. Every community has people who have become specialists in certain areas of nature study through participation in lifelong hobbies and interests. These people almost always are willing to share their enthusiasm and knowledge with anyone who shows interest. Frequently these people can be used effectively in leadership roles for programs, giving demonstrations or presenting a specific point of view. Many of these people have valuable and interesting collections and are eager to help others start collections of their own. They may serve as sponsors for youth hobby clubs.

A number of different areas that contribute to nature programs and serve as resources and places to go on field trips can be found in almost every community. The personnel of these areas are glad to help you, but it is a good policy to let them know your plans ahead of time and to make proper arrangements. Every field trip or excursion needs to be planned. The leader and the group must have their objectives in mind and plan the trip in such a way that these goals can be attained. It helps to have prepared a series of questions to which you are seeking answers. These questions may grow out of outdoor explorations and hikes.

BIRD SANCTUARIES AND WILDLIFE PRESERVES

Many communities are near areas set aside as wildlife preserves. An effort is made to provide the type of habitat that will attract and hold wildlife. Hunting is not permitted in these areas and animals show less fear than they do in other settings. This then becomes an excellent place to observe wildlife in its natural environment. Many communities or organizations maintain their own bird sanctuaries and feeding stations. Making a list of locations of sanctuaries and feeding stations in a community is a good project.

FARMS

For many city children few experiences are as thrilling as spending some time on a farm exploring its areas. On the farm they can have firsthand experiences with domesticated animals and can learn their living habits as well as how they are cared for.

Most farms contain a variety of intriguing areas which offer opportunities for nature study. In a small wooded area one can become familiar with the woodland plants and life. In pastures one becomes acquainted with prairie flowers and animal life. Almost all farms have either a pond, stream, or lake in which one can try his hand at fishing or studying water life.

Carefully choose the farm to which you take your group. Be sure that the farm contains the kinds of things that will help you to achieve your objectives. Some farms are highly specialized in such areas as poultry or dairying, and you may be disappointed if you expect to find a diversified farm. If the farmer is enthusiastic about his work, likes people, and has the knack for creating interest, he can add a great deal to your group's trip to the farm.

Visits to specialized "farms" can be most educational and interesting. Such farms might raise minks, hamsters, guinea pigs, bees, or domesticated rabbits.

Some schools operate small farms as a part of either their environmental education program or their agricultural education program. Also, some public and private agencies, such as county parks through their interpretive programs, may operate certain farm activities or have areas of farm animals. These are sometimes referred to as children's farms because they are frequently composed of baby animals.

FORESTS AND WOODLANDS

Forest areas may not be as easily accessible as parks, for usually they will be found outside the city limits. They do, however, offer unique opportunities to people interested in nature. The importance of maintaining forest areas is being recognized by many civic leaders, and they are setting aside areas known as forest preserves which are within a reasonable distance from heavily populated areas. The Cook County Forest Preserve, Chicago, has a number of these areas set aside which are visited by many residents.

The purpose of the forest is to insure the wise use and management of our native woodland. The managers of forests practice good conservation methods — permitting lumbering, hunting, grazing, and other activities which are not commonly permitted in parks. Forests tend to be larger in size and not as highly developed as parks, but they contain picnic areas and campgrounds.

Forests provide opportunities to conduct explorations as well as to carry on individual study in the nature-related areas. Since most of the forests are located in areas which are not suitable for farming, they usually contain hilly and rough areas and frequently are dotted with lakes and streams.

Occasionally, forests also may be owned and maintained by community groups. Usually these are located on marginal land that was available at a low cost. Woodlands may also be maintained by Conservation Districts to protect watersheds, and "natural areas" may be preserved by the Nature Conservancy or other private organizations. These lands are usually available for educational and recreational activities.

Woodlands adequate for many nature activities are also owned by individual farmers and "second home" developments. Some of the larger metropolitan, county, and regional parks have areas of natural woods which can be easily utilized and are usually accessible.

In certain regions in the United States, schools own and maintain forests. These are regarded as being important educational tools serving as outdoor education centers. Here, students learn conservation of natural resources and have an opportunity to do research. The profits from these forests are used to help meet the cost of the educational program.

GARDENS AND GREENHOUSES

In pioneer days, gardens were necessary as the family's primary source of vegetables. They were family enterprises with each member of the family contributing a fair share of the labor. This meant that almost everyone had direct experiences with soil and seeds and growing plants. This is not true today, for now a family can purchase frozen vegetables the year around for less effort than it takes to maintain a garden.

The garden is not a thing of the past; in fact, it is gaining in popularity. Gardens are maintained today not because of necessity, but rather for the recreational benefits that they bring to people. Today the gardener plants the things that he enjoys having in his garden, and frequently today's gardens have more flowers than vegetables. Gardens have become areas of beauty, and as these areas are multiplied they do their bit in making beautiful cities. Gardens vary in size. Some small private gardens are kept indoors, while some cities have botanical and flower gardens that cover large areas and contain a great variety of plants. Arboretums, under both private and public auspices, are found in many communities and provide a wide diversity of trees, shrubs, and other plants.

Children should have the opportunity to participate in gardening activities. (See the section on gardening in Chapter V.) If this is impossible, then they should at least have opportunities to visit gardens and learn of the plant life that they contain. Greenhouses basically are indoor gardens, and the owners usually are happy to help people start their own gardens by providing them with seeds and plants. Why not take your group to visit a greenhouse and have the people there explain their program?

Commercial nurseries, as well as state nurseries, are excellent resources. These can be used to discuss home landscaping and the growth of woody plants, including Christmas trees.

HISTORICAL RESOURCES

The Bicentennial Celebration of the founding of the United States, with its focus on colonial history, has highlighted the importance of cultural and historical interpretation as a vital part of understanding the environment. Some public parks, school environmental education programs, and historical societies have established "living crafts" or "pioneer crafts" centers. In these centers individuals may practice the various skills in which the pioneers engaged. Visits to these centers and actual participation in their crafts are excellent opportunities for nature activities for people of all ages. Village people specializing in the rural craft arts are also a fine community resource.

Further, most communities have areas and structures of historical significance that may be used to interpret the culture of times past. The local historical society is usually most willing to provide both personnel and literature resources. An increasing number of archeological "digs" have also been taking place and you may be fortunate to have one in your community or within easy field trip distance. A nearby college anthropology/archeology department may be able to help you in this type of activity. See Historical-Cultural Activities in Chapter V.

MUSEUMS

Museums of some type can be found in almost every city. Most of these contain materials which help to interpret natural history and can be used to illustrate relationships. Museums are excellent places to obtain help in identifying materials gathered on field trips or to find detailed information concerning things you may have merely glimpsed while out in the field. Many museums have displays using native mounted animals and birds which may be inspected from close range. They also contain rock and mineral collections which can be helpful in identifying rocks.

Recently, museums have been attempting to make their programs become truly alive and have added naturalists to their staffs to help visitors. Museums often will send out specimens for nature museum use. Some museums have workshops and offer courses related to nature study.

OBSERVATORIES AND PLANETARIUMS

For individuals who are interested in exploring the heavens, a trip to the observatory and the planetarium is a must. An observatory is a dome-shaped building usually set on a high hill. It contains such equipment as telescopes for the purpose of observing and studying heavenly bodies. The planetarium, on the other hand, usually has a dome-shaped ceiling which is used as a screen on which are shown pictures of stars and planets as they are seen in the sky. While the program emphasis at the observatory is primarily on research, the program at the planetarium is educational. The planetarium staff will hold regularly scheduled lectures for visitors, and classes for those who are interested in astronomy or in the making of telescopes. Many of them have workshops equipped to grind lenses. They also have many displays and exhibits.

While planetariums usually are found only in larger cities, many smaller communities have observatories. Frequently the observatory is connected with a college and used in their astronomy department.

PARKS

Parks vary greatly in purpose, size, and content, but almost every community has a park of one type or another. It may be the small neighborhood park which consists primarily of a playground for the children; or it may be a large city park complete with playgrounds, picnic areas, nature trails, and zoos. Outside the city one may find county, state, or national parks, some of which may contain thousands of acres of natural areas. Many of these parks provide the opportunity to study unique geological formations, plant and animal life, and natural history.

A primary purpose of parks is to preserve areas of natural and historic importance in such a manner that they can be enjoyed and used by the growing population. To do this they need constantly to carry on an interpretive program of educating the people who come to the park, encouraging them to establish good conservation practices and to become interested in absorbing some knowledge about the materials contained in the park.

Many of the larger parks and cities have interpretive services. They have made available nature trails, trailside museums, and conducted tours as part of their nature programs. Also, many of the parks have nature centers (see previous section) and provide full time environmental interpreters who not only conduct programs for all ages on site but also frequently will assist with in-service education programs for teachers and club leaders.

Parks and other small parklike spaces in urban environments should not be overlooked for nature activities—from individual aesthetic enjoyment, bird walks, and care of plants to day camping and field plot studies.

ROCK QUARRIES

Working with rocks and minerals is a hobby that is developing an ever-growing number of enthusiastic supporters. Interests include rock and fossil collections, rock polishing, and gem making. Rock quarries are excellent hunting grounds for specimens. Permission should be obtained before entering, and safety precautions should be observed if you are taking a group of children to a quarry on a field trip. Sand pits also make interesting field trips.

WATER AREAS

Water areas should not be overlooked in searching the community for areas in which to conduct your nature program. Usually the land bordering rivers, streams, and lakes is not suitable for farming. When these lands are not within the limits of a park or forest, they may provide you with an area undisturbed by people. Frequently, these will contain backwater, lagoons, and swamps which attract numerous species of animal life.

In addition to these areas (usually on private property) do not overlook public properties owned by the Corps of Engineers and other federal government agencies, as well as those owned by state agencies. Fish hatcheries are especially good educational field trips. And don't forget the water supply reservoir areas.

ZOOS

Children always enjoy visits to the zoo. Here they have the opportunity to observe animals at close range where they can study in detail their shapes, colors, and movement. In modern zoos the animals are kept in areas that give the impression of their native habitat. Many zoos now have children's areas with domesticated animals which children are permitted to pet and fondle.

REFERENCES

Audio-visual Materials and Presentation Techniques

Bale, R. O. *Conservation for Camp and Classroom.* Burgess Publishing Company, Minneapolis, 1962.

Brown, Vinson. *How To Make a Home Nature Museum.* Little, Brown, and Company, Boston, 1954. Has chapters on collecting, classifying, mounting and labeling specimens; molds and models, drawings, charts, diagrams, and paintings; arranging displays; pictures and photographs.

Gilbert, Douglas L. *Public Relations in Natural Resources Management.* The Wildlife Society, Washington, D.C., 1971.

Hanna, John, *Interpretive Skills for Environmental Communicators.* Department of Recreation and Parks, Texas A & M University, College Park, 1975, 2nd edition.

Hilker, Gordon. *The Audience and You.* Office of Publications, National Park Service, U.S. Dept. of Interior, Washington, D.C., 1974. Available through Superintendent of Documents, U.S. Government Printing Office 20402.

Hillcourt, William. *The New Field Book of Nature Activities and Hobbies.* G. P. Putnam's Sons, New York, 1970. Particularly good for ideas for displays and exhibits.

Minor, Ed, and Frye, Harvey R. *Techniques for Producing Visual Instructional Media.* McGraw-Hill Book Company, New York, 1970.

Neal, Arminta. *Help! for the Small Museum.* Handbook of Exhibit Ideas and Methods. (Denver Museum of Natural History) Pruett Publishing, Boulder, Colo., 1969. Paperback.

Nickelsburg, Janet. *The Nature Program at Camp.* Burgess Publishing Company, Minneapolis, 1960. Material especially on bulletin boards at camp, some exhibits.

Park Practice Program materials are especially good. See references for Interpretive Programs.

Sharpe, Grant. *Interpreting the Environment.* John Wiley and Sons, New York, 1976.

Strung, Norman, editor. *Communicating the Outdoor Experience.* Outdoor Writers Association of America, 4141 West Bradley Road, Milwaukee 53209, 1975.

Field Trips

Brown, Robert E., and Mouser, G. W. *Techniques for Teaching Conservation Education.* Burgess Publishing Company, Minneapolis, 1964.

Hammerman, D. R., and Hammerman, W. M. *Teaching in the Outdoors.*
    Burgess Publishing Company, Minneapolis, second edition, 1973.
Hillcourt, William. *The New Field Book of Nature Activities and Hobbies.*
    G. P. Putnam's Sons, New York, 1970, pp. 9ff and 36ff.
Mohr, Charles E. *How To Lead a Field Trip.* Audubon Nature Bulletin,
    National Audubon Society, New York, 1957.
Nickelsburg, Janet. *Field Trips.* Burgess Publishing Company, Min-
    neapolis, 1966.
Russell, Helen Ross. *Ten-Minute Field Trips.* J. G. Ferguson Publishing
    Company, Chicago, 1973.

Interpretive Programs (General)

Association of Interpretive Naturalists. Central Office. 6700 Needwood
    Road, Derwood, Md. 20855.
Brown, Vinson. *The Explorer Naturalist.* Stackpole Books, Harrisburg, Pa.,
    1976.
Bunce, Frank H., et al. *Arboreta, Botanical Gardens, Special Gardens.*
    NRPA Management Aids Bulletin No. 90, National Recreation and Parks
    Association, Washington, D.C. 1971.
Frieswyk, Siebolt H. *Mobile and Portable Recreation Facilities in Parks and
    Recreation.* National Recreation and Park Association, Washington,
    D.C., 1966, pp. 36-42.
Hillcourt, William. *The New Field Book of Nature Activities and Hobbies.*
    G. P. Putnam's Sons, New York, 1970.
National Audubon Society. Education-Information Series. See Nature
    Centers reference section.
Nickelsburg, Janet. *The Nature Program at Camp.* Burgess Publishing
    Company, Minneapolis, 1960.
Park Practice Program. National Conference on State Parks in cooperation
    with the National Park Service and the National Recreation and Park
    Association. In *Guideline,* the section on Interpretation; in *Grist,* the
    March-April issue is the annual Interpretation issue but helpful
    suggestions are carried in all issues; in *Design,* a few construction helps.
Schneider, Gail. *Children's Zoos.* NRPA Management Aids Bulletin, No. 87,
    National Recreation and Park Association, Washington, D.C., 1970.
Sharpe, Grant. *Interpreting the Environment.* John Wiley and Sons, New
    York, 1976.
Strung, Norman (editor). *Communicating the Outdoor Experience.* Outdoor
    Writers Association of America, 4141 West Bradley Road, Milwaukee
    53209, 1975.
Tilden, Freeman. *Interpreting Our Heritage.* University of North Carolina,
    Chapel Hill, 1957.
Vinal, William G. "The Technique of Nature-Club Leadership," *Nature
    Recreation,* second edition. Dover Publications, New York, 1963.
Wallin, Harold. *Interpretation: A Manual and Survey on Establishing a
    Naturalist Program.* AIPE Management Aids Series #22, National
    Recreation and Park Association, Washington, D.C., 1963.

Nature Centers

National Audubon Society, 1130 Fifth Ave., New York, N.Y. 10028. Education-Information Series.

(1) Shomon, Joseph J. *A Nature Center for Your Community.* 1962.
(2) Ashbaugh, Byron L. *Planning a Nature Center.* 1963.
(3) Shomon, Joseph J. *Manual of Outdoor Conservation Education.* 1964.
(4) Ashbaugh, Byron L., and Kordish, Raymond. *Trail Planning and Layout.* 1971.
(5) Shomon, Joseph J.; Ashbaugh, Byron L.; and Tolman, C. D. *Wildlife Habitat Improvement.* 1966.
(6) Shomon, Joseph J. (editor). *Manual of Outdoor Interpretation.* 1968.

Organizations To Help You Plan

American Alliance for Health, Physical Education, and Recreation, 1201 Sixteenth Street, N.W., Washington, D.C. 20036.
American Camping Association, Bradford Woods, Martinsville, Ind. 46151.
American Forestry Association, 919 Seventeenth Street, N.W., Washington, D.C. 20006.
American Youth Hostels, 14 W. 8th Street, New York, N.Y. 10011.
Association of Interpretive Naturalists. (See Interpretive Programs.)
Bicycle Institute of America, 122 E. 42nd St., New York, N.Y. 10017.
Bureau of Outdoor Recreation, Dept. of Interior, 18th and C Sts., N.W., Washington, D.C. 20240.
Conservation Foundation, 1250 Connecticut Ave., N.W., Washington, D.C. 20036.
Daisy Manufacturing Company, Rogers, Ark. 72756.
4-H Clubs, local County Extension Office.
Garden Clubs of America, 598 Madison Avenue, New York, N.Y. 10022.
Izaak Walton League of America, P.O. Box 368, Crystal Lake, Ill. 60014.
National Association of Casting and Angling Clubs, Box 51, Nashville, Tenn. 37202.
National Audubon Society, 1130 Fifth Avenue, New York, N.Y. 10028.
National Campers and Hikers Association, 7172 Transit Road, Buffalo, N.Y. 14221.
National Conference on State Parks, 1601 N. Kent St., Arlington, Va. 22209.
National Field Archery Association, Box 514, Redlands, Calif. 92373.
National Foundation for Junior Museums, 151 Potrero Street, San Francisco, Calif. 94103.
National Park Service, Dept. of Interior, Washington, D.C. 20240.
National Recreation and Park Association, 1601 N. Kent St., Arlington, Va. 22209.
National Riflery Association, 1600 Rhode Island Avenue, N.W., Washington, D.C. 20036.

National Speleological Society, Inc., 2318 North Kenmore Street, Arlington,
    Va. 22201.
National Wildlife Federation, 1412 Sixteenth Street, N.W., Washington,
    D.C. 20036.
Natural Science for Youth Foundation, 114 East 30th Street, New York, N.Y.
    10016.
Science Clubs of America, 1719 N Street, N.W., Washington, D.C. 20036.
Soil Conservation Service (see local district)
State Conservation Commission, local State House
U.S. Forest Service, Dept. of Agriculture, Washington, D.C. 20250
See also the annual edition of *Conservation Directory,* published by the
    National Wildlife Federation, 1412 Sixteenth Street, N.W., Washington,
    D.C. 20036. Extensive listing of organizations and agencies with ad-
    dresses, officials, et al.

Trails

Hillcourt, William. *The New Field Book of Nature Activities and Hobbies.*
    G. P. Putnam's Sons, New York, 1970.
Grist and *Design.* Part of the Park Practice Program series. See under In-
    terpretive Services (General).
Mohr, Charles E. *How To Build a Nature Trail.* Audubon Nature Bulletin.
    National Audubon Society, New York, 1953.
Sharpe, Grant. *Interpreting the Environment.* John Wiley and Sons, New
    York, 1976.

Periodicals

There are many specialized and specific topic periodicals. The following
periodicals are of a general nature and include publications of some
organizations listed above.

American Forests
Audubon
Backpacker
Camping Magazine
Canadian Camping
Christian Camping
Conservation News
Conservation Report
The Conservationist (New York)
Extension Service Review
Journal of Environmental Educa-
    tion
Journal of Interpretation
Living Wilderness
Minnesota Volunteer

National Geographic
National Geographic World
National Parks and Conservation
    Magazine
National Wildlife
Natural History Magazine
Nature Study
New Jersey Outdoors
Our Public Lands
Outdoor America
Outdoor World
Ranger Rick
Soil Conservation
Trailer Travel
Wilderness Camping

PART TWO

Activities

All community nature-oriented programs, regardless
of organization, have activities as components. These
activities can be used as a total program event or may
be integrated into other program aspects. The chapters
in this part give, in some detail, suggested activities
in nature crafts, nature games, and outdoor-living skills,
and in lesser detail, activities related to Indian life,
nighttime, winter, family and day camping, and campfire programs. Adventure activities and outing sports,
as well as nature projects and hobbies, are included also.

CHAPTER II

Nature Crafts

P HILIP JAMES BAILEY ONCE SAID, "ART IS MAN'S
NATURE; NATURE IS GOD'S ART." It has been said
again and again that mechanical devices increasingly
are depriving human beings of creative expression. Work with
natural materials, where mechanical devices are at a minimum,
offers just such a chance for personal expression. Originality and
ingenuity constantly are being challenged. Valuable, too, is the
concomitant learning found in this type of craft. Since crafts dealing
with native materials are really the oldest we have, they can arouse
an interest in primitive people and the history of crafts. The idea of
creating beautiful and useful articles from pine cones, shells, or
acorns is a novel and interesting one to most groups.

Then, too, it is much cheaper to work with seeds and grasses
than it is to work with leather and metals. Such materials are
inexpensive, frequently free, and easy to find wherever one may live,
although they may vary greatly from one part of the country to
another. In making things from native materials, the individual
learns to work with raw materials and to feel the response of clay,
sand, and other natural materials. Design ideas are everywhere if
one can learn to recognize them. Nature in its beauty and variety
provides a limitless source of design inspirations, but one must
develop awareness in order to become sensitive to its possibilities.
As one becomes aware of the variety of beautiful shapes, colors, and
textures in nature, good taste and feeling for making beautiful things
will develop.

Even though nature has provided an abundance of colorful and
interesting craft materials, it is of utmost importance that serious
consideration be given to conservation principles if this supply is to
remain for future use. Groups should be cautioned not to take

materials that will result in a lasting injury to the area. Some areas once rich with wild flowers and saplings have lost their ability to contribute to the craft program because of ruthless and indiscriminate cutting. Respect for sources of craft materials may be developed by having the group set aside an area in which plants are grown specifically for use in the craft program.

This section is not meant to be exhaustive, but only suggestive of the vast scope of nature crafts. As used here, nature crafts include those objects made by hand using native materials and reproductions of native materials in the various art forms.

MATERIALS FROM TREES

Trees furnish a great variety of materials that can be used effectively in a nature craft program. All parts of the tree including its roots, bark, twigs, nuts, and flowers can be used. But for many craft activities no substitute material can bring the same satisfactions that working with wood itself does. The following is a list of some woods frequently used in making craft items from native materials:

Basswood—best of the carving woods for ease and for beginners. Inner bark is excellent for fiber material used in making cordage; it can be used also for the same purposes as raffia. Green basswood is one of the best woods for making whistles.

Cedar—an excellent whittling wood, has a beautiful color to the heartwood. Old trees have interesting roots and gnarled sections. Wood is very resistant to decay. Used in fire-by-friction sets as fireboard and drill.

Hickory—one of the best woods for making coals for broiling. Inner bark is used for lashing. Slender green branches may be bent for making toasters and frames. Some nuts are excellent food. A preferred wood for axe handles. Used by the Indians for making bows.

Sassafras—roots are famous as a source of sassafras tea. Bark can be removed and the green wood may be pounded for splints for use in basketry.

Willow—may use young shoots for basketry, particularly where sharp bends are not required. Used for whistles. Bark can be used for binding material on chair bottoms. Straight shoots often are used for making willow beds.

Witch hazel—best of the woods for making "pulled" whisk brooms. See Page 58 for instructions.

How To Carve Wood

Whittling and wood carving belong to the group of the truly great crafts that are rapidly disappearing. During the pioneer days almost everyone knew how to use a knife and had developed enough skill in wood carving so that tools and implements could be made as needed.

While many children have pocketknives, few know how to use them safely or with any degree of real skill. Few adults, for that matter, have such skills. Most people, however, become very enthusiastic about wood carving once they get started and learn some of the basic skills.

Following are some tips for beginners:

1. Get a good quality knife that has several blades of various shapes and sizes. The handle should fit comfortably in the hand.

2. Sharpen the knife on a carborundum stone. New knives are seldom very sharp. You will be less likely to cut yourself with a sharp blade than with a dull one which is difficult to control and will easily slip.

3. Select a piece of soft wood such as basswood or white pine for your first project. Start with a simple design of an animal and use a jig saw or coping saw to cut the wood down to its approximate shape.

4. Begin to round off the edges and to shape the wood into the design. In rounding off the edges one learns quickly how to hold the knife for good control and that the knife cuts better when you cut with the grain rather than against it. Hold the knife so that the thumb of your cutting hand can serve as a brace and a guide. Take bold strokes at the beginning and smaller ones when you are completing the shaping.

5. Use sandpaper to smooth out the rough edges. Begin with a medium-grain paper and finish with a fine-grain paper.

6. Use a paste floor wax or linseed oil for a finish. Apply directly to sanded surface and rub it in with your fingers. Repeat this operation until the desired luster is obtained. Avoid using finishes that cover or destroy the natural beauty of the wood. Varnishes and shellacs are suitable, but take time to dry. When you are working with groups, remember they are likely to leave messy

brushes; and they must have a drying place where they can leave the project.

You can experience great satisfaction when you find a piece of wood or a branch in the outdoors and start to work on it. After looking over the piece that you have picked up you will begin to get some ideas of possible design. You may see in the wood a letter opener or a little squirrel. Only you and your pocketknife can take away the excess wood and release the letter opener or the squirrel from its prison.

The following are good whittling woods:

Apple—brownish wood that takes a beautiful polish.
Basswood—one of the best for beginners.
Cherry—reddish-brown wood excellent for whittling.
Osage orange—difficult to carve, but one of the most beautiful carving woods.
Red cedar—excellent for whittling, but splits easily.
Walnut—a harder wood, but extremely beautiful when polished.
White pine—excellent for beginners.

Driftwood

Use driftwood in its natural state. Scrub and clean the wood. It is preferable to leave driftwood in this natural, clean state with no finish; however, it may be rubbed down with oil or wax. *Driftwood should never be painted or varnished.* Use driftwood for decorative purposes or carve into statuary, jewelry, lamp bases, centerpieces, mobiles, or totem poles.

Roots and Burls

These can be used for carving into jewelry, figures, candelabra, or used in natural shape (burls) for containers or dishes.

Twigs and Branches

By whittling and carving twigs and branches you can make buttons, buckles, matchholders, candleholders, shepherd pipes, soap dishes, camp furniture, coat hangers, birdhouses, whisk brooms, spoons, forks, cooking utensils, animals, name tags, or

pins. The possibilities are limitless. Equipment also can be made for
various games such as tic-tac-toe and checkers from slices of twigs
and branches. Another interesting project is to make a twig belt or
necklace. Hiking sticks can be carved from branches. A shepherd
pipe, whistle, or a bird or animal call can be made from willow or
elderberry.

How To Make a Willow Whistle

Step 1. Cut a 2 1/2''-3'' straight section of willow branch, el-
       derberry, or basswood (or other similar wood which
       will permit the bark to be removed easily) without
       knots or joints and about 3/8''-1/2'' in diameter. (Late fall
       and winter are not good times to make whistles as the
       sap isn't flowing.)

Step 2. Using a closed pocketknife, hammer the whole
       length of the branch, crushing the cells between
       bark and wood (inner), until you can slide the bark
       off in one piece. Be careful not to mutilate the bark,
       since it will be used as a slide; it should have no
       cracks through which the air could escape as the
       whistle is blown.

Step 3. With your pocketknife carefully make a vertical cut
       about 5/8'' from the smallest end to a point about
       one-third through the wood and a diagonal cut about
       1/4'' farther back, completing the notch as shown in
       diagram above.

Step 4. Now, slide the bark off, removing core through the
       larger end, opposite the notch, to avoid splitting the
       bark.

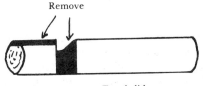

Remove

Mouthpiece   Tonal slide

Step 5. Cut the wood (core removed from bark) into two
       pieces where the notch was made, as shown. The

space left after removing the notched portion serves as the music box. The smaller piece is the mouthpiece and the larger one the tonal slide. Slice a thin piece (1/16'' or less depending on the size of branch used) off the top of the mouthpiece for the air channel.

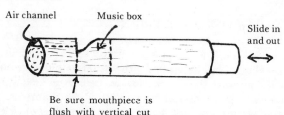

Step 6. Replace the mouthpiece in the end of the bark cylinder and the long tonal slide in the other end. Be sure the end of the mouthpiece is flush with the vertical cut in the bark, as indicated in the diagram. Leave the long piece (tonal slide) extended slightly so it can be held for sliding back and forth.

Step 7. Now blow—you should have a whistle! If you slide the tonal slide in and out slowly, you will have a multitoned whistle of three or more tones depending upon the length you have used. Experiment with whistles of different lengths and diameters.

How To Make A Whisk Broom

Select a freshly cut stick of ash, witch hazel, or sassafras which has a natural handle about ½'' in diameter and 12'' long (can vary in length). Cut away bark (peel off) from shaded area shown in diagram above. At brush end, peel wood fibers back (about toothpick size or smaller) to the band of bark. Peel around the stick until all the end is stripped into bristles. Then begin pulling fibers at the handle point down toward the band of bark. Peel about halfway through the stick.

Fold this portion over the band and bind with cordage. The length of the upper part of the peeling should be the length of the lower part plus the bark band, and a tiny bit extra for the fold.

Bark

Bark can be used for pictures, collages, greeting cards, block printing, and containers of all types. Birch bark is the best suited for bark crafts. *Bark should* not, *however, be taken promiscuously.* Good conservation principles must be observed! To secure bark, make a straight cut down the trunk of the tree or limb and work the bark off with a wedge. In preparing it for use, soak it in hot water if you wish to make it pliable. Bark bookmarks, book covers, hatbands, and pocketbooks all are easy to make. Just cut the bark, soak it, punch holes, sew it together, and then carve your own design. Bark duck floats, animals, whistles, and various bird calls can be made with a little effort and interest.

The Making of Cordage

The inner bark of some woods, such as basswood, and roots of certain trees and shrubs, as well as weeds (Indian hemp, milkweed stem, yucca, stinging nettle) provided the Indian with materials for making cordage for lacings, rope, nets, and fishlines. See references for technique.

Nuts

Such nuts as walnuts, hickory nuts, butternuts, and acorns can be used for jewelry, belts, lapel pixies, etc. Lapel pins may be made by glueing shells together or by carving. Nut buttons are made by using the whole nut or by cutting it into sections. Belts may be made by slicing a nut with a hacksaw, holding the nut in vise. Clean the nut first with wire brush. Sandpaper the cut, and wax, oil, or shellac. For belts, string on throngs. Bracelets, brooches, and earrings in matching sets also may be made from nuts.

Pine Needles (long)

Use long pine needles for weaving basketry and making pillows and brooms.

Basketry

The making of useful and beautiful containers from native materials is one of the oldest known crafts. Primitive man had few tools but he was able to make many things by twisting and knotting pliable plants. Native materials suitable for making baskets are to be found in every country. Because materials are readily available, basketry has become an important part of many nature craft programs.

Some of the materials found in the United States include honeysuckle, willow, woodbine or Virginia creeper, pine needles, and such nontree materials as cornhusks, sweet grass, rye, broom straw, cattails, and rushes. Most of these materials should be gathered while they are still green and then dried slowly, turning them at frequent intervals. Most of these will have to be moistened at the time they are to be used. The following woods may be pounded for splints for pack baskets and other similar basketry weaves: black ash, sassafras, American ash, hickory, basket oak.

Primarily three basic techniques are used in the construction of baskets: braiding, plaiting, and coiling.

Pine Cones

Christmas tree ornaments, fantastic animals, mobiles, bird feeders, dolls, and collages can be made with pine cones, which can be used in block printing, too.

Nature Pixies

Making nature pixies is a delightful craft which challenges the creativity of both the young and the old. Nature pixies are animals made by combining a variety of seeds, pods, and other natural items.

Making the pixies is not difficult, but one should have a generous supply of materials on hand before beginning. These should include pine cones, acorns, hickory nuts, melon seeds, twigs, cornhusks, bark, feathers, etc. Other materials and tools which may be used to put the pixies together are pipe cleaners, fine wire, quick-drying glue, thin-nosed pliers, hand drill with small bits, and a hacksaw. A wire brush is useful on hickory nuts and walnuts.

It is good to have an idea in mind before you begin to explore the possibilities of putting the materials together to make the figure. Large pine cones make wonderful turkeys, while small pine cones make interesting mice, rabbits, and birds. Swans may be made from milkweed pods.

SEE REFERENCES

MATERIALS FROM PLANTS OTHER THAN TREES

Berries

Use juice for dyeing or staining. String them for ornaments.

Cattails

The leaves can be used for weaving, basketry, or decorative arrangements. The tails can be used in decorative arrangements.

Corn

Cornhusks can be used to make braided sandals, baskets, flowers, brooms, dolls, etc. The best cornhusks for craft work are those from the inner layer of husks next to the silks. Dry husks in the shade for a soft green color, or in the sun for a bleached white. Husks are readily dyed with any fabric dye or with native dyes. Hair, eyebrows, and moustaches for dolls may be made of corn silks or yarn. Baskets are made by taking strands of braided cornhusks and sewing them together. Even brooms can be made from the husks.

Corncobs can be used for dolls, puppets, animals, buttons, and even block printing.

Whistles, animals, and furniture can be made from cornstalks.

Fungi and Lichens

Use flat bracket fungus for whatnot shelves or name plaques. Pick before fungus begins to dry out. Write your name or some message on it. Dry, and then shellac to preserve.

Collect turkey-tail fungus from dead branches or logs, the small shell and larger gray lichens. Dye in permanent ink or Rit dye. *Do not try dyeing with tempera, paint, or shellac* because the texture will be ruined. When dyed with ink or Rit dye each fungus has two intensities of color in rings. Trim fungus end which was attached to the log. Make flowers, such as pansies, for a brooch and matching earrings. Glue pin on back. If a preservative is desired, use a light coat of clear plastic spray.

Gourds

Here, the shape will suggest the object. Table pieces, dishes, salt and pepper shakers, birdhouses, rhythm band instruments, and decorations can be made from gourds.

Grasses

Common wayside grasses may be used to weave beautiful placemats, baskets, or sit-upons. The tall grasses, such as sedge grass, swamp grass, or slough grass are preferred, but over fifty kinds of related grasses found in every part of the United States can be used. The grass should be cut close to the ground to get long lengths of stem. It is best to cut the grass in the summer or fall after it has matured. It should be laid out to dry in a shady place for several days and then may be tied into bundles and stored until you are ready to use it. Grass may need to be soaked before use because of the brittleness caused by drying.

The grass is prepared for weaving by cutting off the wiry tops and peeling the leaves from the stem. A floor or table loom is nice, but a cardboard loom can be substituted for the weaving of place mats. Use a coarse crochet thread or carpet warp for the warp. The weaving process is the same as that used in weaving oat, wheat, or rye straws, and long pine needles.

Grasses also can be used effectively in making dry nature arrangements, basketry, and nature prints. For these purposes you will want to include some of the smaller, finer, and colorful grasses. Grasses may be dyed, although wherever possible the natural color should be retained.

How To Make a Navajo Loom

Use this loom for weaving round-stem rushes, cattails, sedges (triangular stems), or any tall grass.

Cut two 48'' sticks and at least four 18'' stakes. Number of stakes to use depends upon size of mat wanted and closeness of weaving.

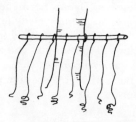

Lash one of the long sticks to a tree about 18''-24'' from the ground. Tie 8 pieces of twine to the stick at equal intervals (alternating 4' and 5' pieces). Use clove hitch to tie to stick.

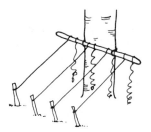

Drive stakes into ground; be sure that at least 12'' is sticking out of the ground. Tie the shorter twine lengths to the top of the stakes. Tie the longer strings to the other 48'' stick. When the strings are tied and pulled taut, the stick should be about 6'' beyond the stakes.

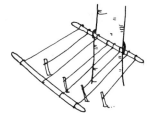

Holding the big stick and its four strings up, lay in grass or whatever material is being used and push up tight against the stick attached to the tree.

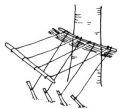

Lower stick to ground, put in another bunch of grass tightly against the next; then raise stick. Continue with this procedure until mat is finished.

Cut strings from sticks and stakes and tie ends in pairs with square knots, holding the grass together firmly.

You can make thicker mats by using larger bunches of grass, and bigger mats by extending the length of twine and number of sticks. Be careful that you get sufficient number of strings to hold the grass firmly.

Mosses

Can be used for models, pictures, and displays.

Pods

Make them into jewelry, holiday decorations, rhythm instruments, mobiles.

Seeds Other Than Nuts

Animals, dolls, bean bags, buttons, jewelry, rhythm instruments, mosaics, collages, blueprints, rubbings, murals, pictures, and signs can be made from seeds.

NONPLANT MATERIALS

Bones

Objects such as pirate ships can be made from the breastbones of chickens or other fowl. Neck bones can be used for neckerchief slides, animals, napkin rings. Bones also can be used for sculpturing.

Clay

Dig clay from stream beds, lake beds, and excavations. Remove foreign matter. Mix in one tablespoon of dextrin or Dexin to help the clay to harden. Mix well; add enough water to make a thick modeling clay. Keep clay covered with wet cloths until used. A primitive kiln may be made for firing.

Feathers

Use for backings of pictures, brooches, decorative arrangements, and decorations on objects.

Horns

Horns can be used in various ways, particularly as neckerchief slides and napkin rings. Large horns may be used for ornamental decorations, lamps, etc.

Rocks

Lapidary, the polishing and cutting of stones, is one of the most interesting of craft activities. Chipping of flint knives and arrowheads can also be an interesting hobby. Other projects include limestone carving, stone mosaics, and rock pictures (using different colors of soft rocks as chalk).

Sand

Most youngsters at one time or another have built castles and other objects in the sand. For crafts, however, sand is used primarily as a casting material for reproductions and for sand painting. See Page 70 for sand casting technique.

Sand Painting

Obtain *fine,* preferably white, clean sand through a collecting trip. To dye the sand use regular all-purpose dye, food coloring, or tempera paints. Experiment with dyes and amount of water until you get the colors you want. Remember that when the sand is wet it will be much darker than when it dries. Dry sand by spreading it out in the sun. Store in jars (so you can see the colors) or in boxes.

To paint: Draw the picture you want to paint in outline and decide on colors. Mix glue (Elmer's or Fuller's) with equal parts of water. Brush glue on design, covering only the area for *one* color at a time — then sprinkle that color of sand on the design. Let stand a few seconds to dry, and shake off excess sand onto a piece of paper so that it may be returned to the jar for use again. Put lighter colors on first. Continue brushing glue and sprinkling sand until all colors are on.

Shells

Trays, artificial flowers, jewelry, Christmas tree ornaments, ash trays, mobiles, mosaics, and block prints are possibilities. Spoons can be made easily from clam and mussel shells.

REPRODUCTIONS

Nature Prints of Leaves, Flowers, Grasses

Although spatter prints, blueprints, and ozalid prints are easy and inexpensive forms of nature printing, they show less detail than other types and are not as useful for identification or notebook collections. Crayon prints and oil and smoke prints can be used for identification, for making attractive note paper, and for making coverings for boxes and containers. Christmas cards, program decorations, and leaf scrapbooks also can be made. Block prints and spray, oil, and spatter prints may be made directly on fabric if suitable inks or paints are used. Heavy materials and materials with a coarse weave do not take the prints as satisfactorily as lighter weight materials. Ink-pad prints are a handy method if for some reason you want to make prints in the field. Leaves also may be reproduced by photographic printing and carbon paper printing.

Blueprinting

You can purchase blueprint paper from shops handling drafting supplies. A 5" x 7" size is preferable. Make a 9" x 12" frame by placing a piece of glass and a cardboard of the same size together and binding with masking tape at one end. All edges of the glass should be bound with masking tape for safety. Place object to be printed between glass and cardboard, with blueprint paper next to cardboard with the blue (sensitive) side up. Hold frame, glass side out, in the sun for several minutes, or until paper is greenish-gray. You will have to experiment on the proper amount of time according to the sun's intensity. Take into the shade and remove paper; immerse in pan of water, exposed side down. A drop of hydrogen peroxide in the water will help bring out the blue color. Be sure the paper is thoroughly wet; leave in water 15-60 seconds. Some blueprint papers need a chemical to fix the color — check on this when purchasing. Take paper out and press on blotter pad of newsprint to absorb water. Dry in shade, weighting down at corners to keep flat. CAUTION: Blueprint paper is highly sensitive to light so you must work with it in the dark, until ready to expose to sun. Extra blueprint paper must be wrapped in heavy paper and kept in a dark place.

Oil Printing

Provide plenty of newspaper plus several old mimeograph stencil backings or similar material that will not soak up ink readily.

Put a pea-sized dab of printer's block printing ink on the stencil backing. You can use either water base or oil base ink. The oil base makes nicer prints, but water base is better for youngsters since they tend to get it on their clothes. Spread ink out to just a bit bigger than the leaf you wish to use, using a wadded piece of newspaper as the spreader. The ink should be even and not very heavy.

Place leaf vein-side (back or underside) down on ink. Place another piece of paper over the leaf and rub thoroughly every vein and edge of leaf to help ink adhere evenly. Remove paper, lift the leaf carefully by the end of its stem. Lay carefully on note paper or whatever paper or fabric you wish to print on. Put a clean piece of newspaper over leaf *being sure that the leaf does not move.* Holding your finger down on center of leaf, rub thoroughly every vein and edge. Remove paper and leaf carefully. There's your print.

Now, take your spreader and even out the ink on the stencil backing. Place leaf vein-side down again and repeat the process. When ink becomes too light, add a *very little* more ink. If prints do not show veins, but just a blotch of ink, the ink is too heavy. You can mix inks to get fall colors. If textile extender is used in the oil ink and the ink then properly set, printing may be done on fabric.

Ozalid Printing

Ozalid printing is similar to blueprinting but can be done in a variety of colors and is a "dry" process. Buy diazo paper (ozalid is a trade name which has come into common usage for this type of process) at shops handling drafting supplies. It usually comes in a roll, so must be cut to size in a dark room. Follow the procedure for blueprints, testing the exposure time — approximately 15-25 seconds for red, 20-35 seconds for blue, 40-50 seconds for black. Remove print from frame in the shade, roll into cylinder, print-face inside, and place in a half-gallon glass jar containing enough concentrated ammonia (stronger ammonia [about 28%] purchased at a drugstore) barely to cover the bottom and a layer of marbles to keep the paper from getting into the ammonia. The ammonia also may be placed in a small jar, like an ink bottle, and set uncapped inside the big jar. Another method is to turn the large-mouthed jar upside down to prevent loss of fumes. Ammonia is placed in a container on the table with the jar over it. The ammonia fumes develop the print by bringing out and setting the color. Ammonia cannot be saved and reused. Use a fresh supply when you wish to print on another day. Remove the print after 3-4 minutes when proper color appears. Underfuming makes prints pale; overfuming makes them harsh and dark. Developing should be done outside or in a well-ventilated room.

Smoke Printing

Cover a piece of typewriting paper or a smooth-surface notepaper with a thin layer of lard or shortening, or you can use a greased paper. Light a candle and smoke the greased paper by moving it back and forth over the flame so that soot forms on the paper. When the surface is black with soot, place soot-side up on a table and lay the leaf vein-side down on the blackened surface. Cover the leaf with another piece of paper, such as newspaper, and rub every vein and edge of leaf well to make soot stick to the leaf. Lift leaf carefully by end of stem and place smoked side down on fresh piece of paper. Lay another piece of paper over it and, holding with finger in center, rub entire leaf carefully. Remove top paper and leaf with care. Smoke prints are delicate. They may be preserved from smudges by spraying lightly with clear plastic spray. Smoke also may be gathered on glass if care is used with the flame so that the glass will not crack.

Spatter Printing

If indoors, or working on a table, cover working area with several layers of newspaper. Select a leaf, flower, fern, or other material to spatter. It is preferable to have previously pressed the object flat. Choose paper and contrasting ink. Pin leaf on cardboard (on top of newspapers), putting pins at points and depressions so that the leaf lies very flat against the paper. Slant pins toward center of leaf or away from edge so pins will not retard spraying. Spatter by one of these methods:

1. With brush and knife or toothpick: Dip old toothbrush in ink or paint mixed to a thin-cream consistency; shake off excess. Hold near paper and leaf. Draw knife blade (or toothpick) across the brush with bristles at slight angle, bringing knife *toward* you making a spray of ink. Move the brush and knife around so ink sprays in desired places and gets desired intensity. Practice will be necessary to get even spattering without blots. Avoid getting too much ink or paint on brush.

2. With brush and screen: Dip brush in paint; shake off excess. Hold piece of fine wire screening in place and ''scrub'' or brush, moving around as above. Practice! A good method for screening which is not quite so messy is to make a frame from a cigar box or other box of similar size; remove top and bottom, using just the sides for a frame. Attach screening to top of box only. Place the

open bottom of box down on paper. Brush across screen, moving brush only to get spatters all over.

If paint quickly and thickly fills squares of the screen, there is too much paint on the brush. To get rid of excess paint on the screen, lay it on newspaper and rub, blotting off the excess paint. Delicate looking leaves with interesting edges and compound leaves make interesting designs. For a shadowing and depth effect do not use pressed leaves.

3. An atomizer or spray also can be used.

Spore Printing

This is a very different kind of printing. Spread a thin coat of a half-mucilage-half-water mixture (or slightly beaten egg white) onto a piece of thin cardboard. Cut off the stem of a mature, fully-opened mushroom directly under the cap. Place the cap, bottom down, in the middle of the cardboard. Cover the layout with a turned-over glass dish, and leave undisturbed for 24 hours. Remove both the dish and the mushroom and air dry.

Casting

Another method of preserving designs and imprints is through "casting." Casts can be made from a variety of materials such as plaster of paris, plastic, or paraffin wax. The casting material is in a liquid form and is poured into the mold. The hardening qualities of these materials cause it to "set" after which the mold can be removed. The result is a three-dimensional reproduction that can be handled and studied. The clear plastic casts permit the preservation of insect and plant life by imbedding them in their natural state in such a manner that they can be viewed from all angles. The discovery of an imprint of the paw of an animal and the making of a cast can be an interesting and educational experience for children and adults alike.

Plaster Casting

Plaster casts of animal tracks, snakes, mushrooms, leaves, fish, etc. may be used for wall plaques, bookends, paperweights, identification boards, and the like. Single tracks are best for plaster casting. Look for distinct tracks along streams, in sand or mud. Put a round or oblong form, or "collar," made of 2"-wide strips of tin or

cardboard (cut before you go into the field) around the track to hold
the plaster in place. The form should be 2-3 inches wider than the
print to be cast. Push this down into the mud or sand, leaving about
one inch above the surface. Mix the plaster of paris and water,
pouring the plaster into the water, to a thick, soupy consistency.
Pour the plaster into the track, filling the form to about one inch in
depth. Leave this in place for 2-3 hours to harden. The thicker the
mix the quicker it hardens. But if you get it too thick it may harden
before you can pour it! To reverse the track, put a cardboard mold
around the plaster of paris track which has been well greased with
petroleum jelly. Pour in some plaster of paris. Let it harden, then
knock it out. (It should drop out because of the petroleum jelly.) Now
you have a track as it appeared in the sand or mud.

Some tips: Stir plaster of paris with a disposable stick, not a
spoon. Sift plaster of paris into water without stirring, letting it sink
to bottom until no more will sink below the water surface, then add a
little more for good measure and stir. If you start to stir right away,
you may have a more difficult time adding more plaster of paris. If
the mixture becomes too hard before pouring, throw it out! Adding
salt will hasten setting; vinegar will retard. You can tint casts of
leaves and flowers with poster paints while plaster of paris is still
moist, or when dry with thinned oil paints. Air bubbles sometimes
are formed in the plaster in the process of stirring and pouring.
Jarring the cast while wet will help break many of these. To help
keep the cast from retaining so much sand or mud, shake talcum
powder into the track before pouring plaster.

Sand Casting

Put sand in a box of sufficient size to hold the object to be cast
and still leave a border on the sides. Dampen sand so the grains will
stick together. Finer sand sticks together better. Draw or carve
design in sand, or sink object to be molded. Use equal amounts of
water and plaster of paris — first placing water in container which can
be thrown away and sifting plaster in slowly so air bubbles will come
to the top. Stir until it starts to thicken. When you have a thick
"gravy," pour plaster into design, filling deepest depressions first.
If you are making plaques, a twisted wire stuck in the back will make
a wall hanger. Remove plaster when hardened, usually about an
hour. Some sand will stick to the plaster. It may be left for texture or
may be removed with a brush. Color (dry tempera) may be added to
the plaster of paris if a colored object is desired.

Plastic Casting

The use of plastics in the preservation of insect and plant specimens is one of the more recent developments to gain widespread popularity. The product can be used either for study or as a memento of an occasion or may serve as a paperweight. The plastic is purchased as a liquid to which a hardener is added, causing it to jell and become hard. The mold is half filled with the liquid; the insect or plant is then placed into the mold and more plastic is poured over the top. Thus the flower or insect is completely surrounded with a protective layer of clear plastic. Be sure that the mold is large enough. Keep the design simple and avoid overcrowding.

Sketching

Charcoal sketching can make use of native materials. Burn thin hardwood sticks in the campfire and then cover them with earth before they are consumed by the flames. This shuts off the air and allows the wood to char completely through. Finger sketching can be done with paints made from berries. Soft limestone and other rocks also may be used for drawing.

PRESERVATION

Drying Flowers

Flowers to be dried should be picked in prime condition just before the peak of bloom, although they may be dried in any stage of development before full bloom. If colors are to be retained the flowers must be perfectly fresh and should be picked when they are free of moisture. You may want to make new stems of florist's wire.

There are two primary materials for drying most flowers — silica gel or borax and corn meal. Silica gel is preferable as it absorbs moisture rapidly and thus retains color better. Also, while the initial cost may be more, it can be used again and again. When it loses its absorbency, it can be placed in a warm oven to restore this quality. It may be purchased at most garden centers and craft stores and is sold under the trade name of Flower-dri. When using silica gel, place the flower in a slanting position in a dish and then cover the flower entirely with silica gel. Cover the dish (a butter tub works well), and leave in a dark place for five to seven days.

For borax drying, pour about one inch of borax (or two inches of borax and corn meal mixture in 1:6 ratio) in a plastic bag or paper sack and place the flower upside down or face down on the borax. Pour more borax (mixture) gently around the flower until well covered (1-2''). Place flowers so they do not touch each other. Flowers and more borax may be added until the bag is almost full. Gather the top of the bag, squeeze the remaining air out of it, and tie with cord. Put in a dry, dark place for one to four weeks, depending on how much water the petals originally contained. Flower petals turn crisp when they are dried. Remove the flowers as soon as they are dried; they will lose their color if left too long. This method works well on marigolds, pansies, single roses, sweet peas, and similar woods flowers.

Pressing Flowers

Simply place flowers or leaves between sheets of absorbent paper under a weight. Leave for several days in a dry place. You may want to change absorbent paper occasionally. May be mounted, as on lampshades, and sprayed with clear plastic. See Pages 160-162 for proper procedures for pressing plants.

Sunbaked Flowers

Remove all leaves from the stems of the flowers. Pour one to two inches of sand in a shallow box, then place the flowers upside down on the sand, carefully pouring more sand over each flower to cover to a depth of about one inch. Be sure the flowers do not touch. Place the box of sand and flowers to bake in the sun. Two or three days will be ample. This method works well on the flowers mentioned above for borax drying.

Parchment

A method of preserving nature specimens to provide a useful product for items such as lampshades, note cards, booklet covers, etc., is to make a semitransparent parchment.

Place upon a piece of household waxed paper various nature specimens, leaves, butterflies, twigs, etc., in a pleasing design. It is preferable to have these objects pressed flat. Cover with a single piece of rice paper or sakuragami paper; a single facial tissue (separate the ordinary tissue into its layers) may also be used with good success. Using a stiff-bristled pastry brush, or other suitable brush, saturate the paper evenly with a tapping motion while applying a diluted mixture of white glue — 50 percent water and 50 percent Elmer's or other similar glue. Dry thoroughly. Iron between layers of brown wrapping paper with iron set for "silk," or press between weights to flatten. Ironing is preferable because it sets the wax into the parchment. Trim edges; a deckle edge can be made by tearing excess, using a straightedge.

Two pieces of rice paper may be used. "Wash" paper with glue after placing specimens between sheets and hang by clothespins to dry. Makes a good opaque "glass" for a door or other object.

DYEING

There is satisfaction and charm in making and using native dyes which are easily obtained from many vegetables, fruits, and trees.

onion skins: red or yellow
raspberries: dark red
bloodroot: red
beets: red violet
strawberries: red

goldenrod: yellow
pear leaves: dull yellow
sumac roots: yellow
celandine: yellow
tanglewood stems: yellow

mountain ash berries: orange
larkspur flowers: blue
pokeweed berries: purple
sassafras roots: pink
walnut hulls: rich dark brown

citron: yellow
blackberries: blue
dandelion roots: magenta
butternut bark: brown
sumac bark: brown

REFERENCES

Booklets and books that refer primarily to a single type of craft are listed under that specific craft. Books that cover a variety of crafts are cited under Nature Crafts (General). Although some references are quite old and out of print, they are still useful and often may be found in public or school libraries. County extension agents also frequently have helpful booklets.

Bark

Jaeger, Ellsworth. *Wildwood Wisdom.* Macmillan Company, New York, 1945.

Basketry

Basketry. Boy Scouts of America Merit Badge Series, New Brunswick, N.J., 1968.

Couch, Osma Palmer. *Basket Pioneering.* Judd Publishing, New York, 1947.

Fitzgerald, Sallie G. *The Priscilla Basketry Book.* American Reedcraft Corporation, Hawthorne, N.J., 1924.

Hammett, Catherine T., and Horrocks, Carol M. *Creative Crafts for Campers.* Association Press, New York, 1957, pp. 65-79.

Hart, Carol, and Hart, Dan. *Natural Basketry.* Watson-Guptill Publications, New York, 1976.

Jaeger, Ellsworth. *Wildwood Wisdom.* Macmillan Company, New York, 1945, pp. 76-80.

Cordage

Jaeger, Ellsworth. *Wildwood Wisdom.* Macmillan Company, New York, 1945.

Metcalf, Harlan G. *Whittlin', Whistles and Thingamajigs.* Stackpole Books, Harrisburg, Pa., 1974.

Driftwood

Ishimoto, Latuso. *The Art of Driftwood and Dried Arrangements.* Crown Publishers, Inc., New York, 1957.

Drying Flowers

Brooklyn Botanic Garden. *Dried Flower Design.* Brooklyn Botanic Garden, 1000 Washington Ave., Brooklyn, N.Y. 11225.

Squires, Mabel. *The Art of Drying Plants and Flowers.* M. Barrows and Company, New York, 1958.

Whitlock, Sarah, and Rankin, Martha. *Dried Flowers: How to Prepare Them.* Dover Publications, Inc., 180 Varick St., New York, N.Y. 10014, 1975. Inexpensive paperback for beginners. Excellent.

Dyeing

Adrosko, Rita J. *Natural Dyes and Home Dyeing.* Dover Publications, Inc., New York, 1971.

Brooklyn Botanical Garden. *Dye Plants and Dyeing—A Handbook.* Brooklyn Botanical Gardens, 1000 Washington Avenue, Brooklyn, N.Y. 11225. Includes plants from throughout the world.

Castino, Ruth. *Spinning and Dyeing the Natural Way.* Van Nostrand Reinhold Co., New York, 1974.

Gourds

Ornamental Gourds, U.S. Department of Agriculture. Farmers Bul. 1849, Washington, D.C., 1940.

Grasses

Shanklin, Margaret Eberhardt. *Use of Native Craft Materials.* Charles A. Bennett Company, Peoria, Ill., 1947.

Nature Crafts (General)

Bale, R. O. *Creative Nature Crafts.* Burgess Publishing Company, Minneapolis, 1959.

Benson, Kenneth, and Frankson, Carl. *Creative Nature Crafts.* Prentice-Hall, Englewood Cliffs, N.J., 1968.

Carlson, Reynold. *Nature Lore Manual for Church Leaders.* No. 60-H, Methodist Publishing House, Nashville, Tenn., 1953. Primarily leaf prints, plaster casts.

Griswold, Lester. *Handicraft.* Prentice-Hall, Englewood Cliffs, N.J., 1963. Basketry, ceramics, cord weaving, lapidary, weaving, leatherwork, metalwork.

Hammett, Catherine, and Horrocks, Carol. *Creative Crafts for Campers.* Association Press, New York, 1957.

Hillcourt, William. *The New Field Book of Nature Activities and Hobbies.* G. P. Putnam's Sons, New York, 1970.

Hunt, Ben W. *The Golden Book of Crafts and Hobbies.* Simon and Schuster, New York, 1957.

Jaeger, Ellsworth. *Nature Crafts.* Macmillan Company, New York, 1953.
————. *Wildwood Wisdom.* Macmillan Company, New York, 1945. Cordage, barkcraft, and camp furnishings only.

Metcalf, Harlan G. *Whittlin', Whistles and Thingamajigs.* Stackpole Books, Harrisburg, Pa., 1974.

Musselman, Virginia W. *Learning About Nature Through Crafts.* Stackpole Books, Harrisburg, Pa., 1969.

Nagle, Avery, and Leeming, Joseph. *Fun With Nature Crafts.* Lippincott, Philadelphia, 1964.

Shanklin, Margaret. *Use of Native Craft Materials.* Charles A. Bennett Company, Peoria, Ill., 1947. Straw, corn, grass, rush, clay, and miscellany.

Spear, Marion R. *Keeping Idle Hands Busy.* Burgess Publishing Company, Minneapolis, 1950. Acorns, bayberries, birch bark, cactus, citrus peel, clay, corks, cornhusks, driftwood, feathers, fish scales and bones, hollyhocks, honeysuckle vines, horsehair, moss, milkweed—some of the lesser known native materials used for crafts.

Vinal, William G. *Nature Recreation,* second edition. Dover Publications, New York, 1963.

Nature Pixies

Jaeger, Ellsworth. *Nature Crafts.* Macmillan Company, New York, 1953.
Spear, Marion R. *Keeping Idle Hands Busy.* Burgess Publishing Company, Minneapolis, 1950.

Pods

Van Rensselaer, Eleanor. *Decorating With Pods and Cones.* Van Nostrand, Princeton, N.J., 1957.

Rocks (Lapidary, Chipping)

Griswold, Lester. *Handicraft.* Prentice-Hall, Englewood Cliffs, N.J., 1963.

Whittling and Woodcarving

Hunt, Ben W. *Whittling With Ben Hunt.* Bruce Publishing Company, 2642 University Ave., St. Paul, Minn. 55114, 1959.
Metcalf, Harlan G. *Whittlin', Whistles and Thingamajigs.* Stackpole Books, Harrisburg, Pa., 1974.
Pynn, LeRoy. *Whittling Is Easy.* Boy Scouts of America, New Brunswick, N.J., 1945.
Waltner, Elma. *Carving Animal Caricatures.* Taplinger, 29 East 10th St., New York, N.Y. 10003, 1958.

CHAPTER III

Nature Games

NATURE-ORIENTED GAMES can serve several useful functions provided they are used appropriately. Games are *not* a substitute for the study of nature, nor should they be considered a necessary device to "sugar-coat" or entice youngsters to learn about nature, implying that nature is not interesting in and of itself. Games can be used in many settings with youth groups, but they should always be used in a supplementary manner to the actual nature study and direct activity. Four functions which games can serve in the nature-oriented program are:

1. Fun in the recreational period and free time.
2. Reinforcement of prior teachings.
3. Teach knowledge, skill, appreciation.
4. Stimulate new interests through introducing new areas of knowledge and skill.

MAP AND COMPASS GAMES
Area Identification

Have a compass course laid out along a circular path. At point #1 have the person list all the objects within a designated area that are foreign to the environment—pieces of paper, foil, cloth, marbles, etc. At point #2 have person identify the leaves within a marked circle. At point #3 have cardboard animals along the path and let the person identify only the animals that are native to the area. Many other points for different types of identification could be added. The player with the most correct answers wins.

Compass Relay

Select team members and station them at certain points along the course, with their locations unknown to the other team members. The first runner has the readings for the entire team. He takes the first reading which will lead him to the second runner who takes the next reading and runs to the third team member, etc. The first team to finish wins. A maximum time limit should be set.

Compass Treasure Hunt

Individuals are given a list of readings (of similar difficulties and distance) which go different ways but all end at the same place. At this place there is a prize hidden for the first one who gets there.

Competitive Compass Game

This game may be played individually or in teams. On a 100' line, beginning positions are marked one to twenty. Each player has a card with a series of three different compass readings, each ending on the beginning line. Each player or team begins with 100 points. In scoring, one point is subtracted for each foot that the player is away from the place on the line where he is supposed to finish. A pack of 20 cards to play the game is available from Silva, Inc., La Porte, Indiana.

Map Search

Teams of two players are given a topographical map and grid and azimuth readings, with instructions to locate a designated point. First team to find that point wins.

Map Symbol Quiz

Give each player a series of map symbols which he must identify. Winner is the one who has the most correct. For variation, give a series of words and ask the participants to draw the symbols.

Square Play

In a large outdoor area each player walks in a straight line for 400 feet; turns left 90 degrees and walks for 400 feet; turns left again and walks 400 feet; and once more repeats the procedure. The player coming closest to his starting point is the winner. You may also use the same procedure with a triangular pattern—40 degrees for 100 feet; 160 degrees for 100 feet; and 280 degrees for 100 feet. Be sure the starting point, which is also the ending point, is not an obvious landmark which the participant can recognize readily and walk to regardless of his compass reading. A twig, small rock, or golf tee pushed into the ground are suitably inconspicuous.

CAMPCRAFT GAMES

With all nature-oriented activities, but especially with camp-craft activities, special concern should be taken for the conservation of the natural environment. For example, on the three games requiring the building of fires, care should be taken to use only the minimum amount of fuel, and for the games requiring chopping of a log or the lashing of sticks, logs and saplings or sticks should be taken from the source with care. Safety should also be paramount in conducting campcraft games.

Bucking Contest

This is a contest to see who can saw a log with a bucksaw the fastest. Use an 8-inch log about 12 feet long resting on two sawbucks. Buckers take turns sawing against time. Each person is called upon to saw off two pieces, one from each end—having sawed one he runs quickly to the other end and repeats. (Try to have saws of comparable sharpness!)

Campcraft Tournament

Suggested events include the contests described in this section on campcraft games. Select those suitable to the skills of the participants and the length of time available. Tournament may be participated in by team groups or by individuals.

Endless Rope

Players stand in a circle of 6-8 players each. Each player has a small length of rope. The leader calls out a certain knot. The first player ties his rope to that of the second player using this knot, the second player ties his to the next, and so on around the circle. When a continuous rope circle is completed, the rope is held up. Time and the correctness of the knots determines the winning circle.

Fire-building Contest

Each player is given two matches; he must find his own tinder and kindling. The first to lay a fire and have it burn for two minutes is the winner.

Fuzz Stick Contest

Each participant using his own knife is given a piece of wood of a certain size (or have him find his own wood) and given a time limit. Judges then decide which individual made the best fuzz stick according to number and length of shavings. Caution safety, particularly when trying to be speedy with a knife. Violation of safety procedures should result in disqualification of the participant.

Hand Axe Accuracy

Place a small stick or match upright on a chopping block. Contestant tries to split the stick or ignite the match with an accurate axe blow. The one who comes closest to performing the task wins.

Knot-tying One Step Forward

Players are arranged along a starting line each with a length of rope. The leader calls the name of a knot and begins to count, setting time limits according to knot difficulty. At the end of the count, players should be done, with the rope on the floor in front of them. If the knot is tied correctly they may advance one step. The player reaching the finish line first becomes the next leader.

Knot-tying Relay

Players are in a circle each holding a small length of rope while "it" walks around the outside of the circle. He calls the name of a knot and taps one of the players. Both run, in opposite directions, around the circle tying the knot on the way. The last player to return to the open space is "it" if the other's knot is tied correctly.

Lashing Contest

Teams of two people lash various kinds of lashings as indicated. Those finishing first with the neatest job receive a point. Winner is the team which accumulates the most points.

One-hand Tie

Two players in a team are to tie the knots indicated by the leader with each using only one hand. Players cannot switch hands after starting. Team that completes the knot first wins. Game can be made competitive by choosing the best knot tyers from each group and having a contest with series of five or more knots.

Overhand Knot

Each player is give a small length of rope and asked to make an overhand knot without releasing either end of rope (the trick is to cross your arms, pick up both ends of rope, and straighten arms).

Pole-chopping Contest

Use log 8 inches thick, cut into 6-foot lengths. Hand axe or regular axe may be used (reduce size of log for hand axe). Person chopping through in least time wins.

Skudding

Teams of four snake or drag a log with a rope for 100 yards against time. Log should be 1 foot in diameter and 10 feet long. (Modify for size of contestants.) Rope is tied to log with a timber hitch.

Square Knot Gamble

Players are in a circle, each with a short length of rope which they hold behind them. They then tie their ropes together behind their backs, using square knots; and when all are finished, they lean back on the completed rope circle. If they all have tied the knot correctly, the rope will hold; if one has tied a "granny," the rope will not hold.

String-burning Contest

Stretch string or binder twine 12'' above the ground (a prepared fire-site area). String must be long enough for 4-6 contestants at a time. Each contestant lays a fire of his choice beneath the twine. He may build it as high as the twine, but no higher. A second string 18'' high is stretched above the first string. Now remove the 12''-high string. At the leader's signal, each contestant lights his fire. He may add additional fuel after it is lighted. Whoever first burns the string in two wins.

Tent Peg and Sliver

Each person must have an axe, a piece of dead wood 2'' thick and 15'' long, and a chopping block. Judges then determine who made the best tent peg and the thinnest sliver in a given length of time.

Tent Pitching

Small, two-person tents are used to have a contest in speed *and neatness* of pitching.

Water-boiling Contest

Each player is given a cupful of water in a coffee can and two matches. The one who can build a fire and boil the water first is the winner. For ease of judging, add one tablespoon of a sudsing detergent. It will foam and boil over the can.

HIKING GAMES

Beeline Hike

A compass bearing is taken and followed to the destination desired. Objects in the path must be climbed over or under, or be pushed through.

Heads and Tails Hike

One person flips a coin at the junction of each trail, road, or street to determine a new direction. Heads — go to the right; tails — to the left.

Hold the Front, or Number-One Spot

The leader is followed by the hikers in single file as they march along the trail. The leader then asks questions about things observed such as "What is the name of that bird?" If the first one (No. 1) in line answers correctly he stays in his position. If he cannot answer correctly, he moves to the rear of the line and No. 2 attempts to answer the question. Each player who fails to give the proper response goes to the rear of the line. The object is to stay in the No. 1 position as long as possible.

Variation: Sentinel

Hikers walk single file. The lead person is the "sentinel." He may find a tree, rock, flower, weed, or any nature object which he can positively identify. He stops. Each hiker passes by and must either whisper correctly the name of the object or go to the end of the line. The new leader becomes the "sentinel" and the old "sentinel" goes behind those who answered correctly but in front of those who answered incorrectly. The object of the game is to get as near the head of the line as possible and to become "sentinel" as often as possible.

I Spy

(For primary grades.) Leader may say "I spy a robin." All children who see the robin may squat; the rest remain standing. The leader then points out the robin or asks one of the squatting children to do so. The group continues hiking until another object of interest is seen.

Variation: Pebble Cribbage

Each person picks up ten small stones which he carries in his hand or pocket. As the group hikes along, the leader points out some nature object. Everyone tries to identify the object. When the correct name is determined, all those identifying it correctly in their minds may drop a stone. The one who has dropped all his stones first wins. All must agree to play fair!

Nature Far and Near

Make a list of twenty or thirty items to be found along the route with a score for each, for example:

bird's nest:	10 points	frog:	60 points
live snake:	15 points	animal track:	5 points
monarch butterfly:	5 points	flying crane:	15 points

Points should reflect difficulty of finding. First player to observe one of these items and report it to the leader gets the points.

Nature Scouting

Designate several points, on a map of the camp, park, or other area, that are about an equal distance from the starting point. Divide the group into teams and send each team on a scouting trip to a different point. About fifteen minutes should be allowed for the trip. When the teams have returned, they are asked to give a report to the group on what they have seen. This serves as an excellent basis upon which to plan a campfire program. The reports are particularly interesting when the groups can describe the things that they saw with such clarity that the leader or someone else can make iden- tifications.

Variation: Signs of History

Find signs of history that are typical to the area. Such objects of history are as follows: old roads and bridges, deserted buildings, old stone fences, rock piles and contents, old trees (must be able to tell how old trees are), arrowheads, cemeteries, historical markers, pieces of glass and metal, and old paths.

Variation: Observation

Children are given a list of things to look for on a hike, perhaps with questions. They write down what they see or the answers to the questions and discuss them when they return.

TRAILING GAMES

Hare and Hounds

One player, the "hare," is given a ten-minute start on the "hounds" and lays a trail by dropping corn, acorns, leaves. The hounds attempt to trail and catch the hare.

Tree Trailing

Hide messages in various places and send out groups 15-30 minutes apart. The first message may read, "Take the valley trail to the east until you see a large yellow willow" with messages of this kind following in order. The object of the game is not to complete the trail in the fastest time, but to follow the trail the greatest distance, so the trail should grow more difficult as it goes along.

HUNTING GAMES

Find the Trees

Players are in groups of six. Give each group the pictures but not the names of ten trees that are in the immediate area. Have a balance between common and lesser-known trees in each set so that every group will have an equal chance to locate them — or have all trees alike in each group.

On signal, each group carefully examines the pictures and then tries to find the corresponding trees in the wooded area. If the players do not know the tree's name but can identify it as being the same as in the picture, they may receive 5 points — or 10 points for a tree which they both identify and name.

After a designated time, call the search to an end. Reassemble the players. Ask the group finding the assigned ten trees, or most of them, to prove their answers by showing the other players the location of each tree for which the members have a picture.

Variation: Bird Nest Hunt

Divide the group into teams. In a limited time, see which group can locate the most bird's nests, for each of which they receive 3 points. If they can tell the kind of bird that built the nest, they get an extra 5 points. NOTE: *Nests should not be disturbed.*

Variation: Curio Collector

Leader gives the group the name of something to be found, for example, a stump of a tree more than one hundred years old or a tree struck by lightning. The individuals scatter to find the object, the first person finding it calling the rest of the group to see the curio. The leader then names the next object to be searched for.

Photography Treasure Hunt

Couples go out on photographic expeditions much after the fashion of the scavenger hunt. Each has a camera and flash bulbs. They are instructed to get pictures of still life (landscapes, trees), animal life (birds, dogs), or the picture taking may be confined to a single kind such as of trees. The couples are to return after a specified time to develop the pictures and put them on display.

Scavenger Hunts

Participants are divided into small groups of 4-6 or into pairs. Each group is given identical lists of things found in nature. First group back with a correct and complete list wins. NOTE: Stress conservation practices.

Variation: Alphabet Scavenger Hunt

Players bring in objects beginning with different letters of the alphabet which have been specified, such as A,B,C,D—acorns, buttercups, cones, and dogwood leaves. First player to get all items wins.

Some suggestions regarding scavenger hunts:

1. Have the people involved use what they can find in the immediate environment.
2. Have some things easy to find and others more difficult so that it is a challenge.
3. You can give identification books if participants are in doubt as to what some things are.
4. Decide on the length of time and then call players in promptly.
5. Supply containers to put things in.
6. Make sure that the groups are divided fairly as to daring, physical vigor, and knowledge about nature.

7. Use the facts previously learned on hikes or in nature study groups.
8. Do not send players anyplace where there are such hazards as poison ivy, marshes, cliffs.
9. There should be at least one adult leader with each group of six or eight children.
10. Suit your hunt to the group's abilities.
11. The things specified should be within the area and able to be secured within the time limit set.
12. After items are collected, they should not merely be thrown away, but should be identified and commented upon.
13. Do not give names only, but sometimes use other identifying factors to elicit more interest or comment.

The following are items which have actually been used in nature scavenger hunts with fifth- and sixth-graders and older children in a summer camp:

tendril from grape vine
3 different-shaped leaves from the *same* tree
pickerelweed leaf
2 kinds of willow leaves
leaf with vein parallel to margin
leaf with more than 9 leaflets
tail of cattail
snail
frog
mosquito
thorn from hawthorn
fungus
leaf with 5 leaflets
ant
cicada skin
leaf of water lily
moth
5-leaf grouping
burdock
grass gone to seed
fragrant seed from tree
dragonfly

dwarf sumac leaf
beetle
mullein leaf
pebble or rock showing effects of erosion
black locust thorn
8-legged animal
flower of Queen Anne's lace
twin cup of acorn
leaf, white on underside with flat stem
dogwood leaf
oak leaf with bristles
sprig of fern
red top of sumac
elm leaf
sycamore leaf
mayfly
clover leaf or flower
milkweed
fly
little round wafer from tree (seed from elm tree)
3-leaf plant that's harmless and good cattle feed

QUIET GAMES: OBSERVATION

Animal Tracks

Use a set of plaster cast animal tracks for a quiz.

Bird Silhouettes

Hold up flash cards of bird silhouettes. Groups may shout out the name, and the first group so doing gets a point; or each group may write down its answer, and at the end the one with the most correct answers wins. This may also be done with tree silhouettes.

Variation: Card Flash

The picture of some nature object is flashed before the group for a brief period and then removed. The members of the group attempt to describe it correctly. After a short time it is again shown to the group. This time they try to see what they missed the first time or what erroneous impressions they received.

Kim's Game

The leader places about 20 nature objects on a table and puts a cover over them. Each team in turn is brought to the table and the cloth removed for one minute. The team goes back to its place and lists all the objects it can recall. One point for each object.

Variation: Name Me

Interesting natural objects, each with a number, are scattered about the room. Each player tries to specifically identify as many as possible. One with the longest list of correct names wins.

Mystery Bag

Have nature items in boxes or bags into which the participant cannot see. Have each person feel the item in each bag and list what he thinks it is. One with longest correct list wins.

Variation: Blind as a Bat

Blindfolded player is led by another to various nature items about the room. As blindfolded person touches objects, he tells "keeper" what he has found. Longest list wins. Several people are blindfolded at the same time. Keeper may not talk to partner to give hints.

Variation: Shadowgraph

Suspend a white sheet as a curtain with a bright light behind it. Pass several objects behind the sheet so that a shadow is cast. Use such nature objects as a small pine tree, a stuffed bird, a pine cone, a cattail, or a large leaf. Let audience use a sheet of paper to write names of objects.

Observation Lotto

Each person is given a card similar to the one shown in the diagram (p. 92). On seeing an object on his card, he may put an X in the appropriate square (or use a marker from nature such as a pebble). Play as in lotto or bingo—the first to fill a row horizontally, vertically, or diagonally wins. May get 2nd, 3rd, etc., places by continuing until others have completed a row. Finding the object may be done in several ways: Outdoors, as you hike along, look around and when someone sees something that is on his card, he calls it out. Photos could be held up, or the leader could just name the various objects from shuffled cards he picks up.

RABBIT	WILD MUSTARD	BIRDHOUSE	ROBIN
STREAM or RIVER	BIRD FEEDER	FLOCK OF SPARROWS	REFORESTATION AREA
PINE TREE	SQUIRREL	BIRD BATH	ERODED LAND
BLACKBIRD	OAK TREE	"DEER CROSSING"	VULTURE

Sounds

While resting, hikers may sit quietly and write down all of the sounds they hear in a designated period of time. The longest list wins.

What Is Wrong With This Picture?

Announce that a certain nature object is to be described and, although most of the characteristics given will be true, a few false ones will be included. See how many can detect the incorrect ones.

Woodcraft Hike

Pictures of birds and constellations; blueprints of leaves; and actual plants, twigs and rocks are placed around the room. The leader explains that all are to take a hike in the room. The teams then draw to see which one starts first. They set off at intervals, the team captains armed with pencils and paper. Each team is to make up a yarn about what they see and note the various plants, twigs, etc. At the end of the hike the teams are given a few minutes to write the stories. These are read and the best one chosen.

QUIET GAMES: ACTION

Bird Description

See who can imitate the call or song of the most birds. Have someone give a description of a bird and see if others can identify it. Describe birds seen on the trail and ask who saw each bird, what kind of flight it had, shape, size of beak, and other questions. Also, name a well-known bird in the locality and see how many interesting things can be told about it. Can also use individually by putting a picture of a bird on each person's back without telling him what bird it is. Each person asks questions of others trying to identify the bird on his own back. Variations: Use fish, animals, or other nature category.

Flower Authors

Use a set of 48 cards with 12 pictures of flowers with corresponding 12 pictures of leaves, 12 family names of leaves, and 12 with place and time of flower's blooming. Four teams are each given 12 cards and the names of 3 flowers. The team selects from its own cards those belonging to the names it was given, then goes to the other teams, trying to trade cards so that they can complete their full three sets for the 3 names of flowers they were given.

Nature Charades

Played like regular charades, either in teams or individually, by acting out the word. Some examples of nature categories:

Flowers

carnation	car-nation
sweetpea	sweet-pea
dogwood	dog-wood
marigold	Mary-gold
lady slipper	lady-slip-her
lady finger	lady-finger
foxglove	fox-glove
touch-me-not	touch-me-not
primrose	prim-rows
four-o'clock	four-oh-clock
bittersweet	bit-her-sweet

Birds

sparrow	spare-row
thrasher	thrash-her
towhee	tow-he
warbler	war-blur
woodpecker	wood-peck-her
vireo	very-oh
kingfisher	king-fisher
killdeer	kill-deer
pintail	pin-tail
catbird	cat-bird
grosbeak	gross-beak

Trees

basswood	bass-wood
hornbeam	horn-beam
buckeye	buck-eye
catalpa	cat-tall-pa
sycamore	sick-ah-more
walnut	wall-nut
tulip tree	two-lip-tree
tamarack	tam-ah-rack
mulberry	mull-berry
chestnut	chest-nut

Variation: Animal Antics

Group is divided into small teams of 6-8 players. Leader tells the name of a mammal, bird, or reptile to two players from each team. First player on the team imitates the locomotion of the animal, the second person the call. The rest of the team attempt to identify the object. First to do so receives one point. For variation, players may draw the object instead of imitating it.

Variation: Rabbit Race

Each player arranges four large leaves in a Y formation on the ground, with one leaf for each upper prong and two on the single stem. Tell the players that the first two leaves at the top represent the location of rabbit's rear feet. Have them race to see who can get in correct rabbit position first (feet on two top leaves with hands between legs on stem of Y). When all are in proper postion, ask them to practice how a rabbit runs (put hands down in their respective tracks in front and then jump so feet will overreach hands, forming a Y again just ahead of the old one. Then race in this manner, doing the hop sequentially.

Nature Crows and Cranes

Group is divided into two teams that face each other along two lines 10-12 feet apart (teams stand behind lines). Twenty-five feet or more behind each line is a goal. The crows are "true" and the cranes "false." The leader makes a statement. If it is true, the "trues" chase the "falses" — the crows chase the cranes. Any crane caught by a crow before he crosses his own goal line becomes a crow and must join the other side. If the statement is false, cranes chase crows, etc. Winner is team with most players at the end or when one team as accumulated all the players. Sample statements:

1. The firefly is a beetle. (T)
2. All bats are blind. (F)
3. All snakes are poisonous. (F)
4. A toad swallows his own skin when shedding. (T)
5. Spiders are insects. (F)
6. Mosquitos have four wings. (T)
7. The North Star is the brightest star in the sky. (F)
8. The earth is the largest planet. (F)
9. Chipmunks sleep in the winter. (T)
10. Toads cause warts. (F)
11. Sheep chew cuds like cows. (T)
12. White pine trees have fine needles in a bundle (fascicle). (T)
13. Only the male mosquito bites. (F)
14. Snakes are slimy. (F)

Be sure each individual knows the correct answer before asking another question.

Variation: Tree Tag

One or more persons are "it." Players are safe only when they are touching a tree of a particular kind designated. Change the kind of tree from time to time.

Star Groups

You can use 18-36 players. Players use outlines of constellations formed by flashlights around the campfire. Divide into two teams, each team having 8 or more players and a captain. A leader with a knowledge of astronomy is the judge. Each player should have a good flashlight, the light end loosely covered with a piece of yellow crepe paper held in place by a rubber band. When leader calls Lyra, each team runs to the fire and holds the flashlights above their heads. Each player takes the position of one star in the constellation named. Captain uses two or three players to form the brightest star in each group, such as stars of the first and second magnitude. When the team captain has his constellation formed and the players who are not required are sent back to the edge of the circle, he calls, "ready." The judge then examines the group to check the correctness of the formation for shape, the number of the stars, and star spacing. The first team to form the most nearly correct group wins 2 points.

Variation: May be done indoors using paper, pebbles, or other objects as stars to make the constellations on the floor.

What Am I?

A player leaves the room and the group decides what animal or other nature object he shall represent. The player returns and tries to discover what he represents by asking questions on characteristics that may be answered by "yes" or "no." When he identifies himself, the person whose answer helped him make the discovery leaves the room next.

Variation: Ask a player to think of an object and write it down on a slip of paper. The rest of the group may then ask him questions which can be answered "yes" or "no" until they find out what the object is.

Variation: Have a panel of 4 who ask questions. They may play as "20 questions" and ask only 20 questions, taking turns, or they may ask any number of questions.

Variation: Have a number of clues describing a nature object written on a card with the most difficult clue listed first and each clue becoming easier or more obvious. Read the clues one at a time until someone guesses what the object is. The player guessing correctly gets to keep the card. If an equal number of clues are used for all objects one might give scores by the number of clues it takes to guess the object.

QUIET GAMES: PENCIL AND PAPER

An Astronomy Test

What planet, star, or constellation do each of the following describe?

1. Worshipped by the Phoenicians as a god. It is a constellation near Vega. It was called "The Phantom" or "The Kneelex" by the Greeks. A hero of Greek mythology who was noted for his strength.

2. A planet discovered in 1846 which is not visible to the naked eye. A Roman god of the sea.

3. The planet nearest to the sun. This smallest planet can best be seen in March, April, August, and September. A mythical god of the Romans who carried messages.

4. This constellation is composed of six stars forming a bowl. It appears to be about halfway up the southern sky in the spring. The opening at the top of a volcano.

5. This constellation contains a cluster of stars known as "The Beehive." It is sometimes known as "The Crab." A dreaded disease.

6. A constellation located in the Milky Way. It is sometimes called the "Northern Cross." The flying swan.

Answers: 1. Hercules   3. Mercury   5. Cancer
Answers: 2. Neptune   4. Crater   6. Cygnus

Building Birds

Start with the name of a bird (or other category) and build horizontally or vertically, like in anagrams. An example is on p. 98.

```
        THRUSH
C    O    C
R    BLUEJAY
O    I    T
WREN      B      O          C
        KINGBIRD            H
    S    B R    I C         I
    TURTLEDOVE O A          C
    A    U      L R         K
    R    E      MEADOWLARK
    L    B          I       D
    I    I          N       E
    N    R          A       E
    G    D          L
```

Buried Birds (Flowers, Trees)

Give each team a series of sentences. Within the sentences are names of birds. Object is to underscore the name of the bird which is "buried." Names should be either in one word or adjacent. For example, in Statement 2, "robin" is found in the words "rob" and "in." Flowers, trees, and birds are given as examples. You may wish to make up your own or have each team make 5-10 sentences of buried words; then, compile and give the total list to all groups for identification of the buried items. The group to find the most wins.

Bird Examples

1. The wolves howled at midnight. (owl)
2. It takes a brave bandit to rob in daylight. (robin)
3. Do doctors always charge so much? (dodo)
4. Do ventilate the new house better. (dove)
5. This pencil is a half-inch longer. (finch)
6. "Hit a fly," catcher Jones shouted from the dugout. (Flycatcher)
7. Fred started up suddenly from his reading. (red start)
8. You can't kill deer without a license. (killdeer)
9. Ralph patted her on the cheek jokingly. (heron)
10. I sent the pastor a Venetian vase. (raven)
11. The boy left the porch with awkward strides. (hawk)

12. The window looks over the garden. (owl)
13. He saw them both rush down the alley. (thrush)
14. Her eyes wandered over the curious crowd. (swan)
15. The crown lay shattered on the granite floor. (crow)
16. Bungalow rents are out of proportion of those of apartments.
     (wren)
17. The old horse seemed to wheeze worse than usual. (towhee)

Flower Examples

1. After you wash the pans, you may prepare lunch. (pansy)
2. I had to pay several taxes on this car: national tax, state tax, and
   city tax. (carnation)
3. Did Chopin know Beethoven? (pink)
4. If this car goes any faster I will fall out. (aster)
5. The plane is now dropping food to the marooned people.
   (snowdrop)
6. Before we knew it, the rhinoceros entered the water. (rose)
7. I believe it is the best plane money can buy. (anemone)
8. That scow slips through the water like a rowboat. (cowslip)
9. I understand that the panda is your favorite animal. (daisy)
10. Is your porch identical to ours? (orchid)

Tree Examples

1. Bring me a long strap, please. (apple)
2. The pin extended under the skin. (pine)
3. A bumblebee chased him about the lawn. (beech)
4. The wind came up so a kite was flown. (oak)
5. The map led us to a lonely swamp. (maple)
6. Does chapel make you sleepy, too? (elm)
7. The ball bounced artistically down the field. (cedar)
8. The plumes waved in the air. (plum)
9. I will owe you the balance. (willow)
10. We found the owl in dense swamp brush. (linden)
11. Nancy pressed Randolph's suit neatly. (cypress)
12. The airplane appeared out of the clouds. (pear)
13. Beautiful arches adorned the walls. (larch)
14. He must leap each hurdle in turn. (peach)
15. He went as hurriedly as possible. (ash)
16. The teacher held erasers to throw at the ruffian. (elder)

Categories, Guggenheim, Nature Squares, Versatility

May play as individuals or in teams or groups. Draw chart as below: (You can change the letters at the top by heading columns with T-R-A-I-L or using the letters of your name. The categories on the left also may be changed.)

	A	B	C	D	E
TREES					
BIRDS					
ANIMALS					
FLOWERS					

Example: Fill in spaces as indicated.
  e.g., first line (trees) — apple, birch, cedar, dogwood, elm
  or if you change the letters at the top to TRAIL, line two might be teal, raven, albatross, ibis, lark.
Give one point for each correct answer.

Variation: Single Letter Categories

List all of one category with names beginning with designated letter, e.g., using N and BIRDS — nuthatch, nighthawk, nutcracker, etc.

Variation: Tail and Head Categories

Any word of the category may be written in the first column; in the second column, though, the word must begin with the last letter of the word in column one; third column word begins with last letter of column-two word, etc., e.g., nuthatch, hawk, killdeer, robin, nutcracker, etc.

Other Variations

Players sit in a circle. One player starts by naming a nature category, such as trees, birds, flowers, etc. Each player going around the circle must then name something in the category, such as trees: oak, maple, cottonwood, etc. Game can be made more difficult by having to name them in alphabetical order: apple, birch, cottownwood, dogwood, etc. A player who cannot name something goes to "end" of circle.

Find the Trees in the Forest

The forest puzzle contains more than twenty species of trees. Can you locate them? The way to find them is to begin with any letter and spell out the trees by moving in any direction without skipping a square. You may go diagonally and repeat a letter if you so desire. Example: Begin with the M in the lower righthand corner and spell MAPLE. When using with a group, enlarge the square to full-sized sheet.

G	F	Y	E	W
I	R	C	H	M
B	A	E	L	O
L	D	B	P	U
I	H	S	A	M

Forest

D	O	T	Y	N	M	T
U	O	R	A	E	L	O
K	C	U	J	B	U	I
U	A	N	I	H	S	G
L	R	E	T	R	D	A
W	E	G	K	I	P	N
H	O	T	L	A	R	E

Aviary

Variation: Aviary

In the aviary there are 20 different bird names in the "pens." List all you can find. Try to learn something distinctive about each bird you find.

A Hiking Romance

Each player fills in blank spaces with names of trees and flowers. One point for each correct answer.

This romance began on a hike one day. It is true that he had met her once before down at the __(beech)__ , where he was a lifeguard, but they had not been formally introduced until the day of the hike.

Her name was   (rose)   Budd, while his name was   (red, cotton, or dog)   Wood.

She was very (poplar) with all the boys. In fact, (phlox) of them hung around her home. Her (poppy) was afraid she would wed some ne'er-do-well. He wanted her to (marigold) so that she could have all of the comforts and luxuries she wanted. She had always said, however, that anyone was (plum) crazy who married for anything but love.

(Red) Wood thought that she was a (peach) and he fell in love with her at first sight. The hike gave him his opportunity to tell her about it. " (Yew) are a real (American) beauty. (Yew) are the (apple) of my eye.'' Thereupon he (aster) to marry him.

She loved him but she pretended to doubt his faithfulness. "What (lady's slipper) did I see in your possession the other day?'' she parried. "Oh, that belonged to my brother, (Sweet) William. It was his wife's,'' he replied earnestly. "Oh, (rosemary) me or I'll have a (bleeding heart). It is near to breaking now. If you only knew how I (pine) for you.''

Just then her little brother Johnny fell down. He continued to lie where he had fallen and sure did   (balsam)   . His big sister called to him: "(Johnny-jump-up)   you're not hurt.'' "Oh, sis,'' he yelled back at her, "How can you   (lilac)   that?''

(Red) resumed his courting, and thought of a little French that he had learned in his four years at college. "Mon (cherry) (cherie) je t'aime.'' Since that was all the French he could remember he fell back on perfectly good English. "Let me press your (tulips)   to mine.'' Johnny thought he was a big   (prune) , but she thought he was wonderful. "You're a (daisy) ,'' she said as she cuddled in his arms. "We will be married at (four-o'clock) tomorrow.

So   (jack-in-the-pulpit)   performed the ceremony, and all of their days were blessed.

Name These Trees

Give players sheets of paper with pictures of leaves from trees common in your locale. Players are to identify the trees. Twelve common leaves are pictured here. You may reproduce these or substitute others. (Names are put on for convenience; remove when preparing for actual use.)

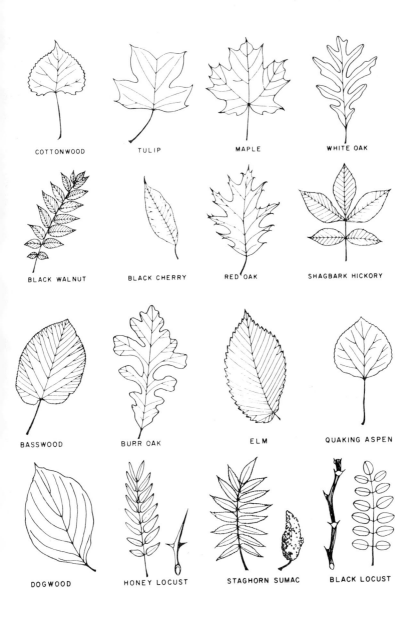

COTTONWOOD TULIP MAPLE WHITE OAK

BLACK WALNUT BLACK CHERRY RED OAK SHAGBARK HICKORY

BASSWOOD BURR OAK ELM QUAKING ASPEN

DOGWOOD HONEY LOCUST STAGHORN SUMAC BLACK LOCUST

Nature Riddles

Bird Riddles

Each individual or team group writes down answers as leader reads riddle. Winner: person or team with highest correct total.

1. A bright bird, whose first name is that of a city. (Baltimore oriole)
2. To peddle. (hawk)
3. Less than the whole and a long line of hills. (partridge)
4. The period of darkness, the reverse of out, and a high wind. (night-in-gale)
5. An instrument for driving horses, impecunious, and a boy's name. (whip-poor-will)
6. A monarch and an angler. (king-fisher)
7. A boy's nickname, an exclamation, and a part of a chain. (bob-o-link)
8. The bird of imitations. (mocking bird)
9. A tree, an insect product, and part of a bird. (cedar-waxwing)
10. A young fowl and two letters of the alphabet. (chick-a-dee)

Tree Riddles

1. What tree always sighs and languishes? (pine)
2. What tree is made of stone? (lime)
3. What tree grows nearest the sea? (beech)
4. What tree always has a partner? (pear)
5. What tree is pulled from the water with a hook? (bass)
6. What tree is often found in bottles? (cork)
7. What is the straightest tree that grows? (plum)
8. What tree is older than most other trees? (elder)
9. What tree is always found after a fire? (ash)
10. What tree do ladies wear around their necks? (fir)
11. What tree wages a war on crops? (locust)
12. What tree is the neatest tree that grows? (spruce)
13. What tree is often found in people's mouths? (gum)
14. What tree runs over the meadows and pastures? (yew)
15. What tree does everyone carry in his hand? (palm)
16. What tree is an awful grouch? (crab)
17. What tree is particularly useful in snow and rain? (rubber)
18. What tree grieves more than any other? (weeping willow)
19. What tree is worn in the Orient? (sandal)
20. What tree describes a pretty girl? (peach)
21. What tree is used in kissing? (tulip)

Flower Riddles

1. What flower do ladies tread under foot? (lady's slipper)
2. What flower is most used by cooks? (buttercup)
3. What flower tells how a man may get rich quick? (marigold)
4. What flower indicates late afternoon? (four-o'clock)
5. What flower tells what father says when he wants an errand run? (johnny-jump-up)
6. A parting remark to a friend? (forget-me-not)
7. What flower do people get up early to enjoy? (morning glory)
8. What flower do young men like to touch? (lady finger)
9. What flower often hangs on the laundry line? (Dutchman's breeches)
10. What flower reminds one of church? (jack-in-the-pulpit)
11. What flower goes with the easy chair and the paper? (Dutchman's pipe)
12. What flower describes a beautiful specimen of an animal? (dandelion)
13. What flower is both pleasant and distasteful to the palate? (bittersweet)
14. What flower reminds one of winter weather? (snowdrops)
15. What flower tells what George Washington was to his country? (poppy)
16. What flower reminds one of birds in a group? (phlox)
17. What flower suggest neat lines? (primrose)
18. What flower suggests a feline bite? (catnip)
19. What flower is a child's delight in winter? (snowball)

Nature Symbolism Race

Name the nature object best symbolized by the words below. For variation the form may be changed, for example:

slyness   fox   or   sly as a   (fox)

Animals

slyness—fox
fleetness (or swift)—deer
industry (or busy)—beaver
hunger—wolf
gentleness—sheep or lamb
Easter—rabbit
stillness—mouse
stealthiness—panther

fidelity (or faithful)—dog
majesty—lion, moose
strength—ox
coolness—polar bear
spring—woodchuck
thirsty—camel
fierce—tiger
big—elephant

Birds

happiness — lark
spring — bluebird
cheer — robin
summer — swallow
persistence — woodpecker

wisdom — owl
courage — eagle
craziness — loon
trumpeter — wild goose

Flowers

purity — lily
modesty — violet
spring — pussy willow
love — rose
Mother's   day — carnation
peace — poppy
cheerfulness —
   chrysanthemum
sympathy — rose
sweet — rose

Easter — lily
remembrance — forget-me-not
he loves me, he loves me not —
   daisy
innocence — daisy, pansy
virtue — lily
contentment — morning   glory
Christmas — holly,   poinsettia
courage — carnation

Scrambles

Rearrange the letters to form the name of a bird or tree.

Birds

1.	obbthiew	(bobwhite)	11. abelrrw	(warbler)
2.	diigrbnk	(kingbird)	12. ceedkooprw	(woodpecker)
3.	eebhop	(phoebe)	13. hhrstu	(thrush)
4.	accefhlrty	(flycatcher)	14. adenpprsi	(sandpiper)
5.	cdfhignlo	(goldfinch)	15. aecukpssr	(sapsucker)
6.	ahkwtihgn	(nighthawk)	16. bidgikmnroc	(mockingbird)
7.	acegklr	(grackle)	17. cjnou	(junco)
8.	achhnttu	(nuthatch)	18. abbcdiklr	(blackbird)
9.	arprswo	(sparrow)	19. abcdirt	(catbird)
10.	eiorv	(vireo)	20. accdiheek	(chickadee)

Trees

1. north	(thorn)		8. lpaaact	(catalpa)
2. panes	(aspen)		9. amcus	(sumac)
3. clouts	(locust)		10. redreylerb	(elderberry)
4. ample	(maple)		11. reegvneer	(evergreen)
5. has	(ash)		12. usthcten	(chestnut)
6. cared	(cedar)		13. rayecoms	(sycamore)
7. mug	(gum)		14. gernaipve	(grapevine)

REFERENCES

Campcraft Games

Smith, Charles F. *Games and Recreational Methods*. Dodd, Mead, and Company, New York, 1937.

Map and Compass Games

Disley, John. *Your Way With Map and Compass*. Canadian Orienteering Service, Willowdale, Ontario, 1973.

Kjellstrom, Bjorn. *Be Expert With Map and Compass*. Charles Scribner's Sons, New York, new enlarged edition, 1976.

Mooers, Robert L. *Finding Your Way in the Outdoors*. E. P. Dutton and Company, New York, 1972.

Silva, Inc., La Porte, Ind. Cards for competitive compass game.

Vinal, William Gould. *Nature Recreation*, second edition. Dover Publications, New York, 1963.

Nature Games

Berry, Christine. *Field Plot Studies*. Penn State HPER Series No. 4. College of Health, Physical Education and Recreation, The Pennsylvania State University, University Park, 1974. Many of the activities are presented as games.

Frankel, Lillian, and Frankel, Godfrey. *101 Best Nature Games and Projects*. Sterling Publication Company, New York, 1959.

Hillcourt, William. *The New Field Book of Nature Activities and Hobbies*. G. P. Putnam's Sons, New York, 1970.

Musselman, Virginia W. *Learning About Nature Through Games*. Stackpole Books, Harrisburg, Pa., 1967.

Smith, Charles F. *Games and Recreational Methods*. Dodd, Mead, and Company, New York, 1924.

CHAPTER IV

Outdoor Living Skills

WITH THE RAPIDLY INCREASING POPULATION and increased interest in camping and outdoor recreation pursuits, observation of good conservation practices becomes mandatory; otherwise, our streams and natural areas will become polluted and stripped of their natural beauty and will cease to be of benefit to humanity.

Plant life, particularly wild flowers, is to be preserved in its natural state wherever possible. It takes years for a tree to grow and mature, but only one careless stroke of an axe or a hatchet can destroy or mar it for the rest of its life. Every flower that is picked disturbs the reproductive cycle of the plant and it is no wonder that many of the beautiful wild flowers are disappearing.

The motto for people who enjoy the outdoors could well be, "Let Living Things Live!" The outdoors and its beauty does not belong to any one individual and is not there for us to destroy or use in such a way that will deny its use and observation by others. Most of the plant life, animal life, and other materials found in the outdoors can be observed and studied in their natural environments and can be left there to be enjoyed by others now and in generations to follow.

This may mean that we need to modify some of our present practices in such heavily used areas as national and state parks. The indigenous materials will soon be exhausted if each camper uses them too freely and indiscriminately. Instead of destroying trees in search of firewood, it may be necessary to purchase wood or to use charcoal or petroleum stoves for cooking.

Dead twigs or branches frequently can be used as substitutes for green sticks. This is certainly true in the roasting of weiners or marshmallows. Bread twists can be made on dry sticks which are first wrapped with aluminum foil. The foil is placed on the stick only over the portion to be used for the twist. Besides protecting the food from the stick, the aluminum foil also acts as a conductor of heat and helps the bread to bake from the inside. If such camp furniture as tables and chairs is to be made by lashing, dead wood should be used instead of destroying live plants.

Some of the more primitive (wilderness) areas, away from the population centers, still have enough wood and other materials which may be used for camping purposes without upsetting the balance of nature. Even here, however, good conservation practices, such as selective cutting, should be followed. A campfire carelessly left can develop into a blazing forest fire, destroying valuable property which cannot possibly be replaced or restored during our lifetime.

Outdoor living skills as a program activity are increasing in popularity. No longer are they considered "campcraft" and the exclusive domain of the children's camp. They are found in many of the outdoor recreation pursuits today—family camping, outings, playgrounds, day camping, special clubs, backyard cooking, special events, hunting, and fishing.

Outdoor cookery, firecraft, ropecraft, toolcraft, gear, and shelter are the skills most frequently identified as outdoor living skills. As with other program activities, these may be utilized as a single activity or integrated into other events, into club groups, and into instructional situations.

Although many individuals have experience with outdoor living skills through their own camping, the American Camping Association campcraft program can be of considerable assistance on the instructional organization and content aspects. The program is an achievement program with certification for ratings as a camp-crafter, advanced campcrafter, and tripcrafter. The A.C.A. also qualifies instructors to conduct the program; however, anyone may use the general outline. An instructor's manual may be obtained for a small charge from the American Camping Association, Bradford Woods, Martinsville, Indiana. Your local section of the A.C.A. will also be glad to work with you in developing your outdoor living skills program. If you do not know the section leadership chairman, write to the national office for his name and address.

GEAR AND SHELTER

Sleeping out in the open or under a simple tent or native-material shelter is one of the thrills of youth, and the romance of such an adventure remains for many into adulthood. However, to receive maximum enjoyment from such outdoor living, you must be comfortable. Comfort comes from knowing "how"—how to make a soft bed on the ground, how to keep the rain from getting all your belongings wet inside the tent, how to stay warm in your sleeping bag or blanket roll, how to erect your shelter so that it stays up in a wind and rain storm, how to pack everything you need properly in your backpack, how to select your site so you're not sleeping downhill, how to pitch your tent so that the morning sun does its job. These are just a few of the many skills which must be learned—and can be learned through your outdoor living skills program.

Another very popular activity is making gear and shelters. For example, the Milwaukee recreation department has long offered a tentmaking class, and others integrate gearmaking into their craft program.

FIRECRAFT

Firecraft skills are valuable for outdoor cookery and for campfires. Suggestions for special fire-building structures, methods of lighting campfires, making colored flames, and woods for campfires may be found in the section on Campfires.

Different types of outdoor cooking require different fire lays and woods. Special suggestions are given under the various cooking methods. It is a real art to build exactly the right fire for proper cooking.

Besides the fire-building games listed in the Campcraft Games section, one sometimes likes to have a few special activities:

1. Use fine steel wool as tinder in starting a fire with flint and steel. Many people will not believe that steel wool will burn until you prove it to them. Once a spark is caught, blow on it and it will become red hot to start your other tinder and kindling. Also, you may wish to find your own flint among the rocks.

2. Try making fire by friction, using the methods of the Indians.

3. A magnifying glass will also start a fire and can be used to do wood burning instead of an electric wood-burning needle. The sun, however, must be bright, hot, and clear.

4. Make fireplace candles and campfire logs. The latter are described in the Campfire section. Buddy burners and fire starters

also may be made. Instructions for making buddy burners are included in Outdoor Cookery under Hobo Stoves.

To make fire starters (particularly useful on damp or rainy days): Roll newspaper tightly into a roll until 1'' in diameter. Tie with string. Cut in 3'' lengths. Soak in paraffin (old melted candles will be fine); place rolls in coffee tin, standing on end, and pour melted paraffin over them until completely saturated. Let cool.

An essential part of every firecraft program should be instruction on fire control, including proper preparation of site, appropriate equipment for fire control, and procedures for extinguishing a fire.

ROPECRAFT

Handling a rope appears to be a lost art among people today. In outdoor living the rope is used primarily in erecting the shelter and for sailing, and basic knots for these purposes certainly should be learned. Knot-tying games and contests are included in the Campcraft Games section.

Ropemaking is an interesting activity for playground or day camp. Rope may be made by hand braiding or by a homemade machine. For making rope, binder's twine or India hemp is the best, unless one wishes to use native materials in the making of cordage (see Nature Crafts).

Here's how to make your own rope machine. Attach two boards at right angles as shown in the diagram. Use screws for more security. Boards should be 3/4''-1'' pine, approximately 5'' in width. Drill 3/16'' holes in both the upright board and handle as diagrammed, with middle hole slightly above the other two. A forked stick may be used in place of the strand separator board. Make hooks out of rigid 1/8'' wire in form shown. These hooks should move freely in the holes. Insert hooks and the machine is ready to be strung for rope making. Attach twine to one hook and take it out around the awl (the length depending upon how long a rope you wish to make). Return to second hook, back to awl, and then tie back at third hook. Insert strand separator and put handle on. Turn handle and the strands will begin to twist, both individually and into a single rope. Hold on to the awl and keep the rope somewhat taut — you will be able to feel the pull necessary to get an even rope twist. Some prefer to substitute for the awl a small piece of board (3'' square) with a single hook, but with no handle-insert portion. The rope is attached to the single hook which should be free to move. For

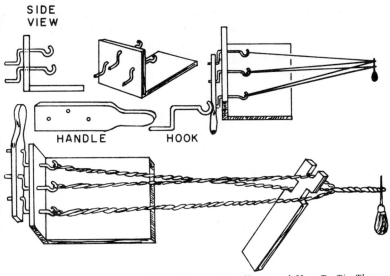

SIDE
VIEW

HANDLE   HOOK

Illustration courtesy *Knots and How To Tie Them,*
Boy Scouts of America, New Brunswick, N.J.

stability, the base board can be fastened to a table with a C clamp.
Some do not bother to have this base board but just hold the end
board with the hooks and the handle by hand.

Adventurous boys and girls may wish to
go into pioneering projects such as rope
bridges, sometimes referred to as "monkey
bridges."

TOOLCRAFT

Unless one is using charcoal, it is rather difficult to have an
outdoor fire without the use of tools, either saw or axe. Certainly
youngsters should be taught proper care and use of axes, saws, and
knives. Safety procedures cannot be overemphasized. In many
camps and for use with youth, the saw is preferred to the axe as a
beginning tool because of safety. Also, in selecting an axe for the
young person, the intermediate size is recommended. Sometimes
referred to as the Hudson Bay style, it has a 2-2¼ lb. head and a
24"-28" handle. This lightweight axe
serves very well in doing the work of both
the hatchet and the regular axe.

Use of the knife can be integrated very well into a crafts program. In contests using saws and axes (see Campcraft Games), as well as in whittling and woodcutting, it is important to teach basic skills first and insist strongly on proper safety principles.

OUTDOOR COOKERY

Half the fun of campin' out
    And trampin' here and there
Is buildin' up your appetite
    'Til you're hungry as a bear.

Then sittin' down at mess time
    With swell victuals all about—
Boy! that's livin' what is livin'
    And you get it campin' out!

Cooking is more than a necessity; it is an activity—it is a time for fun, sharing, and adventure.

The purpose of this section is to suggest a number of ways in which different types of cooking may be used—these are meant only as *starters*—you will want to try many variations and new ideas of your own. The menus, for the most part, have not included beverage and bread; these you will want to add. At the beginning are some general pointers regarding equipment, sanitation, fire sites, etc.

While many of the books on outdoor living contain a section on cooking, if you wish a single, specialized book, probably the best reference is the Girl Scouts' *Cooking Out-of-Doors*.

Basic Equipment

Basic equipment for all groups doing outdoor cookery on the wood fire includes:

Heavy cotton work gloves or pot holders.

Pail and folding trench shovel or other equipment useful in case of fire and to extinguish fire.

First aid kit (can be hung on tree for easy accessibility).

Twine or other small rope—comes in handy when you least expect it!

Soap (liquid is much easier to use, although bar soap or detergent made into a paste can also be used) to soap outside of kettles to make dishwashing easier. Steel wool pads.

Dishwashing equipment (see Sanitation).

Silverware bag—cloth sewn with pockets helps to keep it together.

Paper toweling—helps keep things clean, including your hands, tea towels, etc.

Charcoal may be substituted whenever cooking requires coals, *if* obtaining wood for a fire is a problem. Also, most family campers use a Coleman gas stove for the majority of their cooking.

Dutch oven.

Reflector oven (see section on Reflector Cooking) or Coleman oven, both of which fold very compactly, may be secured for baking. The latter can be used especially well on hunter-trapper fires. Of course, foil and other methods of baking which do not require oven equipment may also be used.

Kitchen fly (large plastic sheet at least 10'x10') for family campers which serves like a "porch"—big enough to cook, eat, and sit under when it rains!

Refrigeration (see Sanitation).

Saw and/or Hudson Bay style axe.

Pots and dishes. A very compact commercial cook kit, called a "nesting kit," may be used. They come in various sizes—those for 4, 6, 8, and 12 people are most common. A heavy aluminum set is a good buy. It will last longer and cook better. Most kits contain 2 frying pans (one is the lid), one or two pots besides the large container for everything, a coffee pot, and cups and plates. Some have plastic cups, while others have aluminum. There are advantages and disadvantages to both. The heavy plastic type cup which does not melt when placed next to the fire or when it contains very hot food is preferable.

If packing space is not much of a problem, a miscellaneous

assortment of old pots, pans, and other utensils can be gathered and carried in an old suitcase or in a backpack. Usually a coffee pot, 2 pots, a mixing bowl, and a frying pan are taken, besides cups and plates.

It is also helpful to have these utensils: can opener, paring knife (jack knife), spatula, mixing spoon. Plastic bags also are convenient to have around for such things as mixing Bisquick dough for bread twists and for storing things.

Packs. A backpack may be useful for packing equipment and food. Either frame or knapsack packs may be used.

In using pack baskets, backpacks or knapsacks, or kettles to carry food for outdoor meals, pack heaviest things in the bottom. Pack so that there is no room for the various articles to shift around. Each item should be in its own container, in proper quantity needed, and well labeled on side and top.

Bags of assorted sizes are desirable for dry materials. The best are made from sailcloth, waterproofed with paraffin, and double-stitched at all seams with a wide hem and a drawstring at the top long enough to tie with a half hitch and use as a handle. For fine materials such as flour, bags should be double thickness or you may use two bags. The inside bag might be a plastic one. Make bags short and broad, with round bottoms, so they'll stand upright with minimum danger of tipping over. Label contents with wax crayon, which will wash out, or India ink, which is permanent.

Liquids should be carried in metal or plastic containers rather than in glass. Semiliquid materials, such as jam and peanut butter, may be carried in heavy, round cardboard cartons with tight-fitting lids, for example, cottage cheese cartons.

Such breakable items as eggs can be carried inside flour bags.

Sanitation and Food Preservation

Sanitation and preservation of food are also important. Here are some tips:

Wash dishes in hot soapy water; put them in a loosely knit nylon bag (easily homemade); place (dip) in boiling water; and hang up in bag to dry.

As much of the garbage and refuse as possible should be burned. Spread out aluminum foil and place in *hot* fire—it will burn to ashes. Foil, if not burned, should be carried out. If a garbage container is not provided in the area where you are cooking, garbage should be *carried out* rather than buried. Cans may be burned out and smashed flat to conserve space. Grease pits should be used for excess grease.

Foods should be planned which need a minimum of refrigeration. Where cooler temperatures are needed, a stream-cooled or air-cooled homemade "refrigerator" will frequently suffice. A watertight jar or cream can may be anchored in a stream. An aircooled refrigerator may be made by constructing a tree pantry wrapped in burlap. Place a 2-gallon can on top with holes which permit water to drip slowly down the burlap. The air will cause evaporation and cooling. An ice chest, of course, can be purchased. Check for quality of insulation and resistance of liner to rusting. Usually block ice lasts longer than crushed ice.

Methods of Cooking

On the following pages are various types of cookery—foil, stick, direct coals, one-pot, Dutch oven, reflector oven, tin can, hunter-trapper fire, hole cookery. A menu is given for each. However, the menu was selected to illustrate various parts of the meal that might be used with that type of cookery. You would not necessarily cook an entire meal by the same method, although it could be done. For example, in reflector oven cooking, you might make the main meal a one-pot meal, and then have a pie baked in the reflector for dessert. However, if you had two reflectors, both the main meal and the dessert, as the menu provides, could be done in reflectors.

Besides the menu, recipes, cooking hints, equipment, and food quantities are given for the specific menu for 6-8 people. In addition, several methods of coffee making are given. Because of the interest in lightweight foods for tripping, there is a brief section on dehydrated and quick-frozen foods.

Coffee Making

There are many successful ways of making coffee on the open fire, and each outdoor cook has a favorite method. The prime concern in all methods is how to settle the grounds. Here are a few suggestions to try at your own risk! Use a level tablespoonful of coffee for each cup of water.

1. Put coffee grounds into boiling water. Stir; put in eggshell or dash of cold water; let sit in warm place 5 minutes.

2. Put coffee grounds in cheesecloth bag and place in cold water. Bring to a brisk boil.

3. Put coffee grounds in cheesecloth bag with a few grains of salt. Pour boiling water on it and allow coffee to come again to a full boil. Let stand 20 minutes on low heat. To clear add some cold water.

4. Mix coffee with one egg and just enough water to moisten. Add remaining cold water; cover and slowly bring to boil, stirring occasionally. Remove from fire; let stand in warm place 3-5 minutes; add ¼ cup cold water to settle grounds.

5. Make in any manner and settle grounds by swinging pot with a full arm arc!

Dehydrated and Quick-frozen Foods

Certain dehydrated or specially prepared foods found on most grocery store shelves can be of considerable convenience. Some examples are "quick" type oatmeal, cake mixes, Bisquick, powdered milk, Minute rice, instant potatoes, or various powdered drinks such as chocolate. Most of these come in awkward cartons and for convenience of packing they may be easily transferred to cloth bags. If their texture is very fine they should be put into plastic bags first, then into the cloth bags.

Several camp outfitters also sell dehydrated foods both as complete meals and as single dishes packed for 2, 4, or 6 people, for a meal, or for a whole day. Although the quality of flavor is constantly being improved, one must learn which brands and dishes are the tastiest. Because of the somewhat higher price, there is no real reason to purchase these special camp packs except for novelty or to reduce bulk and weight.

Dehydrated packages require water for use. Some also require presoaking before cooking.

Direct Coals Cookery

Menu

"Buffalo" steak
Corn on the cob
Tossed salad
Macaroons

Food items and quantities (8 persons)

2-3 large pieces steak (to be cut later
  into 8 pieces)
8 ears corn (16 if want 2 apiece)
1 head lettuce
2 carrots
½ stalk celery (small)
4 tomatoes
1 can sweetened, condensed milk
1 pkg. shredded or flaked coconut
salad dressing
¼ lb. butter
1 loaf solid, day-old bread (or buns, or
  other solid bread)

Equipment

2 small containers (coconut, milk)
1 mixing pot (salad)
knife to fix vegetables and cut meat
can opener
shovel and pail (fire control)
matches
2 gloves or pot holders
paper towels and napkins
8 forks, knives, plates, cups
fork to turn meat (long handled)
dish washing equipment
axe

Recipes

"Buffalo" Steak

Make a good bed of hardwood coals. Take a large piece of thick (1½" to 2") boneless steak, marinate 3-4 hours (mixture: oil, salt, pepper, general steak sauce as desired, little catsup, garlic salt, and thyme and marjoram if desired). While marinating use a two-pronged fork and poke holes in the meat every time you turn it over in the marinating sauce. Cut the fat edge of the steak about every 1½" so the steak will not curl when on the coals. Place steak *directly on* hardwood coals. Turn once after about 15 minutes (if steak 1½" thick). Then after about 10 minutes more, those liking rare meat can eat. Leave on slightly longer for other degrees of doneness. When done, blow white ash off and remove any coals which have adhered; cut into individual pieces. Dip in melted butter.

Corn on the Cob

Take corn directly from field if possible, leaving cornhusks intact. Soak for a short time in a bucket of water; place directly on hot coals. Turn on each of four sides. If coals appear to dry out husks too much, just dip in water again; however, do not be alarmed if *outer* husk leaves burn or get black. Steam cooks the corn. Once the corn is heated through (leave on first side longest so steam can generate), it will take only a few minutes (5 perhaps) on each side if corn is tender. To keep until ready to use, just set off a bit, but still near heat. Cannot really get overdone. However, if coals are quite hot you may get "Indian corn," a parched corn some people like very much.

When done, strip off husks. With experience you will be able to strip down husk with all the silks! Butter and eat. To avoid the messiness of individually buttering many ears with a knife, take a deep tin can, e.g., a juice or coffee can, fill it with hot water, and melt butter in it. The butter will come to the surface. Use a stick or whatever amount is needed to produce a generous layer of butter! Dip the ear of corn into the can. As the corn is pulled out it will be completely buttered; merely add salt and eat. No butter need be lost: when the water has cooled, the hardened butter can easily be lifted off the top.

Macaroons. See recipe under Stick Cookery.

Additional Menu Suggestions

Potatoes. See Foil Cookery.

Banana boats. See under One-Pot Meal.

Fish in newspaper. Use fresh fish or *completely* thaw frozen fish. Add lemon, salt and pepper, and onion to add flavor to bland fish. Wrap fish in wax paper. Wrap fish in several layers of newspaper. May wrap in dry newspaper and soak in water or wrap in wet newspaper. Place on coals. Cooks by steam. Does not take long— after steam has started, perhaps 10-15 minutes or less. Need a good bed of very hot coals.

Dutch Oven Cookery

Menu

Roast		Apple salad
Carrots	Potatoes	Cake

Food items and quantities (for 8)

Equipment

2½-3 lb. roast
2-3 small onions
salt and pepper
8 medium potatoes
8 medium carrots
¼-½ lb. butter
4 medium apples
⅓ lb. dates
½ cup mayonnaise
1 cup miniature marshmallows
½ cup chopped nuts
1 large box cake mix or ingredients for cake of your choice

2 Dutch ovens
bowl to mix apple salad (mix cake in bowl first)
knife to pare vegetables and apples
mixing spoon
axe or saw
matches
shovel and pail (fire control)
dish washing equipment
paper towels and napkins
8 forks, cups, plates

Recipes

Roast With Carrots in Dutch Oven

Sear roast. Add salt and pepper, small onions. Place pared potatoes and carrots around roast. Add 1 to 1½ cups water. Heat. Cover with hot lid. Bake until done.

Apple Salad

Cut up 4 medium-sized apples, together with dates and marshmallows. Add nuts. Mix with mayonnaise.

Cake

Mix cake as indicated on package. Place in greased cake tin. Put in Dutch oven either on inverted pie tin or on small rocks, so that it is not directly on bottom of oven. Close oven and bake. For variation put applesauce on the bottom of the cake pan and pour gingerbread batter over it, then bake.

Hints

The Dutch oven has been in use in outdoor cooking longer than almost any other piece of equipment except the green stick. It was the main cooking utensil of our early pioneers, of prospectors, sheepherders, and cowboys. The chuck wagon was incomplete without its Dutch oven for roasting and baking as well as for frying and stewing. For all but those wishing to travel light, this piece of equipment will allow much more variety and interest in the outdoor meals. Veteran cooks would use no other method of baking, for with a little experience it is almost foolproof.

The best Dutch oven is cast iron. Those of aluminum are possibly two pounds lighter but lack the qualities of the cast iron model which make it so ideal for baking and roasting. The oven is from 3 to 4 inches deep and has a flat snug-fitting lid with a turned-up rim which serves to retain coals placed on top. Three stubby legs support the oven, allowing air to circulate underneath to keep coals hot.

The commonest sizes are 12 inches in diameter (7 quarts) and 10 inches in diameter (3 quarts). The 8-inch Dutch oven used by most housewives is usually too small for camp use and has a rounded lid which makes it impossible to put coals on top. The oven is equipped with a handle or bail and the lid has a cast iron handle. A forked stick will enable the cook to take off the lid to stir or check the progress of the food.

If the Dutch oven is to be used for frying or boiling, the type of fire usually used for that type of cooking is advisable. However, for roasting and baking, some care must be taken to avoid direct flame on the oven; all of the heat should be provided by coals. It is important that the oven be hot enough but not too hot; the exact amount of heat can only be determined by experimentation and practice. The commonest error is to have too much heat rather than not enough. Place the oven on hardwood coals raked out from the fire. Top heat is provided by placing coals on the lid. Heat can be adjusted by adding or taking away coals both above and underneath the Dutch oven. Particularly for baking, both the oven and the lid should be preheated.

For all cooking purposes except baking, the food is placed directly in the Dutch oven. Baking, too, may be done this way, but many prefer to place that which is to be baked in a separate pan. When a pan is used, it must be supported away from the bottom of the oven by inverting another pan on the bottom, or by placing several nonexplodable stones under the pan. This allows for air circulation under the pan and prevents burning. When baking pies or cakes, care must be taken to level the oven before the pan is put in. Also, there must be sufficient space on top for rising; if cake touches the lid, it will burn.

When using the oven for moist foods the first several times, grease lightly to prevent rusting until a film forms inside the pot; nonsalt grease is preferable. After use, wash the oven in soapy water, rinse in near-boiling water, and set out to dry. Avoid scouring with cleanser or steel wool since this removes the protective film. For prolonged storage in humid climates, a light greasing inside and out is recommended.

A Dutch oven can be used for any food you wish to bake. The ready mixes are ideal. Follow the directions on the packages for preparation and baking time. Check frequently, since a common error is to use too many coals, resulting in food cooking too quickly. Potatoes and apples can be baked in the Dutch oven, and it is ideal for pot roast and vegetables and for Swiss steak. A deep-dish pie is easily made by lining the oven with dough, baking for about 10 minutes, filling the shell with two cans of prepared pie filling, topping with crust, and baking until the crust is brown and the filling is hot. Fruit cobbler can be made quickly by using prepared pie filling and topping with biscuit dough.

Foil Cookery

Menu

Baked barbecued chicken
Potatoes
Cabbage salad
Pineapple upside-down cake

Food items and quantities (for 8)

3 chickens (cut up)
1 jar barbecue sauce, if desired
8 medium-sized baking potatoes
½ lb. butter
salt
pepper
1 cabbage
1 jar salad dressing (or bring just
    sufficient amount)
1 #2 can pineapple, crushed
½ cup brown sugar
1 cup flour
1 t. baking powder
1 egg
1 t. vanilla
½ cup white granulated sugar
½ cup milk
(See recipes for additional items if you
    wish to "dress up" or modify items.)

Equipment

1 roll heavy-duty aluminum foil
2 knives to cut cabbage, peel potatoes
2 mixing spoons
2 medium-sized mixing pots for salad
    and cake
can opener
axe or saw
2 pot holders or gloves
matches
shovel and pail (fire control)
8 forks, 8 cups, 8 plates
soap (dishes, soap pots)
paper towels and napkins (a few towels
    are handy to keep things from
    getting too messy and add little to
    carry)
dish washing equipment (either dip
    bags or dish cloths and dish towels)
make cake pan from foil

Recipes

Baked Barbecued Chicken

Sprinkle salt and pepper on cut-up chicken. Place in middle of foil and add a little grease or butter. Add barbecue sauce, if desired. Fold aluminum properly (see under hints), leaving air space for steam expansion, particularly if adding sauce. Place package on hot coals (not flame) for 10-15 minutes depending on size of chicken, turn over for another 10-15 minutes. Spread chicken pieces out, making a flat package, if you wish them to get done more quickly.

Potatoes

"Straight" baked—peel or not at your option. Wrap properly in foil, having added salt and pepper if desired plus a few sprinkles of water. Rub unpeeled potatoes with grease to keep skins from drying out. Allow 40-50 minutes.

Shoestring baked—peel or not peel at your option. Cut in shoestrings about ¼ inch across. Put salt, pepper, and butter in package. Wrap. When potatoes are about done, if you wish crispy browned potatoes, put them in hotter coals for a very short time. Allow 30-40 minutes.

Scalloped baked—slice peeled potatoes thinly. Add salt, pepper and butter to package. Wrap and bake. Takes the least time, particularly if flat package is made. 20-30 minutes.

You can usually tell if potatoes are done without opening the package by feeling how soft they are.

Potatoes in salt—take a #10 can and clean rock salt or ice cream salt. Pack clean small- to medium-sized potatoes into can. Surround each potato with salt. In packing, be sure to have ½ inch of salt insulation around perimeter of can; *do not have any potatoes touch each other or the can.* The potatoes will have a good salty flavor on the outside skin and it may penetrate a little into the potato. (Won't be too salty, though.) Place can near fire if blazing and in coals when flame is down. Clean, damp sand may be substituted for salt, but then of course you will not have a salty flavor. Salt may be used over and over.

Cabbage Salad

Shred (cut) cabbage into bowl or pot. Mix in mayonnaise. Serve. To "dress up," add 1 cup miniature marshmallows and a small can of crushed pineapple. May need dash of salt.

Pineapple Upside-down Cake

3 T. butter
½ cup brown sugar
1 #2 can crushed pineapple
1 cup flour
1 t. baking powder
¼ t. salt

1 egg
½ cup sugar
2 T. melted shortening or butter
⅓ cup milk
1 t. vanilla

Make foil pan. Two small pans are better than one big. Do not seal top, but make a dome-shaped lid from foil. Dome should extend over edges of pan. Heat in top part of oven can be controlled by the amount of coals on the outside of the pan. May serve with spoon instead of inverting onto platter (cut cake, spoon pineapple goodie).

Melt butter in pan, add brown sugar, and remove from heat. Sprinkle pineapple over sugar mixture. Sift flour, baking powder, and salt into bowl (this could be mixed before going on trip). Add rest of ingredients and beat until blended. Pour batter over fruit and bake before moderate fire 30-35 minutes. Loosen cake from sides and invert. (From Campcraft Conference, Camp Blazing Trail.)

Variation: Although many youngsters do not have the opportunity to mix a cake from "scratch" (that's why it is done above), white cake mix can be used instead of making the batter. Other fruits may be used; for some you may wish to substitute white sugar. Or you can make cobbler (see recipe under Reflectors).

Additional Menu Suggestions

Ham and sweet potatoes (see Reflector baking recipes). Just bake in foil.

Hamburgers. Instead of just a plain hamburger in foil, why not try it with a cabbage leaf on the outside and a slice of cheese making a cheeseburger. Cheese and cabbage go well together; cabbage makes a nice moist sandwich. Put all in bun to eat.

Casserole. Thinly slice potatoes, dice or cut carrots in thin strips, crumble up some hamburger (¼ lb. per person), add onion, salt, pepper, few sprinkles of water. Put in foil package. If patted out to make a thin baking package, it cooks more quickly. This gives better flavor (according to some) than putting each in separately without mixing casserole fashion.

Rolatun. Take large piece of round steak, smear with mustard, garnish with thinly sliced dill pickles. Roll or fold steak. Place in foil and cook. Some prefer to tie and barbecue over coals until nicely brown. Tastes better than it sounds—be brave and try something different!

Apples. One of the easiest and surest of desserts is the baked apple. Core apple, fill center with butter, sugar, cinnamon; may also add marshmallows, currants, raisins, or other desired filling. Takes only 5 minutes on a side. Be especially careful to seal foil well.

Biscuits, fish, and many other things can be cooked in foil. Be adventuresome. Try different things.

Hints

One of the easiest and most successful methods of cookery is by aluminum foil. Cooking is based on the principle of steaming. For that reason add some sprinkles of water to "dry" foods such as hamburger to give some moisture for steam. The package must be sealed well so no steam or juices can escape. Use the "drugstore" wrap. Place food in center of foil; bring both sides up and fold down together. Flatten foil package, fold ends several times together. Package should be able to be placed in any position and not leak! Allow a little space when folding down package for steam expansion. When turning the package over in the coals, *do not* use a stick as it is likely to puncture foil, letting steam escape. Use gloves to turn. If puncture occurs, reseal by putting another layer of foil around package. On food items you wish to brown on top and not have soggy, such as cake, use a dome lid as described in upside-down cake recipe.

Foil cookery takes time and should be done on coals; therefore make a hardwood fire if possible, since these coals stay hot longer and give an evener heat. *Be sure foil package is not placed in flames;* be sure wood has burned to coals. Cooking time varies with degree of heat, type of wood, thickness of package. For better protection, heavy-duty aluminum should be used; if not available, double the lightweight aluminum. Except for upside-down cakes and similar foods, turn over when you estimate food is half done. With apples, do not turn over, just turn a different side toward the fire or place in coals with heat all around. Packages should be flattened to cook more quickly, rather than leaving a big roll of food all in one place.

If foil is opened carefully, it may be laid back and used for a plate. Various utensils may be made from heavy-duty aluminum foil, for instance, frying pans, pots, and cups. *Do not wad up foil and be a litter bug. Foil will burn!* Spread out foil in single layer and place on *hot* fire to burn into ashes, or carry out with nonburnable trash.

For greater success with children particularly, let each child make his own package, including paring and slicing. (Instruct in use of knife.) This allows for individuality. Suggest that the child make his main meal package and place it in fire. Then he can have "rabbit food" of celery and carrots for a "tider-over." The child could fix an apple for dessert. By the time this has taken place, the foil meal is ready to eat and the apple can be put in the coals. By the time the meal is eaten, dessert is ready.

Hole Cookery

Menu

Baked beans
Dill pickles
Ice cream

Food items and quantities (for 8)   *Equipment*

2 cups navy beans   pot with tight cover for beans
salt and pepper   hay or straw to line one hole
½ t. dry or prepared mustard   bricks or stones to line other hole
½ cup brown sugar   30 lb. frozen food or lard can
½ cup molasses   cylindrical fruit juice can or 2 lb. coffee
2 small onions   can
1 lb. ham   crushed ice
½ cup white sugar   ice cream salt
1 pt. cream   2 pot holders or padded gloves
2 eggs   matches
2 t. vanilla   axe or saw
approx. 1 qt. milk   shovel and pail (fire control)
jar dill pickles   8 forks, cups, plates
                                           soap (for dishes, and for soaping pots)
                                           paper towels and napkins
                                           dish cloths and towels

Recipes

Baked Beans

Dig hole that is twice the size of the bean pot in both depth and
width. Line with rocks or bricks. Build fire in hole, crisscrossing logs
on top. Let coals fall into hole and keep fire going until hole is about
⅔ full of coals. Hardwood is best for coals. Take out part of coals;
insert bean pot. Cover pot with coals on all sides and top. Seal in heat
by covering coals with dirt. Bean pot should be a kettle with tight-
fitting lid. Leave beans in hole about 6 hours. Fix them after break-
fast, have for supper on return from all-day hike.

Beans: Soak 2 cups beans overnight. Pour off water. Mix ½ t.
salt, ½ t. mustard (more if wet mustard), pepper, ½ cup brown
sugar, ½ cup molasses. Pour onto beans in pot. Put in ham (½ lb.
salt pork may be substituted) and 2 small onions diced. Cover with

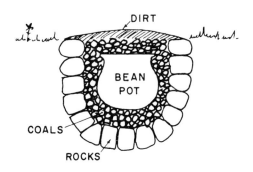

DIRT

BEAN
POT

COALS

ROCKS

water about 1'' above beans; put in bean hole to cook. You can save cooking time by hanging the pot of beans on a crane over the fire while you are waiting for the fire to burn down to coals. If you forget to soak beans overnight, put in pot and bring to boil. Cover and remove from heat. Allow to sit one hour.

Ice Cream

Dig a hole large enough to pack 6'' of hay or straw below and around a 30-lb. can. Put ice cream mixture in a juice can or 2-lb. coffee tin. Place smaller can containing the mixture inside the larger can with crushed ice and plenty of salt underneath and all around. Put a few nail holes in the larger can just below the top of the mixture can so that the salt water will drain to the outside, not into mixture! Cover hole with dirt to keep cold in. Allow 3-4 hours for freezing. May stir once if desired. *Be generous with the salt.*

Mixture (for 2 qts.): ¾ cup white sugar, 1 pt. cream, 2 eggs, 1 t. vanilla. Add milk to fill container (approx. 1 qt.). Half-and-half cream may be used instead of cream and milk.

Hunter-Trapper Fire

Menu

Sausage
Apple pancakes
Celery and carrot sticks
Chocolate tapioca pudding

Food items and quantities (for 8)

1 sq. Baker's chocolate or cocoa equiv.
24 sausages or 2 lb. bulk sausage
1½ cups flour
3 t. baking powder
salt
⅔ cup sugar
3 eggs
1 qt. milk
1 cup shortening
½ t. nutmeg
6 medium apples
¼ lb. butter
1 stalk celery (small)
6 carrots
1 pt. syrup
3 T. tapioca
1 t. vanilla

Equipment

1 medium-sized frying pan (pancakes)
pail and shovel (fire control)
2 pot holders or gloves
axe or saw
2 medium kettles or pots
knives to pare apples, cut celery and
    carrots
2 mixing spoons
1 spatula
1 cooking fork
matches
8 forks, spoons, cups, plates
paper napkins and a few paper towels
dish washing equipment
soap, to soap pots

Recipes

Sausage

Just fry sausages in pan over flame. Be sure they are done.

Apple Pancakes

1½ cups flour
3 t. baking powder
½ t. salt
5 T. sugar
2 eggs
1 cup milk
3 T. shortening (melted)
½ t. nutmeg
6 medium apples (cut finely)

Mix dry ingredients (preferably before you go out). Combine with liquid (milk), shortening, and beaten egg. Add apples chopped quite fine. Cooked apples will also work. Fry in frying pan over moderate-heat coals; must not be too hot or will not get done in middle. Serve with butter and syrup. Variation: other fruits such as blueberries may be added instead of apples.

Variation: Bisquick may be used instead of making own mixture. Mix with milk, add one egg for better flavor, add 3-4 T. sugar depending on tartness of apples; add nutmeg.

Chocolate Tapioca Pudding

1 egg beaten
3 T. tapioca
2 3/4 cup milk
1/3 cup sugar
1/8 t. salt
1 t. vanilla
1 chocolate square

Mix all ingredients except chocolate square (mix in cocoa if used to replace chocolate and add ½ t. butter) and bring to boil. Cook 6-8 minutes; stir in chocolate square; cool 15-20 minutes. Serve either warm or cold. For fluffier pudding separate yolk and white of egg. Beat whites and add last. Use yolk as before.

Hints

The hunter-trapper fire is really a type of fireplace, rather than a type of cooking. This fireplace is constructed from logs about 3 feet long and 6 inches thick. Logs are placed close enough together to support cooking pots; they may be placed in a V shape as diagrammed. The open end is toward the wind. If more draft is needed, a "damper stick" might be placed under one of the support logs. Variations: If logs are not big enough, dig out some dirt in a semitrench to give more depth. Stones may be used in place of logs. The trench fireplace is also basically the same; however, the end toward the wind should be slanted to allow more draft (see diagram).

Set pots on the dirt sides of a trench (trench may have rocks lining edge if desired).

Build fire between logs, beginning with teepee style. If you wish to bake, burn down to coals and push coals into the V of the logs; then, you may have another small teepee fire towards the open end for frying and preparing other foods in a pot. This dual purpose fire is excellent for conserving fire space. Also, a small fire can go a long way in cooking and the fire is protected somewhat. Anything which can be baked, fried, or boiled can be done on a hunter-trapper fire.

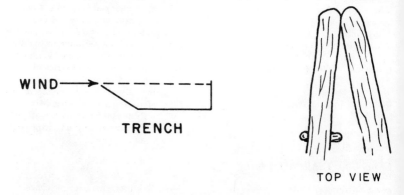

WIND⟶ TRENCH

TOP VIEW

One-Pot Meal

Menu

Slumgullion
Celery and carrot sticks
Dill pickles
Plank bread
Banana boats

Food items and quantities (for 8)

2 lbs. hamburger
½ lb. bacon
2 large onions
4 cans tomatoes
½ lb. American cheese
6 carrots
1 stalk celery (actually ½ is all that's
   needed)
1 small box Bisquick
8 bananas
4 Hershey bars, 16 marshmallows
salt
pepper

Equipment

1 large cooking pot
1 small mixing pot or plastic bag for
   bread dough
1 wooden cooking spoon
can opener
2 ft. of heavy-duty aluminum foil
2 pot holders or gloves
shovel and pail (fire control)
8 plates, cups, knives, forks, spoons
knife for fixing vegetables, cutting
   bacon
matches
paper towels and napkins
dishwashing equipment
soap, especially for soaping pot

Recipes

Slumgullion

Soap kettle well on outside. Dice ½ lb. bacon, fry until crisp in bottom of kettle. Chop onion and add to bacon along with the 2 lbs. of hamburger. When meat is done, add tomatoes and simmer about 15 minutes. Add cubed cheese last and let melt. When just melted, serve. Don't forget salt and pepper added to meat.

Plank Bread

Mix Bisquick and water to biscuit consistency — semisticky dough. Cover split log (plank) with foil. Drop dough onto plank with spoon, or if you have stiffer dough you can make molded biscuits. Prop up plank so biscuits bake in heat of reflected fire. Frying pan may also be used.

Banana Boats

Slit banana skin from end to end, but not over the ends. Open carefully, and holding back the peel, remove a strip of banana on each side with knife. Fill sides with cut-up marshmallows and Hershey bar. Set like a little boat alongside the fire. When side facing fire is all melted, turn around and heat other side. When nice and gooey, eat. Be sure to get Hershey and marshmallow to ends. If the banana is very ripe or does not have a firm peeling, you may need to tie the banana boat together to keep things in (tie with top partially open).

Additional Menu Suggestions

Almost any kind of one-pot meal can be made by using bacon, onion, and hamburger as the base. Get character into the one-pot meal by the additional ingredients used. Some suggestions:

American chop suey. Add 2 cans spaghetti with tomato sauce, green pepper. For a little different flavor, add a bit of sausage to the hamburger and some cooked celery.

Chili. Add to the bacon, onion, hamburger base — 2 cans tomatoes, 2 cans kidney beans, and chili powder.

Campfire stew. Add 2 cans concentrated vegetable soup and enough liquid to keep from sticking.

Ring-tum-diddy. Add 2 cans tomatoes, 3 cans corn, green pepper, ½ lb. cheese. Variation: Omit hamburger and add 1 to 1½ lb. bacon.

Bags-of-gold. Heat tomato soup almost to a boil. Drop in small balls of Bisquick dough that have been wrapped around cubes of cheese. Simmer until dumplings are done.

Hints

Make a substantial crane on which to hang pot. Diagrams illustrate three ways.

Soap pot well on outside with liquid soap (easiest), or make a paste of soap flakes, or use bar of soap with water. By doing this you will make dishwashing *easy.* Be generous with the soap and be sure to get everything covered, but be careful not to get soap on interior.

Fry out bacon first in pot to avoid sticking of other foods. Meat must be cooked almost done before other items already cooked are added. If adding raw vegetables, allow a long time to cook.

CROSSBAR CRANE   TRIANGULAR CRANE   SINGULAR CRANE

When placing kettle over teepee type fire, do *not* set down into flame; the hottest portion of the flame is *at* the tip, not *in* it.

For some fun. Place an egg in a paper cup full of water and place right in the fire. It will not burn as long as water remains. As the water boils away the top edge will also burn. Boil as long as you like — hard- or soft-boiled egg. Most people won't believe it — you'll have to show them!

Reflector Baking

Menu

Sliced ham baked with sweet potatoes
and pineapple slices
Cabbage salad
Cherry pie

Food items and quantities (for 8)

2½ lb. canned ham or equivalent
1 #3 can sweet potatoes or fresh
12 slices pineapple
1 small cabbage
1 cup brown sugar
½ cup or jar of salad dressing
2 cans pie cherries (red, sour), 2 T. tapioca, and ½-⅔ cup sugar or 1 can sweetened pie filling (cherry)
½ lb. butter
salt
pepper
2 cups Bisquick (or make pie dough from flour, shortening, salt)

Equipment

2 reflector cake pans (for ham) or one larger oblong (but then be sure it will fit in reflector)
2 pie tins
2 bowls or pots for mixing
2 mixing spoons
knives for paring and cutting
2 reflector ovens
can opener
axe or saw
matches
pail and shovel (fire control)
2 pot holders or gloves
8 plates, cups, forks, knives
paper napkins and toweling
dishwashing equipment

Recipes

Ham and Sweet Potatoes

Lay ¼'' slices of boiled or canned sweet potatoes in greased pan. Alternate with ham or Spam. Sprinkle generously with brown sugar and butter chunks. Add pineapple slices. Bake before a moderate fire until thoroughly heated and brown sugar begins to make a syrup. May reduce quantity of pineapple or omit altogether.

Cabbage Salad. See Foil Cookery menu.

Cherry Pie

The quickest way to make a pie is to use Bisquick or pie crust mix for the crust. Moisten with water or milk and put in pie tin (greased). Can make pie dough from flour, shortening, salt, and water (see special recipe). For filling use canned cherry pie filling (just put in, need nothing additional) or sour red cherries to which must be added 2 tablespoons of tapioca for thickening and ½-⅔ cup sugar to sweeten. Instead of pie, cobbler can be made merely by putting filling in bottom of cake pan and putting Bisquick mix on top—add a little sugar to it. Bake pie ''open face,'' or make sufficient dough to have a top. If a top is used, sprinkle with melted butter and sugar.

Pie Crust Recipe

Use at least ⅓ cup shortening per cup sifted flour. Blend shortening and flour mixture with water, being careful not to overmix. It should just hold together and is usually a little lumpy. For a 9'' pie tin, use: 1⅓ cup flour sifted, ½ teaspoon salt, ½ cup shortening, 3 tablespoons water.

Additional Menu Suggestions

Anything that can be baked in the oven at home can be made with a reflector oven.

Hints

For reflector baking, one must have a fire bank, fire, and baker. The fire bank may be constructed on a semipermanent basis by using flat stones or green logs supported by a dirt bank or logs. A temporary fire bank may be made by placing another baker across from the first—they reflect back to each other—or use a sliding-saucer sled. A reflector of heavy foil may also be made. The fire bank should face the wind so that flames and ashes will not be blown into the food in the baker.

The fire should be on the same level as the baker. Build the fire as high and wide as the baker you are using. If the fire is too low, bottom of food in baker will burn before top is cooked; if too high, bottom does not cook properly. Keep fire even and steady. Someone should constantly tend fire. The big disadvantage of a reflector fire is that it consumes a great deal of fuel since a flame must be maintained at all times.

There are many types of bakers. Bakers must be level so food inside will not tilt, particularly if item baking is a cake or pie! Sturdy bakers may be made from sheet metal or cookie tins (large rectangular ones). A temporary one may be made by setting pan on grate or sticks 6''-8'' off the ground and placing foil in angular position as other reflectors do. A 30-lb. lard or frozen-food can may be cut in half lengthwise; insert two long rods on which pans may be placed. Individual reflector bakers may be made by using frying pans set up before the fire, pie tins, etc.

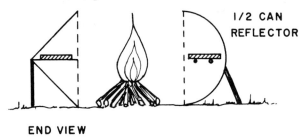

1/2 CAN REFLECTOR

END VIEW

Stick Cookery

Menu

Pioneer drumsticks
Bread twists
Apple salad
Macaroons

Food items and quantities (for 8)	*Equipment*
2 lbs. ground beef	8 green sticks (thumb size)
1 cup cornflakes, crumbled fine	2 mixing pots for salad and drumsticks
2 eggs	4-8 plastic bags (see bread twist recipe)
pepper, onion, salt	knife to cut apples and bread
1 med.-sized box Bisquick	small cereal bowl (see macaroon recipe)
4 medium apples	8 forks, cups, plates
½ lb. grapes	2 mixing spoons
1 cup miniature marshmallows	can opener
1 jar mayonnaise	axe or saw
6 "old" buns	matches
1 can sweetened condensed milk	shovel and pail (fire control)
1 pkg. shredded coconut	dishwashing equipment
¼ lb. butter	paper towels and napkins
1 jar jelly	3 ft. aluminum foil (may be lightweight)

Recipes

Pioneer Drumsticks

2 lbs. hamburger (ground beef)
1 cup cornflakes
2 eggs
onion, salt, pepper

For a good flavor, add a little pork sausage to ground beef. Be sure to cook well.

May also wish to put foil around stick before putting hamburger on to conduct heat inside. Watch that meat doesn't slide off — meat must not be greasy!

Mix beef, seasonings, eggs, and cornflakes thoroughly. Divide into 8 portions. Wrap a portion around a green stick (thumb size) which has been "skinned" (bark peeled off) on one end. If skinned part is short, make two, rather than one thick one. Mold onto stick *thinly*. Cook slowly over coals turning frequently so all sides are evenly cooked. Twist slightly to take off stick. Serve with bread.

Bread Twists

This is probably the commonest stick-cookery food (besides weiners!). It has been found that if the end of the stick is covered with foil, the heat is conducted inside the dough and the bread twist gets done more quickly and the dough rises better, hence a more delicious bread twist. Bisquick is the simplest ingredient to use — just mix with milk or water. It may be mixed easily and with less mess in a plastic bag. Each child may mix his own (or two share a bag), using about ½ cup Bisquick for each bread twist. If the dough is a little sticky, the stick may be put into the bag, and twisted around, getting a thin coating of dough on the foil-covered stick. If you wish, add more Bisquick (or less water) to get a less sticky dough. Take dough out with hand and roll into a "snake." Then spiral or twist around stick or just mold onto stick — be sure it is *thin*. Be sure to cover end of stick so filling will not come out later! Bake slowly by holding about 6'' away from coals at first, so inside will bake. Turn around gradually so that it will brown evenly on all sides. When bread twist is done, it will be easy to turn loose from the stick. If it is tight, it is not done. Stuff hole with your choice of bacon, jam, jelly, cheese, butter, honey, etc. Also delicious is a mixture of butter (melted), cinnamon, and sugar. A cooked (roasted) weiner or small sausage may also be inserted into hole. You may mix grated cheese or orange rind in the dough before baking to get a cheese or orange bread twist. P.S. Be sure sticks are at least thumb-size.

Apple Salad

Cut up 4 medium-sized apples together with grapes and marshmallows. Nuts may be added. Mix in mayonnaise.

Macaroons

Cut "old" buns or bread, preferably solid-loaf Italian or Vienna, into 1" cubes; dip in sweetened condensed milk; roll in shredded coconut. Place on stick and brown slowly so milk caramelizes, making a macaroon. Instead of using a round stick, a pronged or flat sharp-pointed stick will help keep the macaroon from turning around and around on stick. *Do not hurry* baking or milk will *not* caramelize. The coals should be quite hot, but not flaming. You may add a bit of almond extract to milk, if desired. Macaroons can also be made by mixing two bags of shredded coconut and ½ t. almond extract with sweetened condensed milk to a gummy consistency. Drop on foil and bake on coals or in reflector oven. If on foil, coals must not be very hot. Bread cubes spread with white syrup and toasted are good, too.

Additional Menu Suggestions

Kabobs. On end of a thin stick alternately place pieces of steak about 2" square, onion, ¼" sliced potatoes (preferably parboiled), and tomato and green pepper rings if desired. Cook *slowly* over coals, turning frequently. For well-done meat, place pieces about ½" apart and for rare, fairly close together. Baste by interweaving bacon strips. Gives a very fine flavor.

S'mores. A simple old favorite of many. Cook marshmallow slowly until hot and gooey. Place between graham crackers with Hershey bar chocolate (one or more squares). Hot marshmallow will melt chocolate making a delicious, but sweet and messy dessert or snack! Variations: To cut sweetness and add flavor, add slice of apple to "sandwich," or use mint chocolate wafer instead of plain chocolate. Use dried apricots and toasted marshmallow between soda crackers for a variation.

Hints

Stick cooking is a form of cooking over coals and requires *much patience.* It is a slow way to get things *done.* It is not advised for young children, not only because of the time required but also because difficulties frequently occur in keeping food on the stick. To assist "patience," racks may be easily made.

Select sticks that are straight and not too long (approximately 24"). Crooked sticks make even turning difficut, while too long sticks are unwieldy and dangerous. Use one fire for each group of eight people to avoid overcrowding.

INDIVIDUAL PROPS

ROCKS PROP   FORKED
                    STICK PROP

GROUP PROP –
WATCHED BY ONE PERSON
WHO TURNS ALL

COALS IN PIT (TRENCH)
UNDERNEATH

RACK PROP

Often it is not possible to find green sticks nearby but this is no reason why one should be denied the delicacies that can be prepared on a stick. Coat hangers have long been a standby for roasting weiners and marshmallows. Cut off the hook part of the hanger and bend the remainder so that it forms a handle and a two-pronged point which serves to keep food from turning or falling off. For stick cookery which requires a solid, large core, for instance, pioneer drumsticks and bread twists, a ¾" to 1" dowel rod about 18" long may be used. Wrap with aluminum foil on the end where the cooking is being done.

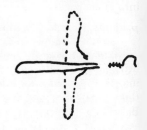

Tin Can Cookery

Menu

Fried ham and potatoes
Tossed salad
Peach cobbler

Food items and quantities (for 8)

2½ lb. ham
8 medium-sized potatoes
1 head lettuce
2 carrots
3 tomatoes
little celery, if available
⅓ cup French or other dressing

1 #2 can sliced peaches
⅓ cup brown sugar, if desired, otherwise white
1 T. butter (for cobbler)
1 cup Bisquick
½ cup shortening
salt

Equipment

10 #10 tin cans	2 mixing spoons
5 tuna fish cans or cans of similar size; tin cups can be used	2 mixing pots (tossed salad and cobbler dough, plastic bag may be substituted for latter)
5 one-lb. coffee tins	
8 knives, forks, spoons, cups, plates	axe
can opener	matches
2 pot holders or gloves	shovel and pail (fire control)
tin snips	dishwashing equipment
knife for cutting potatoes and ham	paper towels and napkins

Recipes

Fried Ham and Potatoes

Nothing special here. Be sure you have sufficient grease on tin can top. Do not put too much food on top or it will spill over and waste. (See Hints—Hobo Stove.)

Tossed Salad

Clean lettuce, carrots, tomatoes, celery. Cut up into pot together. Add dressing. Ingredients may be anything one likes to put into such a salad—green pepper, cucumber, etc.

Peach Cobbler

Use tuna can for baking tin. Grease it. Put some peach slices, a little juice, some sugar, shake of cinnamon if desired, a dot of butter into the can. Mix up some Bisquick and water to form dough. Put thin layer on top of peaches. Sprinkle with sugar and cinnamon. Bake. See following on how to bake on a #10 tin can (hobo stove).

Additional Menu Suggestions

Anything that normally is fried can be made on top of a hobo stove. Particularly good are French toast, apple pancakes, bacon and eggs, hash brown potatoes. For a special sandwich, fry a thick slice of ham, put slice of cheese on top, add a pineapple ring, and, if desired, a little brown sugar. Serve between slices of bread. This sandwich is called "pi-che-am."

Hints

Hobo Stove

A #10 tin can used for cooking is called a "hobo stove." Tin cans can be easily obtained in quantity from school cafeterias, restaurants, or institutions doing quantity cooking. Give them 2 or 3 days notice. If you have a choice, select cans with smooth ends rather than those with circular grooves. If you have a grooved can, you may wish to hammer the grooves smooth for a more easily cleaned and better cooking surface. (The closed end of the can is the cooking surface.) Using tin snips, cut a 3'' doorway in the bottom as shown. You may wish to leave the door attached in order to adjust the amount of air, or it may be cut off and inserted into the end of a stick and used as a spatula. For safety it is desirable to turn the cut edges back with pliers and hammer down until smooth. Punch holes near the top for a chimney. If you burn twigs, you will need more holes for a draft. Cut holes on side opposite the door. Three to 5 holes usually are sufficient. For greater draft on the bottom, raise can on rocks or make tunnel to give a cross draft.

FRONT

Two types of fuel can be used with hobo stoves: natural fuel and buddy burners.

BACK

Buddy Burners

A quick hot fire good for wet weather is provided by the buddy burner. To make, use a tuna fish can, roll a piece of corrugated cardboard the same height as the can, and place inside. Pour paraffin into can. Top of cardboard becomes wick. Usually a buddy burner takes less air than natural fuels. Make as a project before going on cookout.

Natural Fuel

Use dry twigs for fuel, inserting in door of hobo stove. Hard woods are preferable. You may wish to get your *small* teepee fire going and have some coals before placing your hobo stove on the fire. Put sticks in criss-cross to give better air. For the "lazy man," a length of $\frac{1}{4}$'' rubber tubing can be used to direct more air into stove. Fuel must be fed into hobo stove almost continuously.

Cooking

Be sure hobo stove is level. This is both for safety (grease will spill over and blaze up) and to avoid frustration, when frying eggs particularly. Once white begins to spill over, down, down the egg goes *rapidly*. When frying, *do not* fry all bacon at once; it is hard to save the grease (next to impossible!) and it may cause a big fire blaze. Rather, fry out only sufficient grease for the thing you are frying immediately. A good way to fry an egg is to put two pieces of bacon around the outside of the can top and an egg in the middle. Another way to fry eggs is to eat a hole out of the middle of a slice of bread and fry your egg inside the hole. In that way you have eggs and toast ready at the same time and the egg does not spill out as easily. When frying, have one person cook and one person feed the fire (if using natural fuel).

To bake, put three small stones on top of stove. For a more permanent can, insert three stove bolts on top of the hobo stove. This lifts the baking tin (tuna can) off the stove top, permitting circulation of warm air beneath the can. For baking tin use a tuna can, tin cup, small pie tin, or similar container which will fit. Invert a one-pound coffee tin over the baking tin to complete the oven.

For tin can cooking, do not forget the ordinary coffee can stew. Just place small pieces of meat and vegetables in the water in a coffee can with a well-fitting lid. Bring to a boil in coals and then simmer until done.

Blizzard Bucket (also called vagabond stove) and *Safari Grill*

To make a blizzard bucket, take an old bucket, cut slits in both sides and in the bottom for air. Use as a charcoal burner or build a wood fire inside. Place a frying pan on top or cut down a #10 tin can for a frying pan. Anything that can be prepared in a skillet can be cooked. This type of fire has great safety advantage in windy weather or when there is no suitable place to build a fire. Remains also can easily be cleaned up and there is no fire scar left.

A safari grill is very similar. It is made from a metal container about twice the size of a regular bucket. Holes are punched in the bottom for air, as well as about $\frac{1}{3}$ the distance up the side. A hinged grill is placed over the top. Use newspapers for fuel. Crumple four newspaper double sheets (not in tight wad) and light in bottom of grill. The flame will sear the meat in the grill on top. Be sure to turn meat over while flame is still high so both sides are seared to seal in the juices. When newspapers are nearly burnt up, raise the grill and add more crumpled newspaper. It takes about twelve newspapers and 15-20 minutes to roast two half chickens. The safari grill works best when there is a slight wind outside to cause a draft and when the grill on top is covered pretty well with food.

PICNICS

The picnic, an American institution, is the signal for good fun among good friends. Whether it be spring, summer, or fall, the popularity of eating and playing out-of-doors seems never to diminish.

There can never be set rules and regulations for successful picnics, but the suggestions given here should help you to have picnic fun when planning for large groups. Picnics do not just "happen"; many people must work hard to be sure of success. Planning must begin well ahead of time. Some pointers:

Well ahead of the event the general picnic committee should start work on the type of picnic and selection of site, making reservations for date and time and setting up subcommittees.

To help coordination, each subcommittee should be chaired by a member of the general picnic committee. Committees should include publicity, promotion, and invitations; reservations and transportation arrangements; preparation of site (for what is involved in checking facilities see following); program and entertainment; food; cleanup.

There are other things which also must be done. These facilities should be checked: nature and size of game area; waste containers; rest room facilities; water supply; location and sufficiency of picnic tables, benches, and shelters in case of rain; lighting for after-dark activities; firewood; regulations at site. (fires, alcoholic beverages, etc.); parking space; and availability of telephone in case of emergency.

Be sure to have an alternate plan in case of rain. Arrange numerous things for entire group to do together so as to conserve the social values of the picnic. The grounds should be taken care of. Arrange specifically for clean-up; make waste disposal easy; put out whatever fire has been used. Plan to serve the food in a way to prevent long waiting lines. Keep the cost down. Travel time should be kept at a minimum if the length of time available is limited.

Sometimes municipal recreation departments have picnic kits available which may contain such items as 2 softballs and 2 bats, 2 sets horseshoes, box of scratch paper and pencils, first-aid kit, 1 volleyball and net, 1 rubber playground ball, bean bags.

Be sure to take the first-aid kit and Red Cross first-aid book and be sure to have emergency transportation available in case of accident.

REFERENCES

Campcraft Skills

American Camping Association. *Campcraft Instructors' Manual.* American Camping Association, Bradford Woods, Martinsville, Ind. 46151, 1975.

Bales, R. O. *Outdoor Living.* Burgess Publishing Company, Minneapolis, 1961. An inexpensive, simple guide for beginners.

Hammett, Catherine. *Your Own Book of Campcraft.* Pocket Books, Inc., New York, 1950. An inexpensive, simple guide for beginners.

Miracle, Leonard, and Decker, Maurice. *Complete Book of Camping.* Harper and Row, New York, 1961.

Additional program ideas are in Chapter 3, Nature Games, and Chapter 7, Campfire Programs, and Indian Life.

The foregoing books are only a few selected basic references. Bookstores carry many books that teach outdoor skills; be certain the books you choose treat skills suitable to your program. Many books describe survival skills that are not practical in all programs.

Cookery

Angier, Bradford. *Field Guide to Edible Wild Plants.* Stackpole Books, Harrisburg, Pa., 1974.

Cooking Out-of-doors. Girl Scouts of America, New York, 1960.

Most of the campcraft and outdoor living skills books have sections on outdoor cookery. Be certain not to choose books about only backyard barbecueing or game cookery.

Dehydrated and Freeze-dried Food Suppliers

Bernard Food Industries, Inc. (Bernard Kamp Pack), Box 487, St. James Park Station, 22 S. 24th St., San Jose, Calif. 95103.

California Vegetable Concentrates, P.O. Box 3659, Modesto, Calif. 95352.

Chuck Wagon Foods (Chuck Wagon), Dept. CA5, Woburn, Mass. 01801.

Dri-Lite Foods, 11333 Atlantic Ave., Lynwood, Calif. 90262.

Freeze-Dry Foods, Ltd., 201 Savings Bank Bldg., Ithaca, N.Y. 14850.

S. Gumpert Co., Inc. (Trip-Lite), 812 Jersey City, N.J. 07302.

National Packaged Trail Foods, 632 East 185th St., Cleveland, Ohio 44119.

Oregon Freeze-Dry Foods, Inc. (Mountain House and Tea Kettle), P.O. Box 666, Albany, Ore. 97321.

Perma-Pak, 40 East 2430 South, Salt Lake City, Utah 84115.

Rich-Moor, P.O. Box 2728, Van Nuys, Calif. 91404.

Trail Chef, 520 N. Michigan Ave., Chicago, Ill. 60611.
Walnut Acres, Penns Creek, Pa. 17862. (dried fruits and nuts)
Wilson's Certified Foods, 4545 Lincoln Blvd., Oklahoma City, Okla. 73105
      (meats)

Ropecraft

Blandford, Percy W. *Knot End Splices*. ARC Books, Inc., New York, 1965.
Day, Cyrus L. *The Art of Knotting and Splicing*. U.S. Naval Institute, An-
      napolis, Md., second edition, 1955.
Knots and How to Tie Them. Boy Scouts of America, New Brunswick, N.J.
      For making a rope machine, as well as tying knots and splicing rope.
Pioneering. Merit Badge Booklet. Boy Scouts of America, New Brunswick,
      N.J., 1967. For rope bridges.
Rope, Knots, Hitches and Splices. Puritan Mills, Inc., Louisville, Ky., 1968.

CHAPTER V

Projects and Hobbies

MANY PEOPLE FIND that their greatest enjoyment and satisfactions are achieved through projects and hobbies based upon outdoor experiences and materials. These satisfactions and enjoyments are the inherent right of all people including the generations to come. It is of utmost importance, therefore, that good conservation policies and practices be followed during participation in projects and hobbies such as those described in this chapter.

People learn to respect and appreciate the natural environment as they become familiar with the characteristics of natural processes. Keen interest and basic understandings are important factors in the development of attitudes and appreciations. Hobbies and projects are participated in for longer periods than are outings and picnics. For many people they become lifelong interests and therefore provide an excellent opportunity for the development of proper attitudes toward the conservation of natural resources.

Merely because people are in the outdoors or participating in a nature-oriented activity does not mean they are necessarily forming desirable attitudes. If changes are to take place, leaders of outdoor activities will need to plan for these objectives. Everyone interested in the outdoors should assume the responsibility to help others develop appreciation for the natural environment. One approach to ecological involvement that leads to lifelong interests in the outdoors is sensory, based in the affective or "feelings" domain. What is the meaning of the outdoors? How does one foster awareness of a personal relationship with the natural environment? This process has been called by some "acclimatization," and two booklets by Steve Van Matre describe it in very useful detail. They are appropriately entitled *Acclimatization* and *Acclimatizing,* and are published by the

American Camping Association. This kind of awareness program may be used for all types of groups of various ages to introduce them to more meaningful relationships with the environment.

The vast variety of materials found in the outdoors can serve as a basis for hobbies and projects for all people, regardless of age and interest. For the physically active there are rough terrain to be explored and the vigorous activities related to hiking and camping. The outdoors provides a constantly changing scene of natural beauty that invites everyone to observe and enjoy. Nature in winter is as fascinating as in the summer. See Winter Activities in Chapter VII. The serious student is challenged by a never-ending supply of new materials and processes that remain to be discovered, studied, and recorded.

Nature hobbies are not expensive in themselves and few of them require extensive equipment. For their field hobbies most people will want a pocketknife, field guide book and a small notebook in which they can make notations and sketches of what they have observed while on the field trip. The rest is up to the individual. Genuine curiosity, alertness, and a lot of patience are required of the amateur naturalist. He must be ready to develop his senses to the place where he is keenly alert and aware of what is going on around him. In order to fulfill these requirements he will need to put forth an honest effort to improve himself and to find answers to his questions.

Individual activities of a hobby area may be used as projects by the leader of nature-oriented activities. Many types of projects are encompassed by the various fields of nature. Some are self-teaching devices, (electric quiz boards, nature trails, and slides). Others show a process (an ant house or terrarium) or illustrate certain facts (a knot board, leaf board, or a board showing birds identified during the day). Weather prediction or soil testing are projects which test and experiment. Other projects are the making of cages for animals, turtle and reptile pits, and bird banding. There are projects which preserve: pressed leaves and flowers, track casting, mounting butterflies.

The wide range of possible outdoor hobbies and projects makes it impossible to discuss them adequately in this manual. In this section are only a few of the representative areas which have become meaningful to many people who are interested in the outdoors. Additional activities may be found in the sources listed under Nature Study in the References.

Films for interpretation, education, and stimulation are also helpful in developing a nature-oriented program. Check with your own state conservation commission and nearby colleges and universities for pertinent films available from audio-visual libraries. Most of them have excellent films for a nominal rental fee. Because of the many excellent films now available, no effort is made here to give a listing. Watch nature-related and program-oriented periodicals for new films.

CONSERVATION/ENVIRONMENTAL QUALITY

In the decade of the seventies there has been concern for the preservation and improvement of environmental quality, an expanded approach to conservation that involves the total environment. The focus of this concern is on ecological problems, depletion of nonrenewable resources, and the deteriorating quality of elements of the environment such as air and water. There is a real need to help people become more aware of the problems, understand existing solutions and technological capabilities, and become motivated to take appropriate action to enhance environmental quality. Citizen understanding of legislative programs is especially important. There is also a need to develop a respect for the natural environment and an understanding of how nature rules itself through natural laws and how people cause imbalance in the ecological system. Topics through which involvement in conservation and environmental quality concerns can be approached include ecology, air, animals, energy, minerals, plants, soil, water, consumer patterns, environmental ethics, resource use, population, and social implications of conservation. Various sections of this book provide suggestions for activities, projects, and studies on many of these topics. The Conservation Education Association has published an extensive annotated bibliography of resources useful for youth groups and a book *Preserving Man's Environment,* with teaching resource materials.

ANIMALS

The meadows and forests provide homes for many different forms of animal life. Through their regular living activities, these animals (particularly smaller mammals, reptiles and amphibians, and birds [see Bird section]) provide the observant student of nature one of the most interesting of pastimes. Human beings are a part of the animal kingdom; and as such they ought to respect the other forms of animal life, avoiding indiscriminate killing or any manner of injury.

Since many forest animals are nocturnal, the best time to observe them in their natural environment is in the early morning or late afternoon. (See Nighttime Activities, Chapter VII. Even then you need a great deal of patience and the ability to remain quietly in one place for long periods. Most animals, particularly mammals and birds, are afraid of people; a strange scent or noise will often send them on the way before they can be seen. However, the rewards of observing animals in their natural environment as they follow their daily routines are so great that you will consider your time and effort well spent.

The regular placing of food at choice spots and the establishing of feeding stations will attract birds and animals to locations where they can be more easily observed. Once a feeding station is started it should be maintained regularly—particularly in bad weather—for birds and animals will have come to depend upon it for their sustenance. Simple blinds which hide the observer from view will help to get you close enough for detailed observation and for photography.

Tracking and track casting are also enjoyable activities related to animals. You should not forget that tracking can be done as well in the snow during winter as in the warm season. Tracking can be used for finding animals to observe or just for the satisfaction of being able to follow tracks over a considerable distance. Track casting is further discussed in the chapter on Nature Crafts.

Animals from the meadows and forests can make excellent pets and may be kept in a cage or a home or camp zoo. Raccoons, descented skunks, white-footed mice, and others make interesting house pets. Before you obtain an animal, you should learn as much as you can about the animal, its habits and needs, so that you will know how to take care of it and what to feed it. Be familiar with the game laws of your state, for certain animals are protected. In some instances it is possible to secure permits for trapping and keeping animals for scientific study.

Unless you prefer to purchase your animal from a pet shop, or have it given to you by someone, you will probably want to trap it. Live-animal traps that do not hurt the animals are relatively simple to construct. Once these traps are set, they should be checked daily so that captured animals do not suffer unnecessarily. Fully grown animals usually are difficult to tame so you should try to get young ones—preferably of weaning age when they are already eating solid foods.

Give your animals the best care that you can. Newly trapped animals are frightened and should not be handled more than necessary until they are in their cage and accustomed to their new surroundings. Feed them regularly and dispose of their wastes daily. The cage should be thoroughly cleaned once a week. Check the animals for sickness or open sores and see to it that they receive the proper medical attention. Do not touch or attempt to make pets of animals that appear to be sickly or have open sores.

Give the animals some attention, as they, too, need companionship. Be with them during feedings and give them plenty of opportunity to get enough exercise. If an animal refuses to eat, release it into its natural environment. After you have had an animal as a pet for a period of time, it is better to find another home for it than to turn it loose. It will probably have forgotten how to cope with the problems that confront it in the natural world.

ASTRONOMY

The heavens with their brilliant stars and roving planets have attracted people's attention since the earliest times. From ancient carvings and tablets it has been determined that the movements of the planets were fairly well understood as early as 3000 B.C. Astronomy is one of the oldest sciences. There were professional astronomers long before there were such other professional scientists as botanists or biologists. Some of these were given places of royalty and were instructed to chart the courses of the stars and to make predictions of future events based upon their observations.

As in historical times, there are many amateur astronomers today who observe and study the skies. From the stars they can determine time, direction, and location. While this information has been helpful to some people like sailors, most of the modern amateur astronomers observe the sky because of their interest and curiosity and the inner satisfactions that they receive from the activity. Their attention usually is focused on the study of stars, planets, satellites, meteors, comets, star clusters, and nebulae.

Between six and seven thousand stars can be observed with the naked eye, so it is not necessary to have expensive equipment to become an active astronomer and to enjoy the skies. A star guide or a book which shows the location of the stars at the various times of the year is helpful. A pair of binoculars will enable you to see the moons of Jupiter and the craters on Earth's moon. Later, as your interest grows, you may want to purchase or build a telescope which will make it possible for you to see double stars and many other interesting things that are impossible to see with the naked eye.

Making telescopes and other astronomical equipment can become an interesting hobby in itself.

A few stars usually can be seen from any location, but it is advisable to get away from as many lights as possible while you are studying the skies. Do not hurry, for it will take about 15 minutes for your eyes to adjust to the darkness. If you are out with a group of people, you will find a flashlight with a bright beam helpful in pointing out stars and in communicating what you are seeing to others in your party. Set a goal for yourself and try to become familiar enough with the sky so that you can recognize 20 major constellations and 12 of the brighter stars. This knowledge will serve you well as a point of reference in your future study.

The ancient star watchers soon located stars that appeared to be grouped in such a way that, with a bit of imagination, they could see in them the shape of an animal like a horse or a dog. These groups of stars are called constellations and interesting stories and legends were told about them. The telling of these legends and looking for constellations make interesting evening camping and recreation programs. Today the sky has been divided into sections which are named after the constellation that they contain and serve as a point of reference.

Special events such as solar and lunar eclipses have always interested astronomers. These can be predicted to the exact minute of their appearance. Meteor showers with their shooting stars thrill the sky watchers, as do the Northern and Southern Lights. Visits to planetariums and observatories are a good way to interest youth groups in astronomy.

To stimulate interest in astronomy, the Milwaukee, Wisconsin, recreation program developed a Starwagon which is used primarily for the late-hour period on the summer playgrounds, although it could also well be used at other locations and with other groups. The Starwagon is 21 feet in length with a 15-foot (diameter) collapsible dome. Equipment includes a planetarium projector; space interpretation globes; reflector, refractor, and satellite tracking telescopes; charts; and other visual aids. The program usually includes a 30-45 minute lecture followed by viewing of celestial objects through the 'scopes for an hour or more. The interpreter covers such subjects as recognition of constellations, daily and seasonal motion of the stars, planetary motions, position of the moon, fixed stars, and the concept of absolute magnitude. These are related to recent attempts to conquer space as well as to ancient mythology. Public museums and astronomical societies usually are very happy to assist in projects of this type.

Another sometimes overlooked aspect of astronomy is the

finding of directions using the celestial bodies. Location of the North
Star, of course, is the most common. Sundials have also been
popular. A Virginia Boy Scout developed what is known as the
"Shadow Tip Method" of finding direction. It has been field-tried by
the U.S. Army and Air Force and found to be very satisfactory. The
method:

1. Drive a stake vertically into the ground, allowing a minimum
   projection of 3 feet above the ground.
2. Mark the tip of the shadow on the ground.
3. Wait 10 minutes or more.
4. Mark the spot where the tip now is.
5. Draw a line between the two tip marks. This line is always east
   and west and the second point made is always east.

Even on a dull, cloudy day, it is usually
possible to get a shadow if one goes to an open
field and spreads a light-colored material to
catch the shadow.

BIRDS

One of the most interesting and exciting hobbies available to
nature lovers is that of observing birds. They are interesting little
creatures clothed in a variety of colors ranging from a drab gray to
brilliant reds. Their songs have added cheer to many dreary days.
Their ability in homemaking and nest building has amazed even the
most advanced naturalists and held them spellbound as they have
watched the parents prepare for the raising of their young.

Bird watching is probably the activity which is engaged in most
frequently by bird lovers. Many people like to follow this through
with a bird feeding program, or making of a bird sanctuary, or by
entering into the research part of bird study which includes bird
banding.

You do not need expensive equipment to begin bird watching. In
fact, you do not need anything except your eyes and an interest in
birds. There are a few aids which will make bird watching more
enjoyable and will help you to learn about birds more rapidly. The
first of these is a pocket guide such as Peterson's *Field Guide to the
Birds*. This book is so arranged that it not only helps you to identify
the bird but quickly points out its distinguishing characteristics —
size, shape, song, surroundings, sweep (flight), shade (color) —
sometimes referred to as the Six S's. Soon you will also want to take

with you a small notebook in which to jot down observations on your explorations.

A good pair of binoculars is a big help, as they bring the birds close enough so that you can study them in detail. These should be selected with care. Binoculars are expensive, but since this is a lifetime investment it will pay you to get a durable pair with good lenses. Best bird-watching sizes are 7 x 35 or 7 x 50, preferably with central focusing (focusing both lenses simultaneously).

The best time to go looking for birds is in the early morning, when they are most active, or toward evening. Walk away from the sun because it is difficult to see the colors of the birds when you are looking into the sun. The best places to go in search of birds are along the edge of the forest, edges of fields and pastures, marshes and other areas where feed and water are available.

As your interest grows in bird watching, you may want to expand your efforts to include feeding birds in the winter. Simple bird feeders can be constructed. Once you begin setting out feed, birds will come to your area regularly and you may be able to observe them from your window all winter. You should be careful to continue feeding all winter as the birds come to rely on your supply. Suggested food for birds includes suet, sunflower seeds, and a variety of small grains and seeds.

Building birdhouses and setting out nesting materials also are projects which groups or individuals can participate in. Directions for birdhouse construction appear in the references at the end of this chapter. Different species of birds have their own preferences as to size and shape of house, so you should decide upon the kind of bird that you want to attract before beginning to make birdhouses.

Much of what is known about birds has come through the information gathered by amateur bird watchers. There are additional opportunities through participation in the bird banding program of the U.S. Fish and Wildlife Service. In this program birds are captured, banded, and released—the bander doing the identification and record keeping. Information concerning each bird banded—species, sex, age, and place of banding—is reported to the U. S. Fish and Wildlife Service at the end of each year. You must have a permit to participate in this program, and the U.S. Fish and Wildlife Service provides you with instructions, record-keeping forms, and the bands. Further information concerning this program may be obtained by writing this agency.

SEE REFERENCES

CREATIVE EXPRESSION

A common need shared by all human beings is that of being able to give expression to their inner feelings and to their interpretation of their surroundings. In this sense, all of us are artists and have some artistic ability — although the channels through which we give expression may vary greatly in individuals.

People need to learn how to express themselves in a manner which is satisfying to themselves and acceptable to society. We have a responsibility to teach the children of our community acceptable ways of expressing themselves creatively. If we fail to do this we may expect them to develop undesirable habits and to participate in activities that are harmful both to themselves and their community.

The outdoors provides a setting that is conducive to creative expression. The colorful, relaxing scene of the setting sun or the beauty of the dainty spring wild flowers creates the desire to capture the beauty of the moment, retain it for future enjoyment, and share the experience with others. In order to do this we need to be observant so that we see, analyze, and understand what is visible in the natural world. Then we will want to look for the medium through which we can best interpret to others what we see. The following are some forms of creative expression.

Sketching. With such simple and inexpensive materials as a soft lead pencil or a piece of charcoal and some paper it is possible to capture some of the action and beauty of the moment. A gnarled and twisted oak silhouetted against the sky or the sleek form of a deer or other animal make excellent subjects for sketching.

Painting. Oil paints enable the aspiring artist to capture the color of the scene, which is not possible, of course, in sketching. Equipment for oil painting should include an easel, canvas, oil paints, brushes, etc. Many amateur painters have derived hours of pleasure from this rewarding activity. The use of watercolors should not be overlooked.

Prose and poetry. Too many people have the idea that poetry and prose can be written only by a select few who have a talent in this area. This is not true. If you have never had the opportunity to go into the natural world by yourself and try to express your feelings in words, you have missed the opportunity of your lifetime. Many people are writing poetry and prose today for the satisfaction which comes only through creative expression.

Song and music. Some people find it rewarding to express themselves through music, for truly there is magic in the rhythm and music in the natural world. This can be done either through creating new melodies or by creating new words to known melodies. Children of elementary and junior high age particularly enjoy this type of activity.

There are many other ways in which people can express their feelings creatively. Some of these — wood carving, basketry, and photography — are discussed in other chapters.

HISTORICAL-CULTURAL ACTIVITIES

The Bicentennial celebration in the United States has increased emphasis on "heritage activities," and certainly the natural environment provides rich opportunities to engage in them. Through better understanding of what has transpired between people and nature and also of the "monuments" that people have left in the natural environment, perhaps greater insights can be gained into the impacts of present day decisions that must be and are being made on the quality of environment. In Chapter I under Community Resources a number of historical places are suggested for field trips; many of the crafts in Chapter II might be considered "pioneer crafts" of our forefathers. The survival sports of hunting and fishing discussed in Chapter VI, as well as many of the outdoor living skills in Chapter IV, contribute toward historical understandings. In Chapter VII there is also a section on Indian Life. "Heritage activities" should be authentic and scientifically making a contribution, not merely "fun" for the participants.

Homesteading

President Lincoln signed the Homestead Act in 1862. Under it, any adult citizen or intended citizen, male or female, could "take up" a quarter-section (160 acres) or an eighth-section (80 acres), depending on the quality and location of the land, by paying a ten-dollar recording fee. The homesteader had to live on the land, cultivate it, and make certain minimum improvements; at the end of five years the place was his or hers — free. When the pioneers were looking for land, they looked for a place where there was good soil and plenty of water and timber. When they found land that pleased them, they staked their claims. They measured the land by paces; a good-sized step by an adult, or about one yard. Eighty-four paces each way made an acre, and 750 paces each way made 160 acres. The corners of the claim were marked in different ways—with a big rock, a stake with a sign, or a mound of dirt. A stream or a row of trees might be used to mark the boundary of a claim, or as rocks were removed from a field they might be formed into a boundary. In the Midwest the U.S. Government had given the railroads a considerable amount of land, and some of the settlers received land from the railroad. Certain acreage was also set aside for schools.

Look in your community for homesteaded sites; talk with the "old timers" and utilize the records of the courthouse and the historical society. Most areas today have been surveyed and have surveying markers. Check to see where the surveyor marks are (and when they were established), and whether any of the original claim markings remain. Also look for school sites and old railroad beds. If old houses or barns are still standing, see how they were built.

Sometimes you will find family cemeteries or old town or church cemeteries which will help you to identify the pioneers. Try to construct family trees from the markers. Read the epitaphs. See how old the various persons were when they died. In what era did they live (earliest settlers, part of the Civil War times, etc.)? What was the environment like—timber covered, plowed fields, etc.?

Income-producing Activities

The pioneers turned to the environment for their food and clothing and also for "business enterprises" as selling and buying became a part of their life. Study the environment both for remains of agricultural practices and for simulation of pioneer activities. Can you find old logging roads and abandoned railroad beds? Perhaps they are used for hiking trails today. Were the rivers used for barge transportation? Are there old sawmills around yet or iron furnaces with attendant charcoal pits? What about mills that used water wheels? or sand pits and quarries? What agricultural practices were used? Perhaps a visit to a museum that has old implements would be interesting.

Archeological "Digs"

Often a "dig," calls to mind the remains of Indians who first lived on this continent—their homes, tools, etc. But one can also "dig" for more recent remains, such as foundations/basements of pioneer homes, old cabins, etc.

Before attempting a "dig," one should (1) get permission from appropriate persons, (2) study the history of the era carefully, particularly the life style so one can anticipate what type of artifacts might be found, and (3) plan very carefully for the "dig," including learning about the proper techniques.

In preparing the site, it is desirable to establish a boundary and then keep all work within it. The area should be divided into a grid with a number of squares to make keeping records of findings easier. Grids usually have a system of balks, strips of uncut ground running between the squares that make removing the dirt from the grid sections easier. The grid squares and balks should be measured and marked with stakes and strings and a numbering system should be devised. There are several jobs to be done for a "dig" — caring for the tools, keeping records, taking pictures, and removing dirt as well as digging! When artifacts are found they should be labeled with a detailed record made of where they were found, etc., in order to reconstruct the site later.

If sufficient artifacts are found, an archaeological report should be written including documentary history, method of excavation, archaeological evidence, summary about principal artifacts recovered (including pictures, measurements, etc.), and general information about location of the site and acknowledgements of who worked on the "dig." The finding should be shared through presentations, exhibits, and perhaps printed leaflets.

Material remains of past culture tell a great deal about the people who have proceeded us on this continent. Since a "dig" is a systematic destruction of a site, a great deal of caution must be exercised when undertaking a "dig," especially one that excavates more than a partially buried old homestead foundation. The cooperation of a local amateur or professional archaeologist is recommended to help plan and carry out a "dig."

PLANTS, INCLUDING GARDENING

Besides the actual growing of plants in a garden and forest area (see later section, Children's Gardening) the program might also include activities in conservation, garden therapy, horticulture, nature study, civic beautification, flower arranging, food preparation; visits to greenhouses, florists, vegetable markets, nurseries, flower and vegetable shows and exhibits, and fairs; the performing of experiments; tours of the town and visits to private vegetable and flower gardens. For preservation of flowers, leaf prints, and other crafts from native materials, see section on Nature Crafts; also see Nature Photography.

Of particular interest to youngsters, especially those gardening, are other adventures with seeds: how seeds travel (shot from pods, hitch-hikers which steal rides, seeds that fly); seeds used for pixies and pictures; food for birds (set up a bird cafeteria); germination experiments; raising trees from seeds (miniature tree garden); growing seeds in water to eat as sprouts in oriental foods. Mushroom hunts and collecting and preparation of edible wild foods make interesting activities. One can learn many fascianting things while studying the plants normally called "weeds." Wild flower inventories can become as popular a hobby as keeping a bird list.

There are also a host of activities associated with trees, some of which have already been mentioned. Tree stump explorations; study of dendrology and making of a tree calendar; leaf skeletons; identification boards and exhibits of leaves, seeds, winter twigs, wood specimens; and making of leaf keys, as well as nature crafts and other activities, are just a few which can be included in the nature-oriented community recreation program.

Field plot study is one of the most interesting methods of integrating observations of plants, animals, and soils. Such studies encompass those investigative activities that can be carried on within a small, defined land area on or near school grounds, in park areas, or in the backyard. The plot chosen should have considerable variety of features and be away from "heavy traffic" (people trampling). Several plots with contrasting features might be selected for comparative purposes. Plots may be as small as one square yard. The features of the plot are studied in some exploratory depth. Usually a plot is approached from three views — (1) where it is located in relation to its surroundings; relief, topographic, contour maps can be used; (2) biological aspects involving the requirements of living organisms, both plant and animal, to sustain life, the interdependencies and interrelationships of plants and animals, and the characteristics of the organisms under study; and (3) the abiotic influences or physical properties, including the effects of rocks, land forms, soil, water, and climate upon the plot environment and its "inhabitants." An excellent activities guide is *Field Plot Studies* by Berry (see references).

Another popular and interesting project to show environmental interrelationships is the terrarium. Terraria are miniature habitats. Simple, inexpensive containers may be constructed from large-mouthed gallon jars or glass sheets fastened together. The primary types of terraria are desert, woodland, bog, and semiaquatic. Each has different kinds of plants and requires different planting and care.

SEE REFERENCES

Preserving Herbarium Specimens

The collection, preparation, and preservation of plants is a very popular and rewarding activity. The following procedures demonstrate an easy, cheap, and efficient method for preserving herbarium specimens of vascular plants. (Based upon material prepared by the Department of Botany, State University of Iowa.)

1. Carefully select the specimen in the field. It is preferable that the specimen be in flower or fruit. Underground parts of herbaceous plants should be included and carefully dug with a strong trowel, collecting pick, or machete. For woody plants, where it is not feasible to take the root portion, a branch showing leaf, bud, twig, and flower or fruit characteristics should be obtained. Care should be taken not to take sepcemens when there is danger of locally exterminating a rare species.

2. Immediately upon the taking of each specimen, a record should be made in a notebook indicating habitat, location, and date. Notation should be made of petal color, glaucescence, and other characteristics often lost in drying. The height of the plant and the diameter at about 4½ ft. (chest height) should also be noted for woody plants.

3. The pressing of the plant should take place as soon as possible in order to preserve it in its best condition. If a field press is not used, the tagged specimen should be placed in a metal collecting can (vasculum) or plastic bag with moist newspaper to keep the specimen fresh. Pressing can be delayed overnight in cool climates if the specimen is stored in a cool place.

4. To prepare the specimen for pressing, remove the soil and excess moisture from roots and judiciously prune superfluous leaves, being careful not to destroy parts necessary to identify the plant. Place in a folded newspaper. Plants that are longer than a folded half newspaper sheet should be bent accordian-style (V- or N-shaped) with roots at lower left corner of the sheet. Some leaves should be turned over so that both upper and lower surfaces are displayed in the dried specimen. Extra flowers and fruits of the specimen should be included if possible. Collection data should be written directly on the sheets, at least in abbreviated form, in order to avoid confusion of specimens or data later.

5. After plant is placed in the folded newspaper, place newspaper between blotters or felt driers (12" x 18") which are in turn separated from each other by corrugated cardboard or aluminum corrugates which serve as ventilators. The resulting pile of newspapers with plants, blotters, and corrugates is pressed between press frames 12" x 18", usually ash or hickory slats riveted together. The material is put under pressure by tightly tying straps or sash cord around the frames. After the ventilated press is tightly bound, it is placed over a source of dry, heated air. Usually 24 hours of drying suffices for all but the most succulent plants when corrugates and an artificial heat source are used. A good source of dry heat is a series of light bulbs in a wooden frame on top of which the pressing frames are placed with open corrugates down so that the heat will flow up and through the corrugates.

If corrugates are not used, blotters should be alternated with the folded newspapers with specimens inside and must be changed for warm, dry ones every day until the specimens are dry. These moist blotters should be placed in the sun or against radiators to dry.

6. After drying, the specimens may be stored permanently in the labeled newspaper sheets in which they were dried or they may be prepared for mounting. In either instance, specimens should be labeled with neatly written, typed, or printed labels bearing the name of the plant with authorities for the name (as *Buchloe dactyloides* (Nutt.) Engelm. or *Quercus rubra* L.), the habitat, location, date of collection, and other pertinent information, and the collector's name and collection number. The label should be 100 percent rag paper 4" x 2½" or larger. One label should be placed with each specimen sheet.

If mounting specimens, they should be attached to 100 percent rag paper, standard size herbarium sheet (11½" x 16½") which may be obtained from local printer or stationery shop or a biological supply house. Carefully paste label in one corner, preferably lower right-hand. The specimen may be attached to sheet by use of bands of quick-drying liquid plastic, gummed cloth strips, thread, special herbarium paste or glue (such as Special "A" Tin Paste or Improved Process Glue), or combinations of these methods. If glue or paste is used, it is spread in a thin layer over a sheet of glass (14" x 20" or larger) with a small paint brush. The specimen, face upward, is placed firmly (without smearing) on the glue, lifted with tweezers or forceps, and dropped carefully in the desired position on the mounting paper. Excess drops of glue should be removed with a damp cloth. The sheet is then placed between clean, unprinted newspaper sheets (newsprint) in a pile under a light weight. When the glue is dry, the twigs and other heavy parts of the specimen are taped or sewed to the sheet for added reinforcement.

7. The finished sheets are now ready to be inserted with other sheets in standard manila envelopes, each holding a genus, and placed in insectproof and dustproof herbarium cases. Protection from insects and mold can be given by storing in dry places with Paradow (mothballs) or occasional fumigation. Large herbaria often use alcohol solutions of bichloride of mercury for dipping specimens before mounting, or paint specimens after mounting for more permanent protection.

Children's Gardening

Although this section is directed toward children's gardening, gardening is an activity for all age groups, and is particularly suited to families and senior citizens.

Children's gardens are areas where children help plan and maintain the land and the vegetation which is grown. Many children's gardens are school sponsored, but because the growing season extends into summer, frequently this may be in conjunction with a municipal recreation department which can assume supervision after school is out. Some private organizations, such as garden clubs and botanic gardens, also sponsor children's gardens.

Junior Gardeners' Pledge

I promise to help protect birds, plants, trees, and flowers everywhere; to help make my community healthful and beautiful and not throw candy wrappers, fruit peels, or paper on streets, sidewalks, or lawns, no matter whether I am walking or riding in a car. I will be as careful of other people's places and things as I would like them to be of mine; and I will do my best to sow seeds or plant flowers or a tree at least once a year.

You Can Almost Tell

Folks who make a garden,
Who love to weed and hoe,
Always seem less worried
Than other folks I know.

They also seem more gentle,
Their hearts with love abound.
You can almost tell such people
By the look they carry around.

Can it be that gardening
Plays a double role,
Fulfills creative longing
And cultivates the soul?
— Ruth R. Heuter

The values of gardening experience for children are many. Here are a few:

1. For many children this is their first experience with growing plants.
2. They will gain a better understanding of the plant's life cycle by observing its seed sprout, grow, mature, bear fruit, die.
3. It provides an opportunity to accept responsibility, for they will soon learn that they "reap what they sow" and they must take care of their plants if they want them to produce.
4. They will develop new appreciation for the work that goes into the production of the world's food.
5. They will be learning by actually doing, through working with their hands. Safety with tools will also be learned.
6. It assists in the understanding of the need for conservation — the role of fire, insects, disease, water.
7. The opportunity for work experience is particularly important for city children.
8. The chance to work in a group project teaches cooperation on boundaries, paths, equipment, and sharing of joy in the achievement of others.
9. It creates a love and appreciation for beautiful things. This will encourage them to make things beautiful and give them a feeling of joy in the care and propagation of plants.
10. They will develop interests that may grow into valuable lifetime hobbies and wise use of leisure time.

There are various types of gardens. Both vegetable growing and flower growing should be planned for in a children's garden program, although certainly one does not need to insist that a child plant both. Specialty gardens also are valuable.

There are also different kinds of gardens in location and design. The home garden is very common, but when utilized in the community recreation program, certain guidance and visitation should be provided. The commonest type (sponsored by municipalities and schools) is the tract garden where each child has a small plot in a large garden area which he takes care of himself. A third type of garden is the farm or forest garden which may have individual gardens but is usually cared for as a group. This garden is usually away from the city so that transportation must be provided. Specialty gardens are another type—dish gardens, indoor terraria, flats, miniature gardening on a button in a bowl, window boxes, rock gardens, wild flower collections, and the like.

In all gardening activities the children should help in designing or landscaping the area. They should help prepare the land, plant the seeds, care for the garden during the growing season, reap the harvest, use the crop, and then clear the area. They should also learn what the tools are, when and why to use them, and how to care for them. Here are some guiding principles for supervising children's gardens:

1. Children should be from 8-10 years of age to start in a gardening program.
2. Involve the children in all phases of gardening, including planning, purchase of seeds, preparing the ground, planting, hoeing, and reaping.
3. Discuss the items that should be considered in the selection of a garden site—good soil, proper drainage, shade, and sunlight.
4. Plan your garden on paper, including a diagram of the area and a list of the seeds that will be needed.
5. Gardens do not need to be large (8' x 10' minimum). Rectangular plots with well-defined paths around them are preferred to square ones.
6. Include a variety of flowers and vegetables in your plans. Choose those that mature rapidly and are hardy so that the beginners will be assured of success.
7. Children should learn how to start plants and which ones need to be started indoors.
8. Work the soil when it is dry enough so that it does not form mud balls.
9. Plant the seeds at the proper time and depth.

10. The following equipment will be needed in your **gardening** program:

spading fork
iron rake (ladies' size, 8-tine)
sticks or pot labels (for marking end of rows)
yardstick
heavy string
trowel
hand cultivator
hoe (ladies' size)

SEE REFERENCES

INSECTS

Everybody has had some experience with insects and no wonder, for more than one-half of all of the known animals in the world are insects. Too frequently associations with insects have not been under favorable conditions and many people have a negative reaction at the mention of the term. They immediately think of the mosquitoes that they have slapped, the flies that molested their naps, or the ants that were the uninvited guests at their picnics.

Actually, a very small percentage of insects are ''bad,'' and many perform valuable services in the propagation of plant life. Fortunately, nature has provided a system of checks and balances so that natural enemies have pretty well kept the undesirable species under control.

There is a real fascination in the study of these small, six-legged creatures. The brilliant colors of many of the insects, such as the butterfly and beetle, beckon us to take a closer look—and soon we are thrilled with the beauty which we had never before seen. The highly developed social systems of the ants, termites, wasps, and bees continue to amaze even the most ardent student of insects, for they are to the insect world what human beings are to the world of mammals.

The purpose behind watching these little creatures is to learn as much about them and their living habits as possible. There is a real advantage for a beginner to work with someone who has experience in working with insects. Frequently the science teachers in the local school can give you some help or suggest others in the community that share your interest. A good book to help identify and classify insects is almost a must. In addition to this, a few simple homemade materials such as a collecting net, killing jar, mounting boards, and display boxes will be sufficient to get you started.

Killing jar. A homemade killing jar can be made by placing a layer of cotton batting on the bottom of a screw-tip pint jar. Moisten the cotton with carbon tetrachloride or ethyl acetate, which is safer. Cover this with a piece of cardboard cut so that it fits snugly over the cotton. Wrap the bottom 1-1½'' of the jar with masking tape or adhesive tape to prevent shattering in case the jar does happen to drop or hit against something. Killing jars should be used with a great deal of caution. Potassium cyanide, frequently used in killing jars, must *never* be used around children since it is an extremely potent poison.

Collecting net. A serviceable collecting net can be made by bending a coat hanger into a circle, attaching a length of broom handle to the hanger-hook part which has been straightened, attaching cheesecloth (to form a net) to the circular form, and sewing up the side and bottom to make a sack.

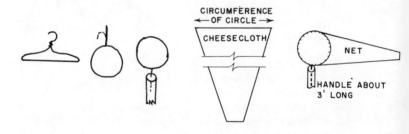

Mounting or spreading boards. Insects such as butterflies and moths should be placed on a spreading board to dry so that the wings will remain in an attractive open position. You can make a spreading board from a paper plate by cutting out a thin strip in the center for the insect's body, and using strips of paper to hold the wings in place. A more permanent spreading board can be made from soft wood, with a strip of balsa wood below the groove to hold the insect pins. Lightweight cardboard strips can be attached to the top to hold the wings in place.

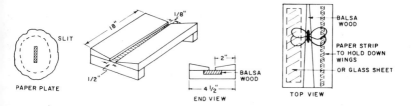

Display boxes. Cigar boxes or hosiery boxes make nice display cases. It is best to use thin dressmaker's pins for insect mounting pins rather than regular straight pins because the latter are too thick. Use #1 pins for most insects, #2 for butterflies, and #3 and #4 for large moths and butterflies. In mounting, the pin should be thrust through the thorax of most insects, slightly to the right of center. Bugs, however, are pinned through the small triangle in the center of the back, while beetles are pinned through the right wing covering. Grasshoppers and crickets are pinned through the saddle.

Beetles (pin through forepart of right wing)
True bugs (pin through triangular patch)
Butterflies, moths, flies, wasps, bees, etc. (pin through thorax).
Grasshoppers, crickets (pin through saddle)

Insects are difficult to identify since there are over 650,000 known species. These are divided into 25 major orders — some of which are known by common names such as beetles, moths, butterflies, flies, termites, etc. Once identification is made, the insect should be properly mounted, labeled, and displayed. Labels should be attached to the mounting pins as shown in the diagram and include besides the name of the insect, the location where found, date, and name of finder if desired.

Insects can be found almost everywhere. The problem of finding the kind that you want is far more difficult. Many different kinds can be found in grassy areas, in gardens, and on trees. Insects have a desire for sweet food, so it is possible to place some food for them

and wait for the insects to come to you. Light also attracts insects and
it is possible to make insect traps using lights to attract them. Insects
may be found during any time of the year, even in midwinter, but are
the most active in the late summer and fall.

There are many other projects related to insect study which are
of interest to adults as well as children. Because of their relatively
short life span, it is possible to capture insects and watch them go
through the entire life cycle in as little as a four-week period. A large
jar containing some leaves makes an excellent cage for a caterpillar.
You can then observe him as he goes through the process called
metamorphosis, emerging as a butterfly. The making of observation
hives in which to keep bees or an ant house in which to keep a colony
of ants is always interesting.

Ant House (formicarium)

Take two pieces of window glass, 10" x 14", 12" x 18", or
whatever size you have available, and insert 1" apart into a
frame grooved to hold the glass. Top of
the frame should be removable so that
the ants can be put in. Two or three
holes should be made through which the
ants are fed and watered. Close holes
with corks or small strips of wood which
turn on a nail or screw. The house may
be put together with adhesive tape. If
desired, place house on wooden blocks.
It is desirable to seal around the glass
fitting with paraffin—ants have a way
of getting out of the smallest crack!
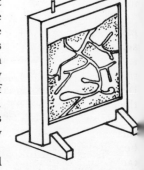
To fill with ants, locate ant hill and
scoop out a couple of handfuls or trowelfuls of ant-dirt mixture. Try
to get eggs, larvae, pupae, and a queen. The queen is especially
important as the ants frequently will not work too well without her.
She is a larger and fatter ant. Pour ant-dirt mixture between glass
panes. Fill to about 2" from the top. Before fastening top, hang two
small sponges under the two openings. One is to be kept moist with
water, the other with sugar water or honey water. Occasionally throw
in a few flies or other insects. Cover with heavy paper or cardboard to
keep dark except when viewing. You will then
be able to observe the ants' tunnel-digging
prowess and how they move things.

NATURE PHOTOGRAPHY

More and more people are becoming interested in nature photography. With the increasing amount of inexpensive photographic equipment and materials available today, many people are beginning to keep pictorial records of their trips into the parks, forests, mountains, and other natural areas. Black and white and color pictures and slides are taken with many different types and sizes of cameras.

Some of these people are primarily interested in documenting the things that they have seen and the places where they have been. Frequently their emphasis will be "artistic" in nature; the photographer will attempt to capture some of the beauty and color to take with him so that he can relive the experiences at a later date. Many teachers and amateur naturalists also are taking pictures for scientific purposes. These pictures may be used for identification purposes or to illustrate some form of nature in its natural setting. Excellent subjects for this kind of photography are birds, animals, wild flowers, insects. Care should be taken to show these animals in their natural habitat and in real-life situations. Do not give false impressions through trick photography or by faking pictures.

It is well for the beginning photographer to spend some time planning his trip before he goes out. He should attempt to get a series of pictures that tell a story rather than to take pictures at random and then try to build a story around the pictures. "A day in the forest" or "exploring a stream" are themes that might be used. Decide what type of pictures will best help you to tell your story and then take them with this purpose in mind.

It is not necessary to have expensive equipment before starting this hobby, since a simple, inexpensive box camera will take beautiful pictures. It does help, though, to have a portrait lens attachment for close-up shots. Single and twin reflex cameras have become popular for nature photography because of the advantages they offer in focusing and composing the picture subject through the same or similar lens that takes the pictures. Most single lens reflex cameras use 35mm film, while the most popular double lens reflex cameras use 2¼" x 2¼" film. Many cameras now offer the versatility of interchangeable lenses which provide telephoto, wide-angle, or close-up shooting in addition to normal picture taking. A sturdy tripod (which helps eliminate camera movement) is helpful for time exposures. Strobe lights or flash bulbs help to get good exposures made in deep forest, shaded areas, or in areas with other poor lighting conditions, as well as in "freezing" action shots.

Select the film that will best serve your purpose. If you are going to be shooting pictures in dim light or of objects that are moving rapidly, a fast film should be used. Color pictures are beautiful but expensive in the larger sizes. The 35mm size is good for transparencies. Small-sized cameras being developed are convenient and take good pictures. Check with your local photography shop for both camera and film recommendations to serve your purposes best— there are always new developments in this area.

There are many subjects in nature that will be a challenge to the best of photographers. Birds are extremely colorful and are always available. It is difficult, however, to get close enough for a good shot without a telephoto lens. Placing a remotely controlled camera so that it covers a spot where birds frequently come will make it possible to get interesting poses. It is a challenge to construct blinds which will enable the photographer to get close enough to animals to take good pictures. Many wild animals are difficult to photograph because they are active only at night or in the late evening. Most animals are afraid of people and will avoid them or any area that contains their scent. This means that great care must be taken in setting up the camera so that everything appears normal to the animal. Triggering devices attached to food can lead to most interesting pictures. Use natural feeding places. Underwater photography is another aspect which offers challenge and adventure.

Many people gain a great deal of satisfaction from the processing of the film and the printing of the pictures. A darkroom can be set up in the basement or other room in the house. Seeing the picture of a bird or an animal coming out on the paper while it is still in the solution is a thrill that is difficult to duplicate. A sense of completion results from not only taking the pictures but also carrying the process through to a final product.

Another activity in photography which most groups enjoy is shooting a sequence of pictures telling the story of their club, of an activity, or of something in nature for publicity and promotion purposes — poster series, transparencies for illustrated talks, motion pictures.

ROCKS AND MINERALS

Collecting rocks and minerals is a popular hobby in America. It appeals to all age groups. Even preschool children like to gather pebbles that are pleasant to the touch and have appealing colors. As you study rocks you become aware that the entire history of the evolvement of our earth is hidden in them. From this time on searching for rocks, minerals, and fossils becomes an exciting adventure where one discovery leads to another.

It is not necessary for you to know much about rocks and minerals before you begin your collection. The important thing is to get started, for your knowledge will grow rapidly once you start working with the materials. As you begin your collection you will want to establish a method of labeling so that you will have a record of the kind of rock and the date and place where it was found.

There are more than 1,500 different species of minerals and well over 100 kinds of rocks. A *mineral* is a chemical element or inorganic compound which occurs naturally, having definite physical properties and chemical composition. A *rock* is an aggregate of two or more minerals. These can be identified in the field on the basis of their appearance.

Rocks are the materials of which the crust of the earth is made and can therefore be found in almost any locality. Rocks usually are divided into three major categories depending upon their origin: igneous, sedimentary, and metamorphic. *Igneous rocks* are those formed at high temperature from molten materials and include rocks such as lava and granite. Limestone and shale are representative of *sedimentary rocks* which are formed by the settlement of fine rock particles which are carried by water or wind and later hardened into rock because of pressure. Much of this type of rock is formed at the bottom of seas. *Metamorphic rocks* are those which have undergone radical change due to high temperatures and extreme pressure, turning limestone into marble and shale into slate.

You do not need expensive equipment to begin your work with rocks but it will help to have some of the basic equipment with you when you go looking for samples:

geologic pick—a hammer will do, but a pick is preferable
magnifying glass—any cheap 8-10 power will be fine
container or collecting sack in which to place your samples
cold chisel for breaking rocks
materials for testing hardness: fingernail, penny, knife, glass
pocketknife
notebook and pencil
adhesive tape and newspaper for marking and wrapping specimens

While rocks may be found in almost every area, there are certain places that are better than others for finding specimens. Places that are usually good are old rock quarries, road cuts with rock on sides exposed, dried-up stream beds, coarse sand beaches, openings to mines and slag piles, tops of hills and mountains where erosion has taken place, and in areas where there has been recent volcanic eruption.

After you have returned from a field trip on which you have collected a variety of rocks you will want to identify them and prepare them for placement in the display case. Rocks and minerals are identified through their distinguishing characteristics which can be determined through observation and simple tests. These characteristics include color, luster, hardness, specific gravity, streak, and fracture. Keys and instructions for rock identification will be found in the references.

Many people like to carry their rock collecting into craft activities. Rocks can be cut and polished and used as semiprecious gems in making jewelry. This craft is known as lapidary.

People collecting rock specimens may also want to be on the lookout for fossils. Fossils are prints, remains, or any other evidence of prehistoric life usually found in or among rocks. These fossils are interesting because of their story and age, and are a help to the scientist in determining the period in which the rock was formed.

SEE REFERENCES

WATER—STREAMS AND PONDS

A nearby pond or stream makes an exciting location for water ecology and water quality activities. For water sports, see Chapter VI, Canoeing and River Running and Casting and Fishing.

Water Ecology

The study of life in fresh water is called *limnology*. To get a sort of overview, take a boat field trip to study ecological succession of plants in a pond. Select an undisturbed stretch of shoreline in a pond. Go out in a boat to the central, deep, dark, barren bottom zone of the lake. As you go you will probably notice that you pass over a number of plant communities in a zonal arrangement. Then as you come back toward shore study the various plant species making up the community of each zone. The first zone after the central, barren one is that of *submergent plants*, that is, those plants rooted to the bottom of the lake or pond with leaves completely below the surface. Plants like water milfoil and coontail can tolerate low levels of incident sunlight and grow in this deep area. Next are plants rooted in the bottom but with their leaves floating on the surface; this zone can be referred to as surface-leafed or *floating-leaf plants*. Pond weed and water lilies are the best known of these plants. Then in shallow water is the *emergent plant* zone where the roots and part of the stems are beneath the surface of the water but the tops protrude above the water. These plants include rushes, pickerelweed, and arrowhead. Finally, at the edge of the pond is the first terrestrial zone, the first habitat without any part of the plant actually in the water. Each zone or plant community has its own characteristic plants—the varieties are few and easily identifiable.

Given enough time, any pond or lake should fill in completely; gradually the central, barren area gives way to submergent plants, then the floating-leaf plants, and the emergent plants. Succession continues on the land, too. There it is apparent in the swamp or bog area, which is really the transition from emergent plants to the first terrestrial zone with its sedge meadow plants such as reed grass, cattail, and sedge. As the soil gets deeper, these plants are followed or replaced by moisture-loving shrubs, like shrub willow and dogwood. The shrubs give way to immature forest and shade tolerant trees, and finally the climax forest. Ask an "old timer" to talk about how an old pond that has a swampy area has changed over time.

Of course, the animal life of a pond as well as plant life is interesting to study. There is much life in a pond, ranging from minute organisms to large animals. The question is, where can you expect to find the various types—a bass, a water strider, a crayfish, for example? The easiest way to start answering that question is to learn about habitats and characteristics—and a good way to begin is by classifying animals according to where they live: in the bottom sediments, on the bottom, on or among vegetation, free swimming, hanging from the surface of the water, or on the water surface. Still other animals live at different levels over the water surface. The "bottom dwellers" show the greatest diversity of form and life style. If you have access to a microscope, you may want to dredge up a sample from the bottom and look at the various fungi and bacteria, as well as the protozoans that occur in almost every drop of water in lake or pond. A variety of animals burrow into the bottom sediments, but there are also foragers, scavengers, and predators on the bottom of the pond. Snails are normally found foraging for algae; crayfish are active scavengers. Another group of creatures spend most of their time in the thick growth of aquatic vegetation in the littoral zones. Then there are many, many species of tiny swimming and drifting plants (phytoplankton) and tiny swimming and drifting animals (zooplankton). Of the many larger animals, the next in size are the air-breathing aquatic insects; and, of course, we all think about fish when we think of ponds. So get a good pond book (see references) and with a collecting net and sediment tube search the bottom of a water area — and then the animals among vegetation, free swimming, and just under, on, and above the water surface.

There are quite a few devices for collecting aquatic organisms. Two things must be considered — the device must be a type of mesh or have holes (not too big!) so that the water can pass through; the fineness of the mesh depends upon the smallness of the animals you are collecting. A kitchen sieve is probably the most useful because it is of fairly sturdy construction and mud can be washed from the sample simply by moving the sieve back and forth in a bucket of water with the top of the sieve just out of the water. Window screen can also be used; a piece approximately 1' x 2' stapled to two pieces of wood on each end for handles can be used very nicely to catch animal life coming downstream. If the screen has a woven edge, place it down; if it does not, fold the screen (like a small hem) before attaching the handles. This type of device works best when two people work together: one person holds the screen in the stream current with the bottom resting on the bottom of the stream, while the other person goes a few feet upstream and turns over rocks, wiping animals off the rocks by hand; the current carries the animals into the screen.

For sampling organisms in the bottom sediment, a large can such as a 3-lb. coffee can can be used. Scoop up a can full of mud and pour into the kitchen sieve, then wash clean of the mud. If the pond is more then an arm's length deep, a coffee can about pint size can be fastened on to the end of a broomstick — be sure to punch a few small holes in the bottom and side of can to allow excess water to pass through. To take a core sample of the bottom of the pond in order to identify stratification or layers of sediment, a tube will hold the sample together better than cans. A plastic or metal pipe 2'' in diameter and 2-3' long works well. Plunge the tube into the bottom sediment, then hold the top of the tube (pipe) closed with the hand so as to prevent the core (sediment) from being lost in the water when brought up to the surface. Then, the sediment can be carefully pushed out with a broomstick or similar object into a pan. Incidentally, a white enameled tray makes a good examining tray not only for sediment core samples, but also for the animals caught with the sieve as they are easily seen against the white background.

Stream beds also have various types of habitats and are usually considered to be of four types: bedrock, rubble and gravel, sand, and silt and mud. Since bedrock stream beds provide very little food and protection, they contain little life. Life will also be affected by the type of rock, type of vegetation on the banks, source of water, etc. A high stream velocity is usually found on rubble or gravel bottoms;

thus there is ample supply of food and oxygen being carried to animals lying in wait among the nooks and crannies provided by the stony bed. Muddy or silt-bottomed streams are usually high in productivity, and with buildup of mud and silt plants root and gradually the stream bed begins to fill in. In extremely slow waters, duckweed may grow in stagnant areas and eventually cover the water's surface. Fish found in slow flowing streams are quite different from those in fast flowing streams. To become good at fishing, one must learn about the habitats of different fish!

Water Qualities

Looking at water qualities in terms of physical and chemical properties can provide many very interesting nature-oriented activities. Some of the chemical properties for which one can test include dissolved oxygen, hardness, alkalinity, suspended and dissolved solids, turbidity, and conductivity. While these tests are not difficult, one may want to ask a local science teacher to help. Color, transparency, water pressure, stream volume of flow, temperature, density of water, etc. are physical properties that help one to understand better water quality.

Environmental temperature is an important regulator of life processes, and is an important factor in determining the distribution of organisms. Water temperature is especially important because most aquatic organisms are cold-blooded, that is, their body temperature is about the same as that of their water habitat. Many aquatic organisms can survive only within certain narrow temperature ranges. Water temperatures change gradually, and water has the capacity to store vast amounts of heat. Water temperature may vary with depth in still ponds or in deep lakes and reservoirs. An interesting activity is to take temperatures of water in different locations and depths and see what type of aquatic life may be found at each temperature. For measuring temperatures near the surface, of course, the thermometer bulb is immersed. Watch that you are not holding the thermometer so that your body heat influences the temperature being recorded. The thermometer bulb should be completely immersed, and the thermometer read while the bulb remains in the water after sufficient time has elapsed for the bulb of the thermometer to come to the temperature of the water. A ''sampler'' bottle can be used to secure water samples from various depths. It is simple and inexpensive to make. Take a one quart bottle and put a net mesh around it. The net can be made by just knotting cord or it can be a mesh bag vegetables and fruits sometimes come in. There should be weights of lead or stones on the bottom, and a

calibrated cord (so you know how deep the bottle is) attached to
lower the bottle to given depths. The bottle should have a cork inserted (not too tight!) with cord leading to the top. When the bottle is
to the desired depth, jerk the cord and uncork the bottle; the bottle
will then fill with water from that specific depth. Allow a few minutes
for the bottle to fill, then bring to the surface and insert thermometer. The water temperature, of course, must be measured
promptly upon bringing the bottle to the surface. It is desirable to
take several readings from the same depth and use an average of the
readings. Recording can be made during different times of day,
especially under different conditions, such as evening, rainy days,
etc.

Another interesting but easy activity is to measure stream
volume of flow. Select a short section of stream that is not too wide,
has fairly straight banks (shoreline), and is mostly free of obstacles
protruding above the surface level of the water. Determine the
length, average width, and average depth of that section of stream.
Compute the volume of water in the "test section" by multiplying
the length x width x depth. Put a small floatable object (stick) at the
upper end of the test section, and using a watch with a second hand,
find the time it takes for the stick to float from one end of the test
section to the other. Divide the volume (which you should convert to
liters or gallons) by the number of seconds and you will have the
number of liters that flow downstream in one
second. Of course, you could also find how
much water flows downstream in a day.

WEATHER

Everyone who participates in outdoor activities is well aware of
the weather and the role that it plays in people's lives. Farmers,
sailors, and pilots, for example, are especially dependent upon
weather conditions and predictions. Frequently outdoor activities
have to be modified or canceled because of a sudden rain or other
unexpected change in the weather. Certainly people on camping and
hunting trips can benefit greatly by knowing something about how
weather works and how weather is predicted. There are a number of
different projects related to weather which make interesting hobbies.
These include building a weather station, keeping a record of daily
weather conditions, and making weather predictions.

Weather is the condition of the earth's atmosphere described in
terms of heat, pressure, moisture, and wind. Changes in weather are
caused through an interplay of the sun, the air, and the rotation of

the earth. As the sun warms the air, the air becomes lighter and begins to move upward. Heavier cold air then rushes in to replace it, causing winds. Warm air also has the ability to take on additional moisture through evaporation. As the warm air rises and cools it loses its ability to hold as much moisture and, therefore, it rains.

Building a weather station is not difficult nor does it require expensive equipment. The box that will contain the equipment should be large enough and have enough ventilation so that the weather conditions inside the box will be the same as outside the box.

The weather station should be placed in an open area and have a roof on it so that the sun does not affect the inside temperatures. A weather station should contain a barometer, hygrometer, high-low thermometer, weather vane, and rain gauge. Some of these instruments can be made in a workshop, but it would probably be better to buy commercially made instruments if you want accuracy. Of the two types of barometers, mercury and aneroid, the aneroid will probably best serve your purpose because it does not require as much room. A hygrometer can be made out of two thermometers by placing a wet wick around the bulb of one in order to keep it moist. The relative humidity can then be computed through a comparison of the wet and dry bulb readings and interpreted through the use of a chart (see chart on page 180).

The weather instruments should be read at about the same time each day. Some weather enthusiasts read their instruments two or three times a day and keep detailed records. A simple chart on which a daily record can be kept is illustrated on page 178.

The following information should be recorded:

Barometric pressure. The barometer indicates air pressure and is calibrated in inches of mercury. A dropping air pressure usually indicates the approach of a low-pressure front which may contain rain or snow. A rise in air pressure suggests the approach of a high-pressure front and fair weather.

Clouds. There are four basic types of clouds: cirrus, cumulus, stratus, and nimbus. The cirrus are those clouds that appear high in the sky (5-10 miles) and are often referred to as "mares tails." The large white puffy clouds are called cumulus and are generally thought of as fair-weather clouds. When the sky becomes overcast so that the entire sky is covered with layers of clouds, the clouds are referred to as stratus. Nimbus refers to any cloud from which rain is falling.

Relative humidity. The hygrometer tells us how much water or moisture is presently contained in the air as compared to the amount that it could hold if saturated. Relative humidity is, therefore, ex-

DAILY WEATHER CHART

Month _____   Place _____

| Date | Time | Barometer | | Relative Humidity | | | Temperature | | | Rainfall | Wind | | Clouds | | Observations or Forecast |
		read.	trend	dry	wet	%	high	low	pres.		dir.	vel.	%	type	

BEAUFORT SCALE – WIND ESTIMATION

Beaufort Number	Mph / Knots	Description	Observation	Weather Map Symbols
0	0-1 / 0-1	calm	smoke rises vertically	⊙
1	1-3 / 1-3	light air	smoke drifts slowly	⊙⌐
2	4-7 / 4-6	slight breeze	leaves rustle	⌐
3	8-12 / 7-10	gentle breeze	leaves and twigs in motion	⊩
4	13-18 / 11-16	moderate breeze	small branches move	⊪
5	19-24 / 17-21	fresh breeze	small trees sway	⊪⌐
6	25-31 / 22-27	strong breeze	large branches sway	⊪⎮
7	32-38 / 28-33	strong breeze	whole trees in motion	⊪⎮⌐
8	39-46 / 34-40	gale	twigs break off trees	⊪⎮⎮
9	47-54 / 41-47	gale	branches break	⊪⎮⎮⌐
10	55-63 / 48-55	whole gale	trees snap and are blown down	⊪⎮⎮⎮
11	64-75 / 56-65	storm	widespread damage	⊪⎮⎮⎮⌐
12	above 75 / above 66	hurricane	extreme damage	⊪⎮⎮⎮⎮

179

RELATIVE HUMIDITY TABLE

No. of Degrees Difference — Wet and Dry Bulb	Dry Bulb Reading — Fahrenheit (Percentage Figures)							
	30°	40°	50°	60°	70°	80°	90°	100°
1	90	92	93	94	95	96	96	97
2	79	84	87	89	90	92	92	93
3	68	76	80	84	86	87	88	90
4	58	68	74	78	81	83	85	86
6	38	52	61	68	72	75	78	80
8	18	37	49	58	64	68	71	74
10		22	37	48	55	61	65	68
12		8	26	39	48	54	59	62
14			16	30	40	47	53	57
16			5	21	33	41	47	51
18				13	26	35	41	47
20				5	19	29	36	42
22					12	23	32	37
24					6	18	26	33

pressed as a percentage. Warm air is able to hold more moisture than cold air. On a warm, muggy day when the relative humidity is high, you may expect showers as the air cools in the evening. A Relative Humidity Table is shown above.

Temperature. The high and low temperatures for the last 24-hour period should be recorded as well as the present temperature at the time of reading. A sudden drop of temperature on a hot humid day could produce thunderstorms.

Wind. Both direction and speed of wind should be recorded. A wind blowing from the east generally indicates approaching rain or snow whereas a wind from the west generally indicates fair weather. The harder the wind blows, the sooner you can expect the change to take place. The Beaufort Scale for wind estimation is shown on page 179.

Weather has importance for more than the interesting hobby of prediction. It is essential to understand something about how the elements make one feel, particularly if one wishes to go hiking or backpacking or other physically active sport. In winter discomfort is measured on the "chill index," which is determined by the wind

TEMPERATURE-HUMIDITY INDEX

Temperature (°F.)	Relative Humidity (%)													
	20	25	30	35	40	45	50	55	60	65	70	75	80	85
100	81	82	83	84	85	86	88	89	90	92	93	94	95	96
95	78	79	80	81	82	83	84	85	86	88	88	90	90	92
90	76	77	77	78	79	80	81	82	83	84	85	86	87	87
85	73	74	74	75	76	76	77	78	78	79	80	81	82	83
80	70	71	71	72	72	73	73	74	74	75	76	77	78	79
75	68	68	68	69	69	70	70	70	71	71	72	72	73	74

On this "Index of Discomfort" almost everyone is uncomfortable at 79 or more. Compute relative humidity from the chart on page 180.

speed and the temperature. The greater the wind speed, the greater the chill factor. This is one reason why it is so important to protect against the wind in very cold temperatures — frostbite is easily gotten when the wind is strong, even if the temperature is not unduly cold. See the wind chill chart on page 182 to figure out just how cold it feels in relation to the wind speed and the thermometer temperature. In summer the wind helps to cool, and discomfort comes from humidity and high temperatures. Sometimes this is called an "index of discomfort." It is really a temperature-humidity index. Areas of the United States that refer to their "dry heat" (and say that thus they do not mind the hot weather) are really talking about low humidity. The point at which people begin to be uncomfortable with the humidity varies; however, the temperature-humidity index chart above indicates the range of discomfort for most people.

Another aspect of weather that is particularly interesting and has importance in energy conservation is the amount of fuel saved by maintaining room temperatures lower than 72°. Fuel units needed to maintain a certain room temperature in a building have been calculated for different outside temperatures. The full saving chart on page 183 does not consider the wind chill factor or the impact of the wind or the "tightness" of the building in retaining heat.

It is interesting to make weather predictions based upon your own observations. Compare your prediction results with those of the weather forecaster on TV or in the newspaper. You should be able to predict weather correctly 80 percent of the time.

SEE REFERENCES

WIND CHILL CHART

Estimated Wind Speed in mph	Actual Thermometer Reading (°F.)															
	35	30	25	20	15	10	5	0	−5	−10	−15	−20	−25	−30	−35	−40
calm	35	30	25	20	15	10	5	0	−5	−10	−15	−20	−25	−30	−35	−40
5	33	27	21	16	12	7	1	−6	−11	−15	−20	−26	−31	−35	−41	−47
10	21	16	9	2	−2	−9	−15	−22	−27	−31	−38	−45	−52	−58	−64	−70
15	16	11	1	−6	−11	−18	−25	−33	−40	−45	−51	−60	−65	−70	−78	−85
20	12	3	−4	−9	−17	−24	−32	−40	−46	−52	−60	−68	−76	−81	−88	−96
25	7	0	−7	−15	−22	−29	−37	−45	−52	−58	−67	−75	−83	−89	−96	−104
30	5	−2	−11	−18	−26	−33	−41	−49	−56	−63	−70	−78	−87	−94	−101	−109
35	3	−4	−13	−20	−27	−35	−43	−52	−60	−67	−72	−83	−90	−98	−105	−113
40	1	−4	−15	−22	−29	−36	−45	−54	−62	−69	−76	−87	−94	−101	−107	−116

wind speeds greater than 40 mph have little additional effect

LITTLE DANGER for properly clothed person

(Very to Bitter Cold)

INCREASING DANGER danger from freezing of exposed flesh

(Extremely Cold)

GREAT DANGER

(Extremely Cold)

Find the temperature on the top line and the wind speed at the extreme left. Where the two intersect, you will find the wind chill factor. For instance, if the temperature is 10 degrees and the wind speed 25 mph, the chill factor is minus 29. A blizzard is usually considered winds of at least 35 mph and considerable falling or blowing snow; a severe blizzard is winds of at least 45 mph with falling or blowing snow and temperatures lower than 10 degrees. Note: various charts will differ by a few degrees for the estimated wind chill. The chart will, however, give a good approximation of what happens when wind increases in relation to temperature.

182

FUEL SAVING CHART

Average Indoor Temperature

Outside Temperature	72 degrees Fuel units		68 degrees Fuel units			66 degrees Fuel units			50 degrees Fuel units		
	needed	saved	needed	saved	Percent saved	needed	saved	Percent saved	needed	saved	Percent saved
70	2	0	0	0	100	0	0	100	0	0	100
60	12	0	8	4	33	6	6	50	0	12	100
50	22	0	18	4	18	16	6	27	0	22	100
40	32	0	28	4	12	26	6	19	10	22	69
30	42	0	38	4	9	36	6	14	20	22	52
20	52	0	48	4	7	46	6	11	30	22	42
10	62	0	58	4	6	56	6	10	40	22	35
0	72	0	68	4	5	66	6	8	50	22	30
−10	82	0	78	4	4	76	6	7	60	22	26
−20	92	0	88	4	4	86	6	6	70	22	23

Table based on straight line relationship of temperature difference to fuel requirement.

Percent saved based on a comparison between the "usual" room temperature of 72 degrees and that indicated.

Chill factor or impact of wind were not considered in calculations.

183

184 PART TWO / ACTIVITIES

REFERENCES

Animals

Animal Tracks. Stackpole Company, Harrisburg, Pa., 1954.

Bevans, Michael H. *The Book of Reptiles and Amphibians.* Garden City Books, Garden City, N.Y., 1956. For identification.

Hickman, Mae, and Guy, Maxine. *Care of the Wild Feathered and Furred* (A Guide to Wildlife Handling and Care). Unity Press, P.O. Box 1037, Santa Cruz, Calif.

Marvels of Animal Behavior. National Geographic Society, Washington, D.C., 1972.

Mason, George F. *Animal Tracks.* William Morrow and Company, New York, 1943. Pettit, Ted S. *Animal Signs and Signals.* Doubleday and Company, Garden City, N.Y., 1961.

Schwartz, Charles W., and Schwartz, Elizabeth R. *The Wild Mammals of* Missouri. University of Missouri Press, Columbia, 1959.

Subarsky, Zachariah. *Living Things in Field and Classroom.* University of Minnesota Press, Minneapolis, 1969.

Astronomy

Baker, Robert H. *Introducing the Constellations.* The Viking Press, New York, 1953.

Inglis, Stuart J. *Planets, Stars, and Galaxies.* John Wiley and Sons, New York, 1976.

Mayall, R. Newton, and Mayall, Margaret W. *Olcott's Field Book of the Skies.* G. P. Putnam's Sons, New York, 1954.

Nicklesburg, Janet. *Star Gazing.* Burgess Publishing Company, Minneapolis, 1964.

Page, Lou Williams. *A Dipper Full of Stars.* Follett Publishing Company, Chicago, 1944, revised 1959.

Rey, H. A. *The Stars, A New Way To See Them.* Houghton Mifflin Company, Boston, 1976, enlarged world-wide edition.

Star Explorer (a star-chart wheel for the four seasons). Star Explorer, c/o Dr. H. S. Rice, American Museum-Hayden Planetarium, New York, N.Y. 10024, periodically revised to keep up to date.

Birds

Bent, Arthur C. *Life Histories of North American Woodpeckers.* Dover Publications, New York, 1964. This is illustrative of a series of life histories of various birds by Bent.

Dennis, John V. *A Complete Guide to Bird Feeding.* Alfred A. Knopf, New York, 1975.

Griffin, Donald R. *Bird Migration.* Dover Publications, New York, 1974.

Headstrom, Richard. *A Complete Field Guide to Nests in the United States.* Ives Washburn, Inc., New York, 1970.

Hillcourt, William. *The New Field Book of Nature Activities and Hobbies.* G. P. Putnam's Sons, New York. 1970, pp. 53-94. Good for projects.

Peterson, Roger Tory. *Field Guide to the Birds* and *Field Guide to Western Birds.* Houghton Mifflin Company, N.Y. For identification. There is a record album of bird songs available which corresponds page by page to the birds identified in the Field Guide: *A Field Guide to Bird Songs,* recorded by the Laboratory of Ornithology, Cornell University. Matching Kodachrome slides for most of the species recorded may be secured from Laboratory of Ornithology, Cornell University, Ithaca, N.Y.

Pettit, Mary P. *My Hobby Is Bird Watching.* Hart Book Company, New York, 1955.

Robbins, Chandler; Bruun, Bertl; and Zim, Herbert S. *A Guide to Field Identification, Birds of North America.* Golden Press, New York, 1966.

Terres, John K. *How Birds Fly.* Hawthorn Books, Inc., New York, 1968. Originally published as *Flashing Wings.*

U.S. Fish and Wildlife Service, Washington, D.C.

Creative Expression

Beautiful pictures and writings, expressions of creativity in book form, should be available for inspiration and encouragement. New books are continually coming out; check your local bookstore periodically. Some of the older favorites include:

Adams, Ansel, and Newhall, Nancy. *This Is the American Earth.* Sierra Club, Mills Tower, San Francisco, 1960. *These We Inherit* (Parklands of America). 1962. Both are beautiful volumes of photographs.

Berger, H. Jean. Inspirational Poetry for Camp and Youth Groups. Burgess Publishing Company, Minneapolis, 1958.

Edgar, Mary S. *Under Open Skies.* Clarke, Irwin, and Company, Toronto, 1955. Collection of chapel talks and verses.

Frostic, Gwen. *These Things Are Ours.* Presscraft Papers, Frankfort, Mich., 1960. Also, *A Walk With Me,* 1958. Also, *A Place on Earth,* 1963. Three very lovely little volumes of prints on various types of paper. For those who love beauty in a book.

Grover, Edwin Osgood (editor). *The Nature Lover's Knapsack.* Thomas Y. Crowell, New York, 1947. An anthology of poems for lovers of the open road.

Hay, John, and Strong, Arline. *A Sense of Nature.* Doubleday and Company, New York, 1962. A picture-story book of photos and captions as the authors followed a group of children on their wanderings one summer on Cape Cod.

Morgan, Barbara. *Summer's Children.* Morgan and Morgan, Scarsdale, N.Y., 1951. Photographs with captions. Photographic cycle of life at a camp.

Phillips, Mary. *The Wonderful World of Nature.* Viking Press, New York, 1961. An excellent introduction to natural history through photographs accompanied by brief, authoritative text.

Porter, Eliot. *In Wildness Is the Preservation of the World.* The Sierra Club,

San Francisco, 1962. Seventy-two beautiful color plates with selections
from Thoreau.

Warmingham, Osbert W. (Kodaya). *Dusk and a Voice Singing.* The Lotus
Publishers, Waban, Mass., 1958. Poetry.

Wright, Cedric. *Words of the Earth.* Sierra Club, San Francisco, 1960.
Beautiful photographs with captions and verses.

Conservation/Environmental Quality

A number of excellent books set forth the problems of conservation and
environmental quality as well as their importance. New titles are continually
being published; check your local bookstore regularly and watch outdoor-
oriented periodicals. Some of the older titles you may want in your library
include:

Brower, David (editor). *The Meaning of Wilderness to Science.* Sierra Club,
San Francisco, 1960. Ecology. Sixth biennial wilderness conference.
Also *Wilderness: America's Living Heritage.* 1961. Conservation.
Seventh wilderness conference.

Brown, William E. *Islands of Hope.* National Recreation and Parks
Association, Arlington, Va., 1971.

Carson, Rachel L. *The Sea Around Us.* Oxford University Press, New York,
1961. Revised edition. Absorbing story of the ocean and of the ways it
affects our lives. Special edition for young readers adapted by Anne
Terry White, Simon and Schuster, New York, 1958. Also *Silent Spring.*
Houghton Mifflin Company, Boston, 1962. Discusses indiscriminate use
of lethal chemicals in nature. Also *The Edge of the Sea.* Houghton
Mifflin Company, Boston, 1955. Paperbound.

Errington, Paul L. *Of Men and Marshes.* Iowa State University Press, Ames,
1957.

George, Jean. *My Side of the Mountain.* E. P. Dutton and Company, New
York, 1959. Story of a boy who runs away from home and masters the
skills of survival as he lives a year in the outdoors. Sixth-grade level.

Grange, Wallace Byron. *Those of the Forest.* Flambeau Publishing Company, Babcock, Wisc., 1953. Each chapter a story. Ecology.

Krutch, Joseph Wood. *The Great Chain of Life.* Houghton Mifflin Company,
Boston, 1956. From the one-celled paramecium to the giant mammals.

McInnis, Noel. *You Are an Environment.* Center for Curriculum Design,
P.O. Box 350, Evanston, Ill. 60204. 1972.

Margolin, Malcolm. *The Earth Manual.* Houghton Mifflin Company,
Boston, 1975.

Milne, Lorus J., and Milne, Margery. *The Balance of Nature.* Alfred A.
Knopf, New York, 1960. Equilibrium among different kinds of animals
and their environment.

Osborn, Fairfield. *Our Plundered planet.* Little, Brown, and Company,
Boston, 1948. Conservation. Paperbound.

Pettit, Ted S. *The Web of Nature.* Garden City Books, Garden City, N.Y., 1960. Colorful volume written for youth. Similar in content to *The Web of Life.*

Schumacher, E. F. *Small is Beautiful.* Harper & Row, Publishers, New York, 1973.

Sears, Paul B. *Deserts on the March,* second edition. University of Oklahoma Press, Norman, 1947. Conservation.

Storer, John H. *The Web of Life.* The New American Library, A Signet Key Book, New York, 1953. Ecology.

Swift, Ernest F. *The Conservation Saga.* National Wildlife Federation, Washington, D.C., 1967.

Udall, Stewart L. *The Quiet Crisis.* Holt, Rinehart, and Winston, New York, 1963. Traces the history of the battle in the United States to save its natural resources—from the Indian to the present generation. Contributions of men such as Thomas Jefferson, Henry Thoreau, George Perkins Marsh, Gifford Pinchot, John Muir, etc.

Watts, May Theilgaard. *Reading the Landscape.* Macmillan Company, New York, 1957. Ecology. Each chapter in storybook fashion presents a specific area of the country; however, it does get somewhat technical.

Conservation Projects

Bale, R. O. *Conservation for Camp and Classroom.* Burgess Publishing Company, Minneapolis, 1962.

Conservation Education Association. *Environmental Conservation Education, A Selected Annotated Bibliography.* Interstate Printers & Publishers, Inc., Danville, Ill., 1974.

Pavoni, Joseph L.; Hagerty, D. Joseph; and Heer, John E. *Preserving Man's Environment.* Data Courier, Inc., Louisville, Ky., 1974.

Gardening

Better Homes and Gardens. *New Garden Book.* Meredith Publishing Company, Des Moines, Ia., 1962.

Boswell, Victor R., and Wester, Robert E. *Growing Vegetables in the Home Garden.* U.S. Dept. of Agriculture Home and Garden Bul. No. 202, Supt. of Documents, U.S. Government Printing Office, Washington, D.C. 20402.

Czufin, Louis F. (editor). *A Child's Garden.* Public Relations, Chevron Chemical Company, 200 Bush Street, San Francisco, 94120. 1974. Paperback. Free.

Femal, Jerome T. *Children's Gardening.* NRPA Management Aids Series, #69, National Recreation and Park Association, Washington, D.C., 1967.

Skelsey, Alice, and Husckaby, Gloria. *Growing Up Green* (Children and

Parents Gardening Together). Workman Publishing Company, New York, 1973.

U.S. Dept. of Agriculture pamphlets. Contact local county extension office or/and Congressman.

Weaver, Richard L. (project leader). *Handbook for Teaching Conservation and Resource Use.* Interstate Printers and Publishers, Danville, Ill., 1955.

Historical-Cultural Activities

Check with your local county historical society and materials prepared for the Bicentennial Celebration of the United States.

Brennan, Louis A. *Beginner's Guide to Archaeology.* Stackpole Books, Harrisburg, Pa., 1973.

Deetz, James. *Invitation to Archaeology.* American Museum Science Books. The Natural History Press, Garden City, N.Y., 1967. Paperback.

Doane, Gilbert H. *Searching for Your Ancestors.* University of Minnesota Press, Minneapolis, 1973 edition.

Robbins, Maurice. *The Amateur Archaeologist's Handbook.* Thomas Y. Crowell Co., rev. ed., 1973.

Insects

Headstrom, Richard. *Adventures With Insects.* J. B. Lippincott Company, Philadelphia, 1963.

Hillcourt, William. *The New Field Book of Nature Activities and Hobbies.* G. P. Putnam's Sons, New York, 1970, pp. 149-94. For projects.

Kellogg, Paul, and Allen, Arthur. "The Songs of Insects." 33⅓ rpm record. The buzzes, trills, chirps, and lisps of the common crickets, grasshoppers, and cicadas of eastern United States. Also record of trills, croaks, and calls of 34 frogs and toads of the U.S. and Canada, "Voices of the Night."

Lutz, F. E. *Field Book of Insects.* G. P. Putnam's Sons, New York, 1948. For identification.

Sterling, Dorothy. *Creatures of the Night.* Doubleday and Company, Garden City, N.Y., 1960.

Teale, Edwin Way. *Grassroot Jungles.* Dodd, Mead, and Company, New York, revised and enlarged edition, 1960.

Zim, Herbert S., and Cottam, Clarence A. *Insects.* Golden Press, New York, 1951.

Nature Study

While there are many books on specific areas of nature here are a few general nature study resources:

Adams, Richard, *Nature Through the Seasons.* Simon & Schuster, New York, 1975.

Brainerd, John W. *Nature Study for Conservation: A Handbook for En-*

vironmental Education. The Macmillan Company, New York, 1971.
―――. *Working with Nature.* Oxford University Press, New York, 1975.
Brown, Vinson. *The Amateur Naturalist's handbook.* Little, Brown, and Company, Boston, 1948.
―――. *The Explorer Naturalist.* Stackpole Books, Harrisburg, Pa., 1976.
Comstock, Anna Botsford. *Handbook of Nature Study.* Comstock Publishing Association, Ithaca, N.Y., 1939.
Hillcourt, William. *The New Field Book of Nature Activities and Hobbies.* G. P. Putnam's Sons, New York, 1970.
Life Nature Library. Time, Inc., New York. This is an especially fine series for general information, with each book on one topic, such as *The Universe, Insects, The Forest, The Earth, The Sea,* etc. Excellent illustrations, many in color.
Our Living World of Nature Series. McGraw-Hill Book Company, New York, 1967. An excellent series for both content and pictorial presentation with individual volumes on the life of prairies, plains, the pond, the seashore, the ocean, mountains, the forest, the cave, the marsh, the desert, and rivers and streams.
Palmer, E. Lawrence, and Fowler, H. Seymour. *Fieldbook of Natural History.* McGraw-Hill Book Company, New York, second edition, 1975.
Partridge, J. A. *Natural Science Through the Seasons.* Macmillan Co., Toronto, 1955. (Available from St. Martin's Press, Inc., New York.)
The Peterson Field Guide Series. Houghton Mifflin Company, Boston. A field book series on many topics for the advanced student.
Putnam's Nature Field Books. G. P. Putnam's Sons, New York. A series of field books on many topics for the advanced student and leader.
Van Matre, Steve. *Acclimatization.* American Camping Association, Bradford Woods, Martinsville, Ind. 46151, 1972.
―――. *Acclimatizing.* American Camping Association, Bradford Woods, Martinsville, Ind. 46151, 1974.
Zim, Herbert S., and others. Golden Nature Guides. Simon and Schuster, New York. Paperback. Excellent series for youth and beginners. Includes books on weather, flowers, stars, mammals, birds, insects, trees, fishes, reptiles, rocks and minerals, and others.

Photography

Bennett, Edna. *Nature Photography.* Universal Photo Books, New York, 1961.
Dunton, Sam. *Guide to Photographing Animals.* Chilton Company, New York, 1959.
Harlow, William M. *Art Forms from Plant Life.* Dover Publications, New York, 1976. Revised and expanded republication of *Patterns of Life: The Unseen World of Plants.*
Hillcourt, William. *The New Field Book of Nature Activities and Hobbies.* G. P. Putnam's Sons, New York, 1970. Has photography helps in the various sections, such as night and underwater photography.

Kinne, Russ. *The Complete Book of Nature Photography.* A. S. Barnes, New York, 1962.

Maye, Patricia. *Field Book of Nature Photography.* Sierra Club, San Francisco, 1974.

Roche, John P., and Roche, Mary Alice. *Photographing Your Flowers.* Chilton Company, New York, 1959.

See also books under Creative Expression.

Plant Activities

Berry, Christine. *Field Plot Studies.* HPER Series No. 4. The Pennsylvania State University, University Park, 1974.

Bland, John H. *Forests of Lilliput, The Realm of Mosses and Lichens.* Prentice-Hall, Inc., Englewood Cliffs, N.J., 1971.

Bold, Harold C. *The Plant Kingdom.* Prentice-Hall, Inc., Englewood Cliffs, N.J., 1970, third edition.

Brown, Lauren. *Weeds in Winter.* W. W. Norton & Company, New York. 1976.

Gibbons, Euell. *Stalking the Wild Asparagus.* D. McKay Co., New York, 1962. Describes recognition, collection, and preparation of natural foods that grow wild.

Hillcourt, William. *The New Field Book of Nature Activities and Hobbies.* G. P. Putnam's Sons, New York, 1970. Chapters on flowers and trees. Projects.

National Audubon Society. Many pertinent charts and bulletins.

Partridge, J. A. *Natural Science Through the Seasons.* Macmillan Company, Toronto, 1955.

Preston, Richard. *North American Trees.* Iowa State University Press, Ames, 1976.

Watts, May T. *Tree Finder.* Nature Study Guild, Naperville, Ill. *Flower Finder.* For identification. Pamphlets.

Weeds of the North Central States. Agriculture Experiment Station, Circular 718, revised edition, University of Illinois, Urbana, 1960.

Rocks and Minerals

Brown, Vinson. *The Amateur Naturalist's Handbook.* Little, Brown, and Company, Boston, 1948, pp. 84-89, 170-88.

Fay, Gordon S. *The Rockhound's Manual.* Harper & Row, New York, 1972.

Fenton, Carroll L., and Fenton, Mildred A. *Rocks and Their Stories.* Doubleday and Company, Garden City, N.Y., 1951.

Jensen, David E. *My Hobby Is Collecting Rocks and Minerals.* Children's Press, Chicago, 1958.

Rhodes, Frank H.; Zim, Herbert S.; and Shaffer, Paul R. *Fossils: A Guide to Prehistoric Life.* A Golden Nature Guide, Golden Press, New York, 1962.

Zim, Herbert S., and Shaffer, Paul R. *Rocks and Minerals.* Simon and Schuster, New York, 1957.

See also Nature Craft, Rocks.

Terrariums

Fitch, Charles M. *The Complete Book of Terrariums*. Hawthorn Books, Inc., New York, 1974.

Hillcourt, William. *The New Field Book* (see Nature Study).

Leavitt, Jerome, and Huntsberger, John. *Terrariums and Aquariums*. Children's Press, Chicago, 1961. For children.

Miniature Environments. Bureau of Outdoor Recreation, U.S. Dept. of Interior. U.S. Government Printing Office (2416-00069), Washington, D.C., revised edition, 1974.

The Terrarium, a Miniature Garden Under Glass. Audubon Nature Bulletin, National Audubon Society, New York, n.d.

Weather

Holmes, David C. *Weather Made Clear*. Sterling Publishing Co., New York, 1965, rev. ed.

Laird, Charles, and Laird, Ruth. *Weathercasting*. Prentice-Hall, Inc., Englewood Cliffs, N.J., 1955.

Schneider, Herman. *Everyday Weather and How It Works*. McGraw-Hill Book Company, New York, 1951.

Zim, Herbert S., and others. *Weather*. Simon and Schuster, New York, 1957.

Water—Streams and Ponds

Andrews, William A. (editor). *A Guide to the Study of Freshwater Ecology*. Prentice-Hall, Inc., Englewood Cliffs, N.J., 1972, paperback.

Buck, Margaret Waring. *In Ponds and Streams*. Abingdon Press, Nashville, Tenn., 1955. For young naturalists, identification.

Hillcourt, William. *The New Field Book of Nature Activities and Hobbies*. G. P. Putnam's Sons, New York, 1970. Chapter 7, Water Life, pp. 195-226.

Leavitt, Jerome, and Huntsberger, John. *Terrariums and Aquariums*. Children's Press, Chicago, 1961. For children.

Lindemann, Edward. *Water Animals for Your Microscope*. Crowell-Collier Press, New York, 1967.

Lubell, Winifred, and Lubell, Cecil. *Exploring a Brook, Life in the Running Water*. Parents' Magazine Press, New York, 1975.

Morgan, Ann Haven. *Field Book of Ponds and Streams*. G. P. Putnam's Sons, New York, 1930. Identification manual.

Needham, J. G., and Needham, P. R. *A Guide to the Study of Freshwater Biology*. Holden-Day, Inc., San Francisco, 1962.

White, William, Jr. *The Edge of the Pond*. Sterling Publishing Company, New York, 1976.

CHAPTER VI

Adventure-Outing Sports

A MERICANS PRIDE THEMSELVES on their ability to successfully meet with the forces of nature at work in the natural environment. The activities and focus of the Bicentennial Celebration of the United States in 1976 helped remind us of the spirit and trials of the early settlers and explorers as they pioneered in the early years of our country. We identify with the characteristics of the pioneers and are challenged by activities that test our abilities in outdoor living skills.

Adventure activities based on challenging experiences, such as rock climbing or cave exploring, can contribute to increased understanding of self and a gain in self-confidence and self-respect. Adventure activities participated in by a group will do much to encourage feelings of unity and compassion and the willingness of individuals to give or accept help. Leadership emerges from within the group as individuals work together to solve problems and perform physical tasks. The wary are encouraged by others in the group; the reckless are warned of the dangers involved.

Adventure activities and sports may appear to be dangerous and to involve a high risk factor. They need not be dangerous, in fact they are quite safe if one takes the proper precaustions. These should include:

1. Qualified leadership
2. Using proper equipment that is in good condition
3. Beginning with simple challenges until skills are developed that enable participation in more difficult endeavors
4. Keeping in good physical condition
5. Never taking unnecessary risks — using safety ropes, spotters, etc.

The purpose of this chapter is to point out various program activities that might be included in the community nature-oriented program and to give some selected references to use in development of a program, not to give detailed instructions in the technique of each sport.

The well-known, popularized, and sometimes commercialized water sports, such as water skiing, motor boating, and sailing, and the winter sports, such as tobogganning, snowshoeing, and ice skating, are not included. The outing sports presented were selected because of their potential for community programming. Few communities have organized programs in these sports although they could contribute greatly to an individual's participation in outdoor recreation.

ADVENTURE ACTIVITIES

Rope Courses

In the early seventies there was a sharp increase in interest in rope courses that challenge physical agility, balance, and mental and emotional attitude. The armed forces have long recognized the value of such challenge activities. Outward Bound and similar groups have capitalized on the potential of rope courses. These rope courses are neither difficult nor expensive to build. They are built with rope and logs, utilizing the nature of the terrain on which they are constructed. The major expense is rope that is strong and will withstand weathering. Some of the items frequently included in rope courses are briefly described below.

Balance Beams

Logs of the same diameter are tied to trees at progressively higher distances from the ground. Logs should be 8-10 inches in diameter and 15-20 feet long. The first one is placed about a foot off the ground, the second about 5 feet, the third about 10 feet, and the fourth 15-20 feet. It is strange how easily one can walk on the logs near the ground, but how small the same log looks at 20 feet off the ground.

Swinging Log

A log 10-15 inches in diameter and 15-20 feet long is suspended about a foot off the ground by ropes that permit it to swing freely. One end of the log is suspended by a single rope while the other end is suspended by two ropes. The freedom of movement in all directions makes it difficult to cross.

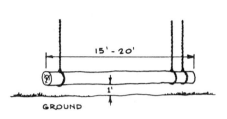

The Wall

There are many ways to construct walls. They can be made of solid boards or a series of logs. The wall should be 8-10 feet wide and 10-12 feet high. If it is made of a series of logs they should be spaced

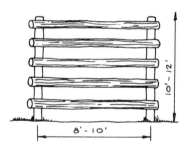

far enough apart so that one can negotiate his body through the openings. The wall presents many challenges, such as the very simple one of climbing up one side and down the other and the very difficult one of doing that without using hands or arms.

Parallel Ropes

Parallel ropes, tied to trees 15-20 feet apart, should be about 12-18 inches apart and about 5 feet above the ground. These ropes need

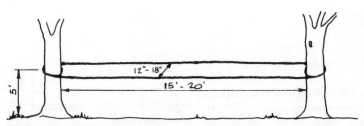

to be quite tight. There are many different ways of negotiating
from one end to the other. Some do it on top — others from below.

These are just a few ideas for rope courses. Other items
frequently included are:
a. Tarzan swing — a swing attached by a single rope to a branch 30-40
   feet above the ground. Can be used to swing across a ravine.
b. Pegs — 3 or 4 inch diameter poles of different heights placed so
   that a person can walk from one to the other.
c. Zip lines — a cable strung across a ravine on an incline; a seat on a
   pulley is used to cross the ravine.
d. Rope bridges
e. Horizontal ladder
f. Stepping stones

INITIATIVE TASKS

Group Activities

Many groups find it helpful to participate in challenging,
problem-solving situations requiring the completion of a physical
task. These initiative tasks may be combined in a series, sometimes
called an Action Socialization Course. The procedure is for the group
to be presented with a task and then left to themselves with no instructions given and no leader appointed. The entire group must
participate. There is no "right" answer or "one way" to perform the
task; groups should be encouraged to try different approaches.

Following are some examples of initiative tasks; they are not
intended to be a complete listing. The environment will suggest
additional tasks.

The Stump

Find a tree stump, preferably 2 or more feet tall, and ask the
group to get everyone on the stump at the same time. Ten or more

people should be able to get on a stump that has a 12-15 inch diameter.

The Wall or Beam

A wall about 9 feet high is constructed of boards. The object is to see if and how each member of the group can get across the wall. The same thing can be done with a beam placed about 8 feet high.

Electric Fence

A wire or string is tied to two posts about 5 feet high. The team is given one pole 8 feet long. The object is to get all members across the "electric" fence without touching the wire and "electrocuting" themselves.

Creating the Monster

A group of ten people are given the responsibility of banding themselves together so that no more than six feet and five arms touch the ground. This monster must be able to walk 10 feet.

BICYCLING AND HOSTELING

Cycling

Few community recreation agencies have recognized the full potentialities of bicycling and hosteling as program activities. Many approach biking solely as a children's activity or as an activity for those adults who have a queer idea of exercise and health, strictly a personal thing. But cycling lends itself to activity of all kinds — activities which can lead to many interesting things.

A safety program is an absolute must in any community. Sometimes a special program is sponsored by schools, civic groups, public recreation departments, or youth agencies. There are many excellent aids available on safety programs, many of which are free.

Many things can be done on bicycles, and they're more fun when planned together and done with friends. The Bicycle Institute of America's pamphlet, *Bicycle Riding Clubs,* is a helpful guide to club organization and activities.

Resources are available that lend themselves to planning bike fun with your bicycle club, your Scout troup, or your friends.

Hosteling

Although many people form their own outing clubs, a good number prefer to organize under a national organization, the American Youth Hostels. An AYH Club brings together individuals interested in outdoor activities which require "traveling under your own steam." This includes hiking, cycling, horseback riding, boating in small craft, and skiing.

One advantage of the AYH affiliation is the network of hostels throughout the United States and Europe.

CANOEING AND RIVER RUNNING

Since the beginning of time, it would seem, canoeing has been an activity for Americans. The light and maneuverable bark and frame craft of the Indians soon became the basis of a favorite recreational activity. Canoeing on lakes or ponds and other sheltered and calm waters has been, and is, an activity enjoyed by thousands of Americans each season. Indeed, canoes are likely to be found in virtually any body of water throughout this country. Canoeing is not only popular in the North Woods wilderness but also is enjoyed on downtown lakes and ponds in many urban areas. Although many people enjoy canoeing activities without ever having had instruction, the Red Cross, Boy Scouts, camps, and other youth-serving agencies have long offered instruction in the basics of canoeing. There is little doubt that the skill gained in such a course adds to the enjoyment and the safety of the paddlers.

Any organized canoe outing should be handled by an individual who is knowledgeable about canoeing and its potential hazards for a group of novices. All members of the group should be swimmers or wear a properly fitted Personal Flotation Device. Whatever the overall intent of the outing, there should be some orientation to and instruction in basic paddling skills and safety practices. The leader should be not only a canoeist but also a knowledgeable lifesaver. All of these precautions may seem to some to be too cautious, but in the few instances where an accident does occur, these simple precautions help ensure that it is only a minor incident and not a tragedy.

Canoeing is not always confined to sheltered and calm waters. The adventuresome will seek out something more exciting, like challenging rivers for the thrill of running whitewater.

River running, whether done in a canoe, kayak, or raft, has

become an increasingly popular sport. Unfortunately, it has also increased the number of fatalities on rivers across the country. The dangers inherent in river running are such that *instruction is a must!* In spite of the potential hazards of river running, more and more people are attracted to the rivers each year. In some cases river use is so intense that quotas are established by governing agencies.

Rivers are classified using an international River Classification Scale, according to their difficulty to paddle. Class I is the easiest; water in that category goes from just barely moving to about the speed you can paddle with small waves and rapids but no real obstructions. Class VI is the hardest; rivers in that category are navigable for teams of experts taking every possible precaution and then at risk of life. In river running, start on Class I and work your way up; always go in a group that includes more experienced people than you; be familiar with the river; and always *wear* a life jacket.

For canoes and kayaks the only source of competent instruction and leadership is through various whitewater clubs and a few commercial schools and outfitters across the country. There are numerous rafting outfitters operating, and they have a very good safety record—however, do select your outfitter with care. One river guide refers to a private one- or two-person raft as being a "suicide **raft**" or a "kamikazi raft." A very high percentage of the fatalities on rivers involve novices in their own or rented boats who did not wear lifejackets, and who were not familiar with the river. Also, the difficulty of a river may change dramatically with an increase or decrease in the amount of water in the river.

River touring is an exciting and challenging activity, but there is no room for ignorance of potential hazards and safety precautions. Ignorance on the river often ends in tragedy.

Several organizations are dedicated to the enjoyment and promotion of canoeing and river touring. Safety codes, technical tips, instruction, and general information are available from:

> The American Canoe Association
> 4260 East Evans Avenue
> Denver, Colorado 80222

> American Whitewater Affiliation
> P.O. Box 321
> Concord, New Hampshire 03301

> United States Canoe Association
> 6338 Hoover Road
> Indianapolis, Indiana 46260

The American National Red Cross
Local Chapter Office

CASTING AND FISHING

"Fishing is the right of every boy — and with no interference from organized recreation!" Yes, fishing *is* the right of every boy and girl, but today every child does not get the opportunity to fish. Perhaps the child has parents who never learned the art of angling and do not enjoy the sport. Or parents may not wish to take time to go fishing with their children. There is a place for angling and casting in the community nature-oriented program. Some recreation departments sponsor casting clubs.

The activities related to fishing are more than just "going fishing," although certainly that is the ultimate purpose! Some of the program activities which will enrich the fishing experience, real or contrived, include the following.

Instructional Program

Instruction in the art of casting should include the technique of the various types of casting (fly, bait, spin-cast, spin), how to handle the rod and reel in landing a fish, and an evaluation of various types of tackle. You may wish to use a certified NAACC (National Association of Angling and Casting Clubs) casting instructor.

Instruction in fishing techniques should include the identification of fish, their habitat and feeding habits, types of bait and lures to use according to species, and how to take fish off the hook and keep them. Embryonic anglers will appreciate information on weather conditions particularly conducive for a good catch, and also weather danger signs when out in small craft. Such regulations as license requirements, bait restrictions, open and closed seasons, catch limits, size limits, and types of equipment that can be used should also be presented. Discussions on conservation and sportsmanship, including their relationship to regulations, the economic aspects of conservation, responsibilities and courtesies to landowners, and the problem of stream pollution, are very important in any program on fishing. There are many helpful films available on most of these subjects.

In addition to your local county conservation officer and state conservation commission, many helpful resources exist.

Competitive Casting Activities

Various informal games for skill improvement, such as roving plug, plug bombardment, box the compass, and challenge, are described in the American Association for Health, Physical Education, and Recreation casting-angling manual.

Tournament dry-casting is becoming more popular. It is developed around the same principles which prevail in fishing, including accuracy in delivery of the lure, distance, selection of tackle, etc. There are two primary tournament programs — tournament fly casting and bait casting, and skish — both managed nationally by the National Association of Angling and Casting Clubs (NAACC), Box 51, Nashville, Tenn. 37202.

The tournament fly and bait casting games officially recognized by NAACC are 5/8 oz. accuracy, 3/8 oz. accuracy, dry fly accuracy, wet fly accuracy, 5/8 oz. distance, 3/8 oz. distance, trout fly distance, and salmon fly distance. Actually the only equipment needed besides the participant's tackle is a set of targets, for all the games consist of hitting a specific target at a given distance with designated tackle. Targets can be made from bicycle tires, plywood discs, oil drum lids, floating aluminum targets, or similar objects. The NAACC *Manual for Tournament Fly and Bait Casting* describes in detail the various events and gives suggestions for club organization and technique improvement as well.

Skish is somewhat similar in that it embodies the same principles of accuracy and distance, but differs in tackle restrictions and in scoring. Skish stresses standard tackle, and the official games include 5/8 oz. bait accuracy using revolving spool and level-wind reel; 1/4 oz. spinning accuracy using fixed-spool reel; accuracy skish fly which includes casting dry fly, wet fly, and roll casting in the same game; skish bait distance 5/8 oz.; spinning distance 3/8 oz.; and skish fly distance. The NAACC *Skish Guide* is obtainable from NAACC.

Special Activities

Crafts such as fly tying.

Field trips to hatcheries, fisheries, and aquariums.

Aquatic life activities, such as studying the plant life in the water, water life photography, water life collections, aquariums, etc.

Earthworm raising.

Minnow propagation.

See also Water Life in Chapter V.

SEE REFERENCES

FIELD ARCHERY

Although archery is almost as old as humanity and has a fascinating history, archery as an organized sport in the United States began in 1828 largely for the elite; however, down through the years it has increased in popularity and since World War II has enjoyed incredible growth.

There are basically two types of archery—target archery and field archery. Although target archery is by far the oldest form, it is not the most popular today. Some people feel it has too many rules and regulations, too much organization, and demands too much perfection from exactly the same position each time with very little physical movement and no vigorous exercise. Some consider target archery a contest, such as riflery matches are; while field archery is a game likened to golf, in which foursomes play a course with varying distances and types of shots.

Although both field archery and target archery have a common source, they are different in many ways. Field archery is based on hunting theory and presumably serves as practice for or a substitute for hunting. As a substitute for hunting, field archery has been organized into different types of rounds and has standards for its field course or range.

Many people think that field archery means going into a field and just shooting at various clumps, stumps, flowers, and whatever is sticking up, but this is called "roving archery." The course in field archery is laid preferably on a scenic, wooded, hilly area. About 10 acres are needed for 14 targets and a full course has two 14-target units. The National Field Archery Association has established recommendations for courses. The target distances range from 20 feet to 80 yards. Shooting may be done from a one, two, or four positions. Some positions may be alongside each other (a "fan"); others may be "walk-up" positions where archers come closer to the target with each arrow shot. The targets vary in size with the length of distance being shot, from 6" to 30". They also vary in style with the type of round, but the two most common are the black and white concentric circle and the animal silhouettes. Each target has only two scoring areas—the inside circle 5 points and the outside 3 points. The solid black "bullseye" does not give additional points but is an aiming spot. A trail system connects the shooting position and the target, then leads to the next shooting position. Frequently one shoots across the ravine or valley area of the hill, making the course one requiring physical stamina. All positions are located for safety so that they can all be shot at the same time without undue hazard to other shooters. The butt backstops or the banks that the targets are set into give good protection. It should be noted that a course may meet the requirements of the National Field Archery Association but not be a nature-oriented course! One should utilize the natural environment to best advantage and minimize the constructed elements; that is, one should not merely set up *butt backstops* at distances specified. Nature trail elements (see Chapter I, section 3) might well be incorporated into a field archery course.

Field archery also differs from target archery in the number of arrows shot (4 in field archery to 6 in target archery for each end—an end being the number of arrows shot at one time at a target), the method of aiming (point of aim in target archery in contrast to instinctive shooting for field archery), and scoring which has already been mentioned. There are also other technique differences.

Field archery is suitable for both men and women and also for children.

If you do not already have a field archery club in your city you may want to initiate one as part of your local nature-oriented program. Be sure to call upon local archers to help; they are usually more than willing to be of assistance. If you do not have any local field archers, write the National Field Archery Association for the nearest club and also the nearest field archery instructor.

In addition to establishing a club, the public recreation department may wish to provide an area and lay out a field course. This may be desirable even when the club is not sponsored by the department. Public recreation and other community agencies would also want to cooperate with any club activities.

Often outdoor activity declines in wintertime, but this is no sign that archery activity must stop! An indoor shooting area might be provided; and certainly a workshop for making equipment, especially bows and arrows, should be made available. The enthusiast will also enjoy some good archery books. See the section on Reading for Pleasure.

Helpful information on technique, course layout, the various tournament rounds, etc. may be found in the suggested references.

FIREARMS SAFETY AND HUNTING

The community program related to firearms safety and hunting can be divided into four major categories of activities.

Instructional Program

The primary function of the community recreation program should be to train for and promote safety. Many states are now adopting a hunter safety program, voluntary for the most part, but required in some states before a young person can obtain a hunting license. State conservation officers usually are trained and willing to assist in such programs. The National Rifle Association also has a firearms safety program and will provide instructional materials or put you in touch with a certified NRA rifle and pistol instructor. For help contact the county conservation officer of your state conservation commission, or the National Rifle Association, 1600 Rhode Island Avenue, N.W., Washington, D.C. 20036.

Instruction in shooting should include a knowledge of the various weapons, as well as proper shooting technique. Again the NRA has excellent materials. An instructional program using air rifles can be particularly effective with young boys and girls.

Knowledge Useful in Hunting

Clothing and equipment for hunting.

How to shoot various animals and birds. Preservation and cleaning. Hides.

Effect of climate, light, wind on hunting.

Regulations — bounties, seasons, limits, protective regulations, carrying and mailing weapons, licenses.

Sportsmanship and conservation.

Outdoor survival/living skills.

Clubs and Competitive Activities

Clubs are organized by various organizations and agencies, such as boys' clubs, police departments, sportsmen's clubs, military department units, public recreation departments, etc. They may be organized either under local autonomy or in affiliation with the National Rifle Association or the Daisy Manufacturing Company program. Both have extensive helps not only for organizing clubs but also for club activities. Crosman Arms Company, Fairport, N.Y., maker of air pellet guns, has various targets with games.

Competitive activities may be sponsored by organized clubs or by organizations indicated above as sponsoring agencies. Such shooting programs include conventional target rifle matches and leagues; shotgun, sporting rifle, and pistol competition; and air rifle and pellet gun activities. The National Rifle Association has a series of ratings, with badges, for various levels of achievement.

The clubs or sponsoring agencies may also wish to have information sessions for parents who contemplate getting their child a firearm.

Skeet and trap shooting are also popular, but they are most frequently sponsored by sportsmen's clubs.

Special Activities Related to Hunting

Dog training, taxidermy, crafts (stock making; plaster casts, etc.; and loading own ammunition), gun collecting, field trips to museums to see gun collections, and trips to game preserves and to gunsmiths are all interesting to those who love hunting and wish to learn the proper use and care of guns.

HIKING AND BACKPACKING

According to the outdoor recreation surveys by the Bureau of Outdoor Recreation, walking for pleasure is the outdoor recreation most frequently engaged in — but a walk is not necessarily a hike. Only too frequently a walk is a saunter or stroll; and this is not a hike in the sense used as part of a community nature-oriented program, for the walk needs no organization. In the hike, a person moves with spirit and some consistency in degree of speed. Usually a destination or purpose of some type involves covering a certain distance. It is this art of hiking that has been lost, for we are a "generation on wheels." Yet some of the finest places of beauty and serenity can be reached only on foot and the thrill and exhilaration of adventuring against the elements can only be experienced by walking.

The community recreation program can stimulate hiking by providing opportunities within its program. Hikes may be organized for the purpose of getting to an area such as a farm, fish hatchery, rock quarry, lake or museum. A hike may also be a special activity in itself, such as a hike through the woods lasting a few hours or a hike on a trail lasting several days. Special backpacking equipment is needed for the latter. Hiking can be done any place, any time! It is something people of all ages can engage in with a great deal of satisfaction in every season of the year.

Here are a few pointers and a couple of resources to help you in your planning:

1. A hike should be planned.

Anticipation is half the activity—looking forward to planning and going. Do not deny the participants this pleasure by planning it all yourself. Every hike taken as a group should involve that group in the organization and operation of the hike. Discuss such things as:

Where to hike to? What is the objective of the hike? Are there activities en route?

How long a hike? Keep in mind the experience of the group and the length of time available.

When to hike? Date, time of day?

What will be suitable clothing to wear; what equipment will be needed, if any; what food shall be taken, if any?

Are permissions needed, such as fire-building permits, permission to go on property, parent permissions?

Review good hiking manners and techniques, and safety precautions to be taken.

Shall we go rain or shine? Warm or cold?

2. The hiking program should have variety and progression.

No person without prior conditioning can enjoyably take a 50-mile hike! The program should provide for progressive experiences for the participants to gain skill, stamina, and endurance. Hikes should at first be short and on fairly easy terrain so that a good pace can be kept and when the end is reached the group would still like to do a little more. Gradually the length and terrain difficulty should be increased. In such progressions the hikers must also learn the differences in clothing needs for varying types of conditions, in changes in pace and rest intervals, in equipment and food, in time and route planning.

While the length of hike and type of terrain do provide for hiking variety, variety should be provided also in the objective for the hike. There are map and compass hikes (see section in this manual on Orienteering), evening hikes, nature hikes to points of natural interest, winter hikes, water hikes where one follows a stream or brook, historical and community hikes where one visits a specific place of interest in the community, rain hikes, etc. Hiking can be done also on established cross-country trails provided by hostels, Scouts, or other groups; in parks and forests; etc.

3. Proper hiking techniques add to the enjoyment.

A hiker is no better than his feet! Get feet in condition by daily walking and progressive conditioning hikes. Toenails should be cut straight across to prevent corners from cutting into skin. Shoes should be well broken in. They should fit well with ample room in front for toes. They should fit snugly in the arch and heel, thus giving support and preventing friction. Light canvas and rubber shoes are not recommended. Socks should *fit well* (not too small or too large) and have no holes or darns where they will irritate the skin. White wool socks are preferable. Powder helps keep feet dry, thus adding to comfort. Immediately attend a spot tender from rubbing. Place adhesive tape over it; if it has already blistered, prick blister and cover with clean bandage. Put on clean socks and change footgear if possible.

Wear clothing that will make you comfortable. For open-country hiking in warm weather, short-sleeved shirts and shorts are suitable; but for cross-country hiking in the woods, tall grasses, or brush, a long-sleeved shirt and long trousers should be worn. Wearing apparel should be of hard finish so that burrs and other natural objects will not adhere as readily. Many people recommend a hat of some type, particularly if hiking is done in the sun. If the weather is apt to get cool, a sweater should be taken. If worn under the shirt, it will provide more warmth because the air spaces of the loose weave serve as an insulator. For very cold weather, do not hesitate to wear heavy underwear. Also, in cool weather, several layers of lighter clothing are warmer than one or two heavy pieces of clothing because of the air-space insulation. If there is any chance of rain at all, take a poncho or raincoat. Don't forget *mittens* if it is cold; they are preferable to gloves. Trousers and shirts *must not* be tight — tight garments not only restrict movement and tire one but also cause rubbing and skin irritation.

Carry only that equipment which is absolutely necessary. When hiking the *hands should be free.* Carry some things in your pockets, but do not make them bulge or have pointed objects which will make you uncomfortable when hiking. Carrying a small backpack is preferable if your load is not too large. If you are going on a longer trip you should have a good backpacking frame to which you can tie your sleeping bag, tent, and cooking equipment.

Some standard equipment for your hike: matches in waterproof container or matches waterproofed by shellacking or waxing; piece of string; a safety pin; two or three adhesive bandages; knife; handkerchief; toilet paper; first-aid kit; snake-bite kit, if necessary in that part of the country; water purification tablets or canteen, if water is unavailable along the way; insect repellent, if a problem of insects exists; flashlight, if hike is of such duration as to extend into dusk. Other specialized equipment needed, such as cooking equipment, map and compass, etc., depend on the nature of the hike.

And don't forget the *food!* Of course, the amount and type depend upon the length and objective of your hike. Sometimes you will want a cold meal prepared beforehand and at other times a hot one, or a cold meal with a hot drink. For hot foods, see section in this manual on Outdoor Cookery. Here are some tips for good trail meals.

Wrap each food item separately. Pack heavy things in the bottom of the sack. Avoid salty, very sweet, and messy foods. Often it is better to take "fixings" for sandwiches and beverages than to prepare beforehand. Sandwiches, especially, will not then be soggy or misshapen. If sandwiches are made before starting, butter the *inside of both* slices of bread to keep bread from becoming soggy. Foods that quench the thirst such as raw vegetables (carrots, celery) and apples are excellent.

A trail lunch high in food value and quick energy (sometimes called a "birdseed" lunch) is a special mixture of sugar-coated cereal (several brands are available), coated chocolate candy of the kind that does not melt in your hand, unsalted peanuts, and raisins. For a group of six or seven, mix about 4 oz. of cereal, one 6 oz. package of candy, 8 oz. of unsalted Spanish peanuts (salted may be used but are not preferred), six 1½ oz. packages of raisins. Mix and carry in plastic bag and eat by the handful.

Other food suggestions are in the sources cited.

Learn to walk correctly. Most of us walk in what is known as the heel-toe style, placing the heel down first, shifting then to the ball of the foot and then to the toes. For hiking, however, many people prefer the "Indian style" which has only enough knee-bend to lift the foot barely clear of the ground. The swing of the leg forward is produced by the powerful hip muscles. Placement of the foot on the ground is almost flat-footed. Toes are pointed straight ahead so that the entire foot does its share of the work and aids in body balance. In going downhill, the knee provides "give." For especially steep slopes, a sideways position tends to give better foot placement on the ground and gives the body more support and balance. A rhythmic and steady pace should be established. Arms should swing easily, your head should be up, and you should be breathing deeply.

While the rate of speed is governed by the slowest hiker, a 3 mph average speed is desirable. A 2-3 minute rest stop every half hour is preferable to longer rest stops less frequently; however longer rest stops of 10-15 minutes should be allowed for approximately each two hours of hiking. An active hiker should attempt to attain at least a 26''-30'' stride — 30'' is the normal army length. The longest-legged hikers should *not* be placed in front of the group for they will "run away" at too fast a pace. Likewise, if the group should be strung out (preferably, keep together with leaders both in front and in back of group), too frequently those in front rest until the stragglers have caught up, then start out again — and the ones who really needed the rest didn't get any!

4. Hikers should observe good outdoor manners.

Good outdoor manners mean courtesy on the road (if hiking there). Keep as far left as possible, facing oncoming traffic. At night something white should be worn to reflect the light of vehicles. It is best, however, *not* to follow roads wherever possible. Ask permission to cross on private property; respect the right of ownership. Watch your fires; do not let them get too large or out of control. practice good conservation principles; do *not* pick everything in sight. Do not litter along the way; take your paper and garbage with you or dispose of it by proper methods.

ORIENTEERING

Although every individual has used a road map with his family to get where he wanted to go, and many backwoods sportsmen have used a map in hunting and fishing, few Americans are familiar with the sport of orienteering so popular in certain parts of Europe.

Orienteering is the skill of finding your way across country with combined map and compass. It is designed for rugged, adventurous persons and demands accuracy, intelligence, and stamina. However, many activities can be carried on not only with combined map and compass but also with map and compass separately. These are suitable for both young boys and girls as well as older youth whether they are in camp, on the playground, or part of a club or troop program.

Maps

Three basic types of maps and map-reading skills can be used in activities related to orienteering—learning to read and to use the common road map (for young beginners), making and using a sketch map, and using a topographical map. This latter map is the one used in orienteering. Topographical maps of many parts of the United States have been done by the U.S. Geological Survey and specific quadrangles are available from them for 30c each. An index to topographic mapping (by states) is available without charge so that you can ascertain whether the specific area you wish to traverse has been mapped and what the number of the quadrangle is. Also available free is *Topographic Maps,* a descriptive pamphlet, which tells you about topographic maps in general.

Fun with maps alone may be found in *Be Expert With Map and Compass.*

Compass

While many members of the armed forces have used a compass, the orienteering compass is designed for easy use by youngsters and for convenience in direction finding and orienting to maps. Its compass housing revolves on a transparent base plate that acts as both a protractor and direction finder. It, like other compasses, comes in different models—air-filled, induction-dampened, and liquid-filled; however, the inexpensive air-filled Type 5 Silva-System Compass has proved to be completely satisfactory for beginners in orienteering. It also will take many hard knocks.

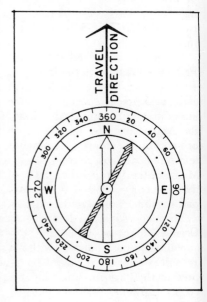

Instructions for use of compass and fun with compass alone can be found in *Be Expert With Map and Compass* which has a number of compass games discussed in the Game section. In addition, the compass treasure hunt and the compass trail to a cookout or other site are excellent activities. In both of these, one group of participants (or the leaders) can lay a compass trail to the treasure or site by getting a series of degree readings and distances between — then, the remainder of the group tries to follow the trail to the proper location. This makes a treasure hunt much more fun and the cookout will seem much more like being out in the woods.

Map and Compass Combined

There are four major types of orienteering activities (using map and compass together).

The Orienteering Hike

The orienteering hike is traveling cross-country using your map and compass. Choose your starting point on the map either where you are or where you can easily get to; then, select one or more points to which you would like to hike. Now, using your map, determine what route you would like to take, get your distances and compass reading. And don't forget to plan the return route unless you plan to have someone pick you up at the other place.

The orienteering hike can be done alone, in pairs, or in small groups. It is not usually good to have many in a group; it is better to have the group broken up into 2-3 with at least one compass per each two participants. The hike can be easy for beginners and then get increasingly difficult. It can be only an hour long or all day.

Project Orienteering

In project orienteering a prelaid route is used, having various stations designated en route. As one reaches each station, there are directions there to do some "project," hence the name project orienteering. The project may be as simple as collecting ten different leaves, or it may be to boil some water, chop some wood, decipher a Morse code. A judge is usually at each station to score the quality of the project done. Route and stations are indicated on the map by the participant as part of the total project.

Orienteering Races

Orienteering as a sport, through orienteering races, has become popular in Europe. A film which shows young men in Sweden competing is *The Sport of Orienteering,* available from Silva, Inc., La Porte, Indiana, on loan or for sale.

The two major types of races are route orienteering and point orienteering. In route orienteering the organizers of the race designate the route to follow on a master map. Participants must transfer this route to their own maps. As they follow the route, they come upon various stations which are then designated on the map. The winner is the participant who has not only found the most stations but also has indicated them correctly on his map.

In point orienteering the participant is given the location of a number of points which must be followed sequentially, but not the route to reach each point. Using the map, the participant decides what is the best (quickest and easiest) route from one point to the next. The points may all be given initially or each point may be revealed one at a time at each station. Time is usually a factor in that the winner is the one who reaches the end first. A variation is called Score Orienteering in which the various points (stations) have score values according to the difficulty of finding them. Then the winner is the one that can amass the greatest number of points from finding the various stations in the given time limit.

Wilderness Orienteering

Ambitious outdoorsmen will eventually use orienteering skills for traveling in unknown wilderness areas as they explore, camp, hunt, and fish. Such adventures must not be undertaken by beginners in orienteering, although the principles of going from map to field are the same as in known territory. They must also have adequate camping skills.

There are also some activities related to orienteering which are both fun and educational and may prove useful in outdoor adventures and camping. These activities are measurements — measures of heights, depths, distances, and volume. In orienteering you will have already learned your own pace and you may wish to know other personal measurements, too.

Some measurements you might like to take without use of traditional measuring instruments are depth of water by soundings, deflection caused by water, locating a spot on a lake for fishing, distance across a river, height of cliffs and trees, age of trees, number of board feet in trees, estimating an acre, a half-mile.

SEE REFERENCES

ROCK CLIMBING

Mountain climbing has been a challenging activity for all who go to or live in the mountains. The grandeur of the peaks dares people to ascend. Most mountain peaks can be reached through routes that will test a person's physical condition, stamina, and the will to conquer, but are relatively safe and not too difficult. There always is that rock, though, or that sheer face of the peak, that dares the individual to test his skill. It dares the adventurer to try to climb it, to take the risk involved both in conquering a dangerous task and testing his courage, for it is difficult for a person to admit defeat in the face of danger. However, to have fun one does not have to scale high and rugged peaks. The techniques of rock climbing can be learned on small cliffs and even structures that present a wall to be negotiated up and down with ropes; then, short weekend trips can be taken to mountains of modest height. Rock climbing is another outing sport that grew rapidly in the early 1970s and gained a large following as is demonstrated by the number of stores that specialize in handling the necessary equipment.

While rock climbing and descending appear frightening to the novice or observer, they really are quite safe if done properly. The best procedure for beginners is to go in small groups with a trained leader. A person seriously interested in climbing extensively should attend a school that offers courses and accreditation upon having attained a certain level of performance.

Rock climbing is more fun and safer if you have the proper equipment and clothes. Clothing should fit close to the body and be flexible and durable enough to protect you from sharp rocks. Knickers are highly recommended. Climbing shoes should be sturdy with a steel shank in the sole, so that if you can get your foot into a toehold you can support your body.

Recommendations concerning ropes, slings, pitons, and wedges can be gotten from the recommended books and reliable stores. Seasoned rock climbers take pride in and care of their equipment. They depend upon their ropes to save their lives and so do not lend them indiscriminately.

Before people interested in rock climbing purchase equipment, it is advisable for them to go climbing with experienced people where they will be introduced to a variety of ropes and other climbing equipment. Then they can purchase what best suits their own needs and interests.

SEE REFERENCES

SKIING—CROSS-COUNTRY

Skiing has often been thought of as a sport restricted to those who live in the mountains or to those with sufficient wealth to help pay for the frills that are associated with ski lodges and resort areas. More recently there has been much more interest shown in downhill skiing by the middle and lower economic classes. This may be due in part to the large number of facilities that have been opened offering a wide range of prices and services. However, in the early 1970s a new type of skiing called cross-country skiing has gained considerable popularity. The equipment for it is not as elaborate or as expensive as that for downhill skiing. Best of all, areas suitable for cross-country skiing are usually within walking distance from the participants' homes. While cross-country skiing does not have some of the inherent physical and mental challenges that some other adventure activities have, participants need to be alert for exhaustion, over-exertion, and frostbite.

Many adventure activity sport shops will rent cross-country skis and shoes at reasonable rates and will conduct clinics where beginners can spend a weekend learning some of the elementary skiing techniques and care of equipment. Attendance at such a clinic is highly recommended.

Cross-country skiing affords people an exciting outdoor activity, good physical exercise, and a unique method of travel enabling them to go places otherwise not accessible. Cross country skiing combines beautifully with outings, picnics, and trips.

SEE REFERENCES

SPELUNKING (CAVE EXPLORING)

Few adventure activities challenge a person's emotional and mental fortitude as does the sport of cave exploration. The complete darkness, the smallness of the crawl spaces, and the cold water through which one must crawl are enough to make all but the most hardy turn back. The sport of spelunking, however, is the type of activity that is so challenging and interesting that once people try it, most want to go again. Spelunking clubs are becoming common over the country.

The better caves for amateur spelunkers are found in limestone areas that have been unlocked by the glaciers. Some of the more frequently visited areas are western Iowa, southern Indiana-Kentucky, and Missouri. The geological story of the formation of caves, caverns, and interesting designs is a fascinating study of its own.

Caving can be a very dangerous sport and every year people get lost, are trapped by rising water, or receive some injury in an accident. Most of these misfortunes, however, are not the fault of the sport itself, but of carelessness on the part of the participants and leaders. Caving can be a safe, pleasant experience if one follows a few commonsense rules. Here are some suggestions:

1. Go with experienced cavers the first few times.
2. Go in small groups—never alone—and go with an experienced leader and "tail." The minimum number recommended is four so that if injury does occur, one can stay with the injured and two go for help.
3. Have proper equipment—coveralls are highly recommended, hard hats, knee pads, three sources of light, canteen.
4. Novices should go only into small and uncomplicated caves.

Because of the even temperatures in a cave, one does not need to worry about outside temperature variations. One does need to be concerned about rain, though, as many caves have water flowing through them and are subject to flooding. The best way to obtain up-to-date information concerning conditions in the interior is to talk with people who have just come out of the cave or whom you meet in a cave.

So, if you are the type of person who thrills with the challenge of attempting to negotiate your body through a crawl space barely large enough to get through, with rocks scraping at the top as well as bottom in complete darkness, and two or three inches of cold water sending shivers up your spine, then you have available to you some of the most beautiful and mystifying sights, and you will be justly rewarded.

REFERENCES

Adventure and Initiative Activities

Rohnke, Karl. *Cowstails and Cobras.* Project Adventure, Hamilton, Mass., 1977.
Simpson, Benjy, editor. *Initiative Games.* Colorado Outward Bound School, 945 Pennsylvania Street, Denver, Colorado 80203, 1974, $3.00. 67 pp., paper.

Teaching through Adventure, A Practical Approach. Project Adventure, Hamilton, Mass., 1976.

Bicycling

Amateur Bicycle League of America, 137 Brunswick Road, Cedar Grove, N.J. 07009. For information on bicycle racing.

Bicycle Institute of America, 122 East 42nd St., New York, N.Y. 10017. For club organization and activities; safety posters, et al.

Cycling. Boy Scouts of America. Merit Badge Series, New Brunswick, N.J. 1971.

Cycling in the School Fitness Program. American Association for Health, Physical Education, and Recreation, Washington, D.C., 1963.

League of American Wheelmen, 19 South Bothwell, Palatine, Ill. 60067. Recreational touring.

National Commission on Safety Education, N.E.A., 1201 Sixteenth St., N.W., Washington, D.C. 20036. Classroom posters on bicycle safety; pamphlets.

National Safety Council, 425 N. Michigan Avenue, Chicago, Ill. 60611.

Sloane, Eugene A. *The New Complete Book of Bicycling.* Simon & Schuster, New York, 1975.

U.S. Dept. of Interior, Washington, D.C. "Bicycling and Hostels," *Outdoor Recreation Action,* No. 34, Winter, 1974.

U.S. Dept. of Transportation. *Bicycling for Everyone.* Stock No. 0-550-719. U.S. Government Printing Office, 1974.

The Wheelman. 32 Dartmouth Circle, Swarthmore, Penn. 19081. Bike history and preservation.

Canoeing and River Running

American Red Cross. *Canoeing.* Doubleday and Co., Garden City, N.Y., 1956.

Canoe. Periodical of the American Canoe Association, P.O. Box 1888W, St. Paul, Minn.

Huser, Verne. *River Running.* Henry Reguery Co., Chicago, 1975.

McGinnis, William. *Whitewater Rafting.* The New York Times Book Co., New York, 1975.

McNair, Robert. *Basic River Canoeing.* American Camping Association, Martinsville, Ind., 1968.

Oar and Paddle. Periodical. P.O. Box 621, Idaho Falls, Idaho.

Urban, John T. *A Whitewater Handbook for Canoe and Kayak.* Appalachian Mountain Club, Boston, 1969.

Whitewater Journal. Periodical of the American Whitewater Association, P.O. Box 321, Concord, N.H.

Casting and Fishing

Blades, William F. *Fishing Flies and Fly Tying,* Stackpole Company, Harrisburg, Pa. 1962.

Brooks, Joseph. *Complete Book of Fly Fishing.* Outdoor Life, distributed by
A. S. Barnes and Company, New York, 1958.

Buck, Margaret Waring. *In Ponds and Streams.* Abingdon Press, Nashville,
Tenn., 1955. For young naturalists, identification.

Casting Clubs in Recreation. American Casting Education Foundation, P.O.
Box 1347, St. Petersburg, Fla. 37202. Free pamphlet.

Flick, Art. *New Streamside Guide.* Crown Publishers, New York, 1969. A
guide to natural aquatic insects and their imitations. Must reading for
every serious fly fisherman.

Gordon, Sid W. *How To Fish From Top to Bottom.* Stackpole Company,
Harrisburg, Pa., 1955.

Hittson, Hamilton, and Jones, Paul H. *Building and Programming Casting
Pools.* Management Aids, No. 12, American Institute of Park
Executives, 1962. Available from National Recreation and Park
Association, 1700 Pennsylvania Ave. N.W., Washington, D.C. 20006.

Hoover, Herbert. *Fishing for Fun . . . and To Wash Your Soul.* Random
House, New York, 1963. Inspirational thought. To be read by every
fishing enthusiast.

Manual for Tournament Fly and Bait Casting. National Association of
Angling and Casting Clubs, Box 51, Nashville, Tenn. 37202.

Marinaro, Vincent. *In the Ring of the Rise.* Crown Publishers, New York,
1976.

McClane, A. J. (editor). *McClane's New Standard Fishing Encyclopedia.*
Holt, Rinehart and Winston, New York, 1975.

Migel, J. Michael (editor). *The Stream Conservation Handbook.* Crown
Publishers, New York, 1974.

Needham, Paul R. *Trout Streams.* Winchester Press, New York, 1969.

Schwiebert, Ernest. *Matching the Hatch.* The Macmillan Company, New
York, 1955.

Shaw, Helen. *Fly-tying.* The Ronald Press, New York, 1963. For beginning
fly-tyers.

Skish Guide. National Association of Angling and Casting Clubs, Box 51,
Nashville, Tenn. 37202. Free.

Walton, Izaak. *The Compleat Angler,* tricentennial edition. Stackpole
Company, Harrisburg, Pa., 1953. A classic. To be read by every fishing
enthusiast.

Zim, Herbert S., and Shoemaker, Hurst H. *Fishes.* Golden Nature Guide,
Simon and Schuster, New York, 1956.

Cross-country Skiing and Snowshoeing

Bridge, Raymond. *The Complete Snow Camper's Guide.* Charles Scribner's
Sons, New York, 1973.

Caldwell, John. *The New Cross-Country Ski Book.* Bantam Books, Inc., New
York, 4th ed., 1974.

Osgood, William, and Hurley, Leslie. *The Snowshoe Book.* The Stephen
Greene Press, Brattleboro, Vermont, 2nd ed., 1975.

Tokle, Art, and Luray, Martin. *The Complete Guide to Cross-Country Skiing & Touring.* Vintage Books, New York, 1973.

Field Archery

Archery. Boy Scouts of America. Merit Badge Series. New Brunswick, N.J., 1941. Not on field archery; useful for equipment making and some special archery activities.

Burke, Edmund H. *Field and Target Archery.* (Fawcett How-To-Do-It-Book), No. 481, Greenwich, Conn.: Fawcett Publications, Inc., 1961.

Burke, Edmund H. *The History of Archery.* William Morrow and Company, New York, 1957.

Grimley, Gordon. *The Book of the Bow.* Distributed in the United States by National Field Archery Association, Redlands, Calif., 1958.

Haugen, Arnold O., and Metcalf, Harlan G. *Field Archery and Bowhunting.* Ronald Press, New York, 1963.

Hill, Howard. *Hunting the Hard Way.* Wilcox and Follett Company, Chicago, 1953.

Love, Albert J. *Field Archery Technique.* Dotson Printing Company, Corpus Christi, Tex., 1956. Available from National Field Archery Association.

National Archery Association. *The Archer's Handbook.* The National Archery Association, Secretary's Office, Lancaster, Pa., 1974.

National Field Archery Association. *Archery* (periodical); *The Basic Technique of Instinctive Field Shooting; Official Handbook of Field Archery.* Route 2, Box 514, Redlands, Calif. 92373.

Perry, Walter. *Bucks and Bows.* Stackpole Company, Harrisburg, Pa., 1953.

Pope, Saxton. *Hunting With Bow and Arrow.* G. P. Putnam's Sons, New York, 1947.

Stalker, Tracy L. *How To Make Modern Archery Tackle.* National Field Archery Association pamphlet, Redlands, Calif., 1954.

Thompson, J. Maurice. *The Witchery of Archery.* Pinehurst edition, The Archers Company, Pinehurst, N.C., 1928. A classic.

Firearms Safety and Hunting

Crosman Arms Company, Fairport, N.Y. 14450. Targets with games.

Daisy Manufacturing Company, Rogers, Ark. Instructional program on air rifles for youth, organizing clubs, and club activities.

National Rifle Association, 1600 Rhode Island Ave. N.W., Washington, D.C. 20036. Firearms safety program, organizing clubs, and club activities.

National Shooting Sports Foundation, Inc., 1975 Post Road, Riverside, Conn. 06878. *Hunting and Shooting Sportmanship; Shooting, Fun for Everyone; How You and Your Friends Can Start a Gun Club.*

O'Connor, Jack. *Complete Book of Rifles and Shotguns.* (Outdoor Life) Harper and Brothers, New York, 1961.

Ormond, Clyde. *Complete Book of Hunting.* (Outdoor Life) Harper and Brothers, New York, 1962.

Remington Arms Company, Inc., Bridgeport, Conn. 06602. Leaflets and pamphlets: *Handbook on Skeet Fundamentals, Handbook on Trap Shooting Fundamentals, Remington Tips on Gun Treatment, Safe Gun Handling, How To Be a Crack Shot.*

Smith, Julian W. *Shooting — Hunting.* American Association of Health, Physical Education, and Recreation, Washington, D.C., 1960.

What Every Parent Should Know . . . When a Boy or Girl Wants a Gun. Sporting Arms and Ammunitions Manufacturers' Institute, 250 East 43rd St., New York, N.Y. 10017.

Winchester-Western Division of Olin Mathieson Chemical Corp., P.O. Box 906, New Haven, Conn. 06704. Gun Charts.

Hiking and Backpacking

Elman, Robert. *The Hiker's Bible.* Doubleday and Company, Inc., Garden City, N.Y., 1973.

Fletcher, Colin. *The New Complete Walker.* Alfred A. Knopf, New York, 1974.

Hiking. Boy Scouts of America Merit Badge Series, New Brunswick, N.J., 1962 revision.

Hiking in Town or Country. Girl Scouts of the U.S.A., New York, 1952.

Learn, C. R., and Tallman, Anne S. *Backpacker's Digest.* Follett Publishing Company, Chicago, 1973.

MacFarlan, Paulette. *The Boy's Book of Hiking.* Stackpole Books, Harrisburg, Pa., 1968.

Manning, Harvey. *Backpacking One Step at a Time.* Vintage Books, New York, 1973.

Merrill, Bill. *The Hiker's and Backpacker's Handbook.* Winchester Press, New York, 1971.

Rethmel, R. C. *Backpacking.* Burgess Publishing Company, Minneapolis, Revised edition, 1972.

VanLear, Denise. *The Best About Backpacking.* Sierra Club, San Francisco, 1974.

Hosteling

American Youth Hostels, Inc., 14 West 8th Street, New York, N.Y. 10011. For general information.

Mountaineering and Climbing

Casewit, Curtis W., and Pownall, Dick. *The Mountaineering Handbook.* J. B. Lippincott Company, New York, 1968.

Evans, Charles. *On Climbing.* Museum Press, Kings Way, London, 1956.

Robbins, Royal. *Basic Rockcraft.* LaSiesta Press, Glendale, Calif., 1971.

Scott, Douglas. *Big Wall Climbing.* Oxford Press, Fair Lawn, N.J., 1974.

Wheelock, Walt. *Ropes, Knots, and Slings for Climbers.* LaSiesta Press, Glendale, Calif., 1971.

Orienteering

By Map and Compass. Silva Inc., La Porte, Ind. 46350. Excellent instructional color film (27 min.) giving basic fundamentals of map and compass use. Suitable for showing to youngsters as well as adults.

Disley, John. *Orienteering.* Stackpole Books, Harrisburg, Pa., 1967.

———. *Your Way With Map and Compass.* Canadian Orienteering Service, Willowdale, Ontario, 1973.

Elementary Map and Compass Instruction. Silva, Inc., La Porte, Ind. 46350. Pamphlet.

Geological Survey. *Topographic Maps.* Denver Distribution Section, Denver, Colo. 80202, if west of the Mississippi River; or Washington Distribution Center, Washington, D.C. 20242, if east of the Mississippi River. Free.

Kjellstrom, Bjorn. *Be Expert with Map and Compass.* Charles Scribner's Sons, New York, new enlarged edition, 1976.

Mooers, Robert L. *Finding Your Way in the Outdoors.* E. P. Dutton and Company, New York, 1972.

The Pathfinding Orienteering Area. Silva, Inc., La Porte, Ind. 46350. Pamphlet.

Ratliff, Donald E. *Map, Compass, and Campfire.* Binfords and Mort, Publishers, Portland, Ore., 1964.

Schoenstein, Roger V. "Organizing Informal Orienteering Meets." U.S. Orienteering Federation.

The Sport of Orienteering. Silva, Inc., La Porte, Ind. 46350. Film, for loan or sale, on orienteering races in Sweden.

Speleology (Caving)

Anderson, Jennifer. *Cave Exploration.* John A. Stellmack Association Press, New York, 1974.

Haliday, William R. *American Caves and Caving.* Harper and Row Publishers, New York, 1974.

McClurg, David R. *The Amateur's Guide to Caves and Caving.* Stackpole Books, Harrisburg, Pa., 1973.

Mohr, Charles E. *The Life of a Cave.* McGraw-Hill Book Company, New York, 1966.

National Speleological Society, Inc., Cave Avenue, Huntsville, Ala. 35810.

CHAPTER VII

Program Varieties

CAMPFIRE PROGRAMS

THE COMMUNITY NATURE-ORIENTED ACTIVITIES PROGRAM should not overlook the campfire program. While the traditions of the summer camp campfire, with all of its special meanings built up through the years, cannot be expected to be established in the park or playground campfire because of the constantly changing participants, the campfire program does have a place in these settings, but with a different function. Usually in the community recreation program, the campfire is used as a single event or as a part of a day's program—not as a symbolic event, as in the summer camp.

Campfires in Parks

Many people have attended an evening campfire in a national park. With the increase in family camping, particularly, these evening campfires are being found more and more in the family camp areas not only of national parks but also state and local parks. Sometimes they are referred to as "interpretive campfires," because their function is to interpret the local natural features as well as to entertain.

The usual pattern of program is a brief welcome to the campground, 10-15 minutes of singing the "old chestnuts," a few announcements of the coming activities in the area, and the remaining time spent in a talk or illustrated lecture about the history of the locale and its people. The ending is precise with "Good night folks. We hope you have enjoyed the evening and tomorrow . . . ," or something similar. People particularly enjoy singing, and singing, enthusiastically conducted, should be an integral part of the program. Sometimes some of the audience like to remain to watch the campfire embers.

The campfire circle design is somewhat different from the summer camp campfire circle. Usually there is a half or three-quarter circle with the fire in the opening and the speaker beside the fire. If slides or films are to be shown, the audience may turn and face the opposite direction for the showing, or a shield may be placed so as to screen out the light of the fire. When the audience becomes very large, a portable loudspeaker system is usually used. While many of the campfire sites have log seats in tiers, there appears to be a trend toward the more formalized outdoor-theater type seating because of the large crowds attending evening programs.

Campfires on the Playground

Sometimes the campfire program is used as a special evening event on the playground. The fire draws attention to the location of the activity and provides a general setting for the program. The program is usually entertainment either by a performing outside group or by the children of that particular playground. Frequently an evening activity may close with toasting of marshmallows or with other refreshments which do not require "cooking."

For a very effective campfire program on a playground, the planners can make use of the fire as a program medium, building around the romance and inspiration of the fire. The playground children can be encouraged to do special creative programming with emphasis upon their own participation rather than performance for parents and friends. An inspirational closing with poetry and singing and watching the embers of the fire can "top off" a very successful evening.

Often the site of the fire is a problem on hard-surfaced playgrounds. The fire itself, in such cases, may need to be portable, such as on a wheelbarrow or top of a steel drum. If possible, the site should be in a secluded wooded area of the playground.

For additional helps for planning the program and preparing the fire, see the sections following.

The Small Group Campfire

The usual concept of the campfire program is that of a large group, or the opposite extreme, the family or a few close friends lingering around the fire. However, one of the finest experiences is that of the small group campfire . . . a Scout troop or patrol, a club, a cabin group in camp, etc. These campfires are informal and spontaneous. The program is one of sharing—sharing in song, poetry, and stories; sharing of oneself. It is in this type of atmosphere that individuals can become better acquainted and feel a part of the group. It is useful at the beginning of some experience and it is also very meaningful as a close to an experience where a group has been together for some time.

Campfires in the Camp Setting

When one says "campfires," most people think of the camp campfire which is full of symbolism and tradition, whether for fun or inspiration. It is usually held in a secluded spot reserved exclusively for campfires. Participation of the campers in the program is an integral aspect, rather than the group's being entertained by outsiders. Singing plays a dominant role.

Planning the Campfire

Whether the campfire is used at day camp, on the playground, in a resident camp, with a small group or with the total group, certain basic principles of planning will help make the campfire more successful.

Physical Arrangements

Selection of Site. While a campfire may be placed anywhere a fire may be laid, usually it is held outdoors. The indoor fireplace loses much of the romanticism of the night with its sounds and lights. However, if natural logs are used, an indoor experience around the fireplace can be an inspirational and enjoyable experience for small groups.

In selecting a site, consider:

1. Should be near enough to the central area to be practical, but remote enough to give some seclusion. Usually the site is reserved only for campfires.
2. Should be well drained and free from insect pests. May be necessary to spray for mosquitoes prior to the campfire.
3. Particularly for large groups, a natural amphitheater (sloping ground) is desirable. See later section on council ring layout. The site should provide sufficient space overhead to prevent fire hazards and be able to be cleared underneath to prevent fire creeping.

4. Access to the site should be by winding trail to give a more secluded feeling in approaching the site. Firewood should be accessible and easy to get to the site. However, selection of the site for other reasons is more important — you can carry firewood! The path should be well constructed so participants will not be likely to stumble in the dark. It should be narrow, although may be wide enough for two.
5. Prevailing winds should be considered, with placement of the fire so that the participants will not have to contend with smoke most of the time. Natural windbreaks also are desirable.

The Campfire Circle. There are quite a few varieties of "campfire circles" — an informal ring of logs around a fire, excavated fire circle, Indian hogan style, on rafts in the water, etc. The following suggestions, though, will be concerned only with the ordinary, common type of campfire circle.

1. The diameter of the circle itself should be no greater than 24-30 feet. To have a larger circle destroys intimacy and group feeling. To provide for more seating, add a second or third row of seats. Some authorities say that there should be no more than three rows. This, of course, limits the size of group which can be accommodated. The additional rows should be raised in tiers.
2. The "circle" may be more elliptical than circular in shape. The seats are ¼ to ¾ the distance around — not completely around, for if there is any performance, part of the audience cannot see what is going on. It is usually better to have semipermanent, sturdy, off-the-ground seats. These may be logs 5-6 feet long and one foot wide which are staked in, planks across log pieces, logs cut flat on top and set in the ground, or other seating material.
3. For better programming, there should be only one entrance — behind the fire. Performances should take place between the fire and the audience. If there is a campfire leader or council chief, he should be seated opposite the entrance. (See diagram.)
4. At all times, the campfire circle should be kept clear of litter.

Structure of the Fire

The focal point of the campfire circle is the fire itself. The success of the program can depend on the success of the fire — does

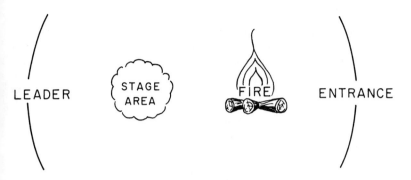

LEADER   STAGE AREA   FIRE   ENTRANCE

it light quickly, burn brightly, and last long enough? Many a fine program has been marred because the fire was a failure.

The purpose of the fire is light, not heat. The ideal fire is not a big bonfire which can be a fire hazard and drive the people away from the fire because of the heat. The fire should be built so that it burns on an outside structure, is self-feeding, and will last 1 to 1½ hours with a minimum of tending. It should be built in a fire pit—an area cleared so that there is no danger of creeping. If there is some difficulty in making such a cleared area, the fire might be built upon a platform of some type. The fire pit usually is encircled or lined by rocks or logs of sufficient size.

There are three commonly used campfire lays: the log cabin fire, the top-lighted fire, and the teepee fire.

Log Cabin Fire

The fire lay rests on two large logs which allows lighting from the bottom. The space between the logs as the lay is built up should be filled with smaller pieces of wood to get a quicker, brighter start on the fire. The ideal log cabin fire has

LIGHT HERE

larger logs on the outside frame which catch fire and burn brightly for the remainder of the campfire.

Top-lighted Fire

This is an adaptation of the log cabin fire with the fire lay (the small teepee of kindling and tinder) placed on the fifth or sixth layer. Several layers are built above this. The fire thus burns at the top first with the coals falling down and igniting the lower platforms. Except for place of lighting, this is constructed similarly to the log cabin fire.

LIGHT HERE

The Teepee Fire

The wood is stacked on end with logs resting together at the top like a teepee. The fire is lighted at the bottom. This style is not as neat looking as the first two.

After building the fire, it is important to pick up all the chips and debris, for neatness greatly adds to the whole effect. Also, *no* debris should be put on the fire. A well-laid fire may be ruined by adding bark, leaves, and chips which cut off the draft. The starting tinder and kindling should be twigs, not leaves or paper.

LIGHT HERE

Someone should be designated as the Keeper of the Fire, and if it needs replenishing with fuel he should quietly and quickly add it. A woodpile of logs of proper size and length should be easily accessible, preferably out of view.

To build and light the fire is only half the job. It is important that the Keeper(s) of the Fire remain after the program to properly extinguish the fire.

Lighting the Fire

Lighting the fire is usually a part of the ceremony of opening the campfire. In such a fire-lighting procedure it is important that the fire lighting be done in a very short time, that an alternate method be ready in case of failure of the planned method, that if a new method is used it be practiced ahead of time, and that there be sufficient tinder and kindling. Some different methods of lighting fires for special occasions:

1. Fireball or blazing stone ("fire from heaven"). Run a thin guide wire from the center of the campfire to a nearby treetop. Saturate the kindling and campfire wood with alcohol or kerosene. Attach a stone which is covered with cotton saturated with alcohol to a spool threaded on the guide wire in such a way that it will slide down the wire into the campfire. Someone atop the tree lights the stone and then sends the ball of fire sliding down the guide wire lighting the fire in a flash.

2. Use of chemicals. a. *Magic quick fire.* Mix 2 tablespoons of potassium chlorate crystals with 2 tablespoons of granulated sugar. Rig up the campfire so that by pulling a wire a 1½ oz. bottle of concentrated sulfuric acid will pour onto the first mixture which will then ignite and start the campfire. An easy way to rig up the acid is to suspend a small bottle like a test tube between two small stakes so that when tipped it will dump into the chlorate and sugar. A short distance in front of the bottle, drive a forked stake. Tying a string to the bottom of the bottle, bring the string over the fork of the stick and out to the edge of the fire circle so it can be pulled at the proper time. Build this rig first, then the campfire lay around it. Safety precautions are extremely important in use of chemicals, which should be handled only by adults. b. *Magic delayed reaction fire.* Place one teaspoon potassium permanganate in cone-shaped paper cup. Set paper cup into fire lay, leaving space at backside so that some one may reach in with eyedropper. When about time for fire to be started, someone should go to fire lay as if checking it and have an eyedropper of glycerine in hand, but shielded from sight. Drop eight drops of glycerine into paper cup. In about two minutes fire bursts into a flame igniting the fire lay. A trip device can be set up so that the glycerine is dumped into paper cup by use of a device similar to that in the quick magic fire. However, one must test the viscosity of glycerine to be sure that eight drops will flow out into the potassium permanganate. This is the safest of the magic fires.

3. Have a torch bearer run in to light the fire.

4. The flaming arrow is the same as #1 above, except that an arrow is attached by two spools to the wire and the tip ignited (sparkler or ball of lightweight material like cotton saturated with alcohol), then fired down into the fire lay.

5. A pipe can be laid underground from the fire lay to a point outside the circle or to the leader's chair. A long fuse may then be used to ignite the fire.

6. The fire snake is made from ¾'' rope, 3' long, wrapped with some dark absorbent cloth which has been lightly dipped in paraffin (old candle wax). Attach the snake by three spools which are threaded on a strong thin black wire about 3'' from the ground. This wire goes from the snake's place of hiding near the edge of the circle to a stake in the fire lay. Be sure it is protected and covered as participants enter the circle. At the proper time, someone lights the snake and a person on the opposite side pulls it into the fire lay by means of thin black wire attached to its nose. When the snake reaches the fire lay, it of course lights the fire.

Colored flames also can be used for special effects by adding chemicals to the campfire directly or in magazine logs. Here is how to make the logs:

Blue Vitriol Magazine Logs

   4 lbs. blue vitriol (copper sulphate powder, not crystals)
   2 lbs. coarse salt
   2½ gal. water

Put the above formula into a 5-gallon, flat-bottomed crockery or earthenware jar. The solution is highly corrosive, so glass or earthenware must be used. Stir slowly with a long-handled wooden spoon, paddle, or stick.

The logs are best made of slick paper magazines rather than newsprint. Roll each magazine as tightly as possible and tie firmly with several turns of strong cord at each end. The larger magazine should be tied in the center as well. Immerse each log endwise into the solution until the jar is filled. Let stand four to six days. At the end of each 12-hour period turn the logs so that the solution will penetrate evenly. At the end of the period, take the logs out of the jar and set up on papers to dry. Any solution left should be stored in large-mouthed glass jars. *Never* pour solution into drains.

Place these dried logs into a low-burning fire or embers of a fire to get best results. These logs will burn blue, green, and purple. Other chemicals may be used in the logs to produce different colored flames. Drugstores which handle prescriptions can obtain chemicals for you or may have them on hand. These chemicals also can be used to soak pine cones, which, when dry, can be added to a fire to give it color.

Chemical	Color
potassium chloride	lavender
common salt	yellow
potassium nitrate	purple
strontium nitrate	crimson
copper ammonium sulfate	light blue
calcium chloride	red
barium nitrate	green

The campfire is many things. It is:

A circle of friendship
A proof of leadership
A place of tradition, history, story
A stage for drama
An arena for fun, games, contests
A focus for music, song
A court for recognition, ceremony, honor
A shrine for memories
A symbol of the soul of the camp.

La Rue A. Thurston
Complete Book of Campfire Programs

Planning

A good campfire program does not "just happen." It, like other good programs, takes planning in considerable detail ahead of time. First, planning should be done *with* the group that is participating. It is not entertainment planned and executed by someone else. Secondly, there must be an alternate program in case of rain when the campfire cannot be held at the site as anticipated.

In program content there should be total group involvement; *everyone* should have a role and participate fully. Stories and poems certainly are acceptable, but there should be no speeches as such. It is helpful to have a theme to "tie things together" and for easier planning. The program should not be just a hodgepodge of activities. Initially the mood should be set, and at the end the participants should be "brought back down" if they have been having an exciting time so that they will not "run wild" upon leaving the campfire area. Forty-five minutes to one hour is usually long enough for a campfire.

Content

Generally speaking, campfires can be classified into three primary types by program content—inspirational, ceremonial, and ritualistic, in addition to fun, although some of each are in every campfire. While the specific content emphasis differs, the sequence of activity is the same for all.

1. Opening—entry into campfire circle (relatively short); lighting of the fire; activity to give a feeling of unity, friendship.
2. Buildup of activity, reaching a climax (main body of program).
3. Quieting period and closing (relatively short).

The closing may use music (taps, musical prayer, goodnight song), friendship circle, organization pledge or benediction said in unison (frequently a short poem or Indian sign language), symbolic ritual, or silence.

Some of the activities often found in the main body of the program include:

Indian ceremonies, legends and lore (see chapter on Indian life)
contests and challenges
dramatics and stunts
songs
storytelling and poetry

OUTINGS AND DAY CAMPING

Outings

Outings can play a very important role in the community nature-oriented program. These are whole-day or part-day jaunts away from the city into a natural environment for various nature-oriented activities, for example, nature study, collecting materials for nature crafts, outdoor cookery, or hiking. This day is complete in itself and usually has several activities, but one central feature such as the exploration of an area rich in Indian lore.

The outing provides a much-needed adventure activity for youth today. It may stem from the playground, community center, youth agency group, or be sponsored on a "sign-up" basis as a special event.

As with any activity, preplanning must be detailed to ensure success. Outings may be taken to many of the community resources discussed earlier in this manual.

Day Camping

Often individuals confuse a day camp and outings. Whereas an outing is complete in itself and may be one day only during the season, the day camp has a series of days, preferably at least five or six, which may be either within one week or one per week for five to six weeks, with continuity of activity from day to day. Each day's activities build upon the preceding one. Usually the youngsters spend at least one mealtime at the campsite, although the time of day may vary.

The day camp may be sponsored by the church, youth agencies, private organizations for special groups, or municipalities.

The day-camp site is not just a shady spot on the playground. It should be a relatively isolated natural area. There should be sufficient acreage to handle the number of children adequately for activities in the natural environment. Some possible sites: large public parks which have an isolated natural area; ranches; farms with nice wooded areas and farm pond; hunting, fishing, or game club sites; lakes with a secluded wooded area; large estates with a woodlot of some size.

The program of the day camp *must not be* the same as activities of the playground or backyard. It should be nature-oriented and include these different types of activities (this manual has helps for each type):

nature activities, including weather, nature study, measuring time and distance, etc.

outdoor living skills, including firemaking, cooking, shelters, toolcraft, ropecraft

adventure-outing sports, such as adventure and initiative activities, boating, fishing, orienteering, hiking

creative arts, including nature crafts, storytelling (especially the legends, myths, and animal stories), music, campfire programs

games, particularly nature games and woodcraft contests

Available from the American Camping Association are minimum standards established for day camps relating to site, health and safety, program, personnel, etc.

FAMILY CAMPING

There are two types of family camping. In one, an agency or organization, such as the "Y" or the church, organizes a program in a resident camp for families. In the other, families camp "on their own" in parks, forests, and other areas with camp sites. Often groups of families with kindred interests camp together. This is called a "camp-out." Sometimes these are referred to as *organized* family camping and *individual* family camping.

Organized Family Camping

This manual does not include organized resident camps as part of nature-oriented programs in the community, although it is recognized that camping is certainly a very integral part of outdoor recreation.

Contact the national office of the YMCA and the church group of your choice. Most organizations carrying on this type of activity have their own resources.

Individual Family Camping

This manual, in including individual family camping, is not concerned so much with the knowledge and techniques needed by the family to go camping as it is in discussing *services* which can be rendered to the family camper by various community groups. Books specifically written for the family camper can be helpful for techniques. There are various periodicals which the individual family camper will find helpful on sites and techniques.

The individual family camper also may belong to national or regional family camping clubs such as the New England Family Campers Association or the National Campers and Hikers Association, 1507 National Newark Building, Newark, N.J. 07102. For local club memberships and activities, see later section. Because family camping has grown so rapidly, many magazines and organizations hoping to capitalize on this interest have ''mushroomed,'' and a good number have ceased publication after a few issues. While many national and regional groups have had only a brief existence, the local family camp club and family camp services have found tremendous popularity.

Program services that are useful to families include:

1. Campground directories, periodicals, and technique books for the family camper available for review in the office or community center. A bibliography (annotated) of these materials should be made available without charge.
2. Free handouts available on family campgrounds describing sights to see in the state or within a reasonable distance from the city.
3. A family camper's bulletin published periodically, carrying information on camp ideas, trading post, camp site information, new publications, festivals, and other events family campers might like to participate in.
4. Demonstrations of equipment either in a special meeting or as a camp show on a weekend. A camp show can be run similarly to many sports shows, although it should usually be held out-of-doors and involve family campers actually camping—for those interested to visit with others and observe their equipment.
5. Sponsored camp-outs for the weekend at a nearby camp site.
6. Trading post — place for people to post notices for what equipment they would like to buy, sell, or exchange.
7. Special instructional sessions or workshop series:

   techniques and helps for beginners in family camping
   tent making (and other gear)
   mobile trailer construction
   nature
   travel trailer techniques

8. Programs for family campers:

   activities for the family camper—''what to do'' ideas
   share equipment ideas, show new equipment
   bring someone in to tell about sites and sights of a certain
       geographical area, perhaps illustrated
   family campers share experiences of where to go and what to do

The Family Camper's Club frequently is sponsored by the local public recreation department; in such instances, many of the following suggested services might take place through the activities of the club. The club may remain unaffiliated with other clubs, or it may wish to join one of the family camp national organizations, such as National Campers and Hikers Association. Purposes of club organization are:

1. Friendship and good fellowship among family campers.
2. Sharing of experiences, tips about camp sites, equipment, activities.
3. Strengthening of family life through camping.
4. Lobbying for site standards and funds for facilities at both the state and federal level to improve conditions on the campgrounds.

INDIAN LIFE

The American Indians and the way they lived before the coming of the white race have been an inspiration to many people. Their great knowledge about the outdoors and the resourcefulness with which they were able to utilize indigenous materials to serve their everyday living needs are truly arts to be envied. The Indians, their skills, and their way of life (customs) have served as an appropriate theme for many camping and recreation programs.

When activities which are centered on Indians are being used in a program, *every effort should be made to make these activities as authentic as possible.* A great deal of injustice and injury has been done to the American Indian when leaders have suggested "let's play cowboy and Indians." In these situations children tend to imitate the Indians of TV fame where they are thought of as bloodthirsty savages with weird, nonsensical dances and chants.

Actually, American Indians had a very wholesome and unique outlook toward the outdoors. They saw themselves as part of every living thing they observed. They did not see themselves as rulers of nature or masters with all living things subject to their whims and desires. Rather they considered themselves related to the living creatures they encountered. This feeling of "kinship" with the animal world led them to develop an attitude of respect and love for all forms of life.

The Indians did not kill game for the sake of killing or just for the sport involved, as did many of the white people. They did not kill more than they needed for food and clothing. There was no room for ruthless slaughter in their approach to the natural environment. It is no wonder they had difficulty in understanding the ways of the white people and that they rose up in protest when they saw unnecessary and wasteful attacks on the buffalo and other forms of wildlife.

With this orientation to the outdoors, it was natural for Indians to look for and find beauty in all of the natural world. They did not recognize as ugly those aspects of nature that seem to impress the white people as being so. The Indians' philosophy concerning the entire outdoor surroundings and all of nature was good and beautiful. Anything natural could not be ugly—if it was ugly, it was so because people had made it so.

The Indians gave expression to their philosophy and feelings through games, crafts, living skills, ceremonials, dances, stories, and legends. Each of these areas offers a wealth of material for use in community and camping programs.

Games

Most of the Indian children's games were based upon the life situations in which adult Indians found themselves. These were games in which the children would imitate or attempt to portray social customs, ceremonies, hunting, warfare, or the skills involved in homemaking. There were no toy shops from which to purchase ready-made toys, so frequently they would turn to the materials found in the outdoors (branches, logs, stones, bones, and shells) from which they would make their toys. Many of the games in which the boys participated were based upon man-to-man combat and included running, throwing, and wrestling.

Crafts

Crafts for the Indians were completely utilitarian and functional rather than recreational. They centered around the making of utensils and equipment for kitchen use, costumes and ornaments for ceremonials, and hunting equipment. Indian crafts can be used in craft programs as well as in preparation for evening campfire and ceremonial programs.

Living Skills

The American Indians developed a high dregree of skill in the areas related to outdoor living. Their abilities to find their way, to hunt animals, and to use native materials to provide comfort for their families were amazing. People can be challenged into trying to develop some of their powers of observation and to gain greater knowledge of the outdoors through studying and participating in projects which demonstrate the Indians' way of life. Indian life can be simulated through building shelters, going on hunts, and looking for edible plant life. Not merely "playing like Indians," but actual authentic practices should be used.

Ceremonials and Dances

Ceremonials played a very important part in the lives of Indians. In these celebrations and ceremonies they were able to give expression to their inner feelings through dances, colorful costumes, and makeup.

Most of the Indians observed ceremonies connected with the changing of the seasons. These were related to the activities of the season such as the celebrating of the planting of crops in the spring. The pilgrims adapted the ceremony of giving thanks at harvest time which later became our "Thanksgiving." Other ceremonies had to do with hunting and warfare or were related to religious practices of driving out evil spirits.

The Indian's dance was composed of intricate but meaningful steps and figures designed for specific purposes. Too frequently Indian dances are thought of as frantic jumping and arm waving and are imitated in this way in recreational programs. Learning Indian dances will give your participants a better understanding of the Indian as well as help develop dancing skills.

Stories and Legends

Tribal traditions were handed down from parent to child through the telling of stories. Most of these were legends and myths describing the creation of the world and such natural events as storms. Some described the experiences of brave warriors and medicine men. Others told how some of the animals got their distinctive features.

SEE REFERENCES

NIGHTTIME ACTIVITIES

In addition to the activities discussed here, you will find other suggestions in the sections on Animals, Astronomy, Campfires, Insects, Nature Photography, Outdoor Living Skills (overnight camp-outs). Only too frequently nature-oriented night activities are not only neglected but often omitted entirely, yet some of the finest hobbies and most fascinating outdoor adventures take place at night.

Creatures of the Night

Nature's nightlife has many fascinating aspects for the curious. There are many creatures who hunt and eat, mate, and raise their families during the night—your evening is their morning! Who are the animal prowlers out in search of food? Have you observed the activity of the beaver building his home? What about the habits of the owls and bats?

Listen! Can you tell who's up? Many people are frightened of the night because of the eery sounds; sounds which are eery because they are unknown. A part of your program could involve identifying the various sounds and then learning something about night creatures' activities and where they might be found. There are records available now on night sounds (see section on Insects).

Who's this at my window? Light draws many insects—they cannot help themselves. This pull of the light is called phototropism. But some insects are negatively phototropic, they skitter away from the light. What is a bug bulb and why doesn't it draw insects? The world of insects is indeed a fascinating one.

Lights in the Night

What makes a firefly light in the night? What is a falling meteor or shooting star—what causes them to travel across the sky? Have you seen the beautiful Northern Lights—why are they more brilliant at certain times of the year? Have you watched for satellites such as Echo? What happens when there is an eclipse of the moon?

Have you seen the moons of Jupiter, the rings of Saturn, or the craters of the moon? Why are the constellations different in the various seasons of the year? What are the "evening star" and the "Milky Way?"

The viewing and discussing of these events and objects will make fascinating activities for your nighttime nature-oriented program. See the section on Astronomy.

Fellowship Around the Campfire

Whether you are camping out all night or just have an evening campfire and then return home, the fellowship of the campfire can be a highlight in your nature-oriented program. Singing and stories, sharing of experiences, and contests and challenges, all go into making up the campfire program. See section on Campfires.

WINTER ACTIVITIES

Do you close up your "outdoor shop" when winter comes and move almost entirely into an indoor program? If you do, you're missing the opportunity of a lifetime! Winter is a wonderful time to be outdoors, and the community nature-oriented program should take advantage of the new and stimulating possibilities—not just the traditional snow and ice sports of skiing, tobogganing, ice-skating, curl-

ing, and ice fishing, but winter activities such as camping, snow games, tracking, snow sculpture and painting, winter carnivals, winter hobbies, and social activities out-of-doors.

Snow Sculpture and Painting

Who hasn't made a snowman—but have you tried your abilities in making other creatures? Snow sculpture is an old art which can be done on any day when the snow packs well. Simple packing of snow is the commonest type of snow sculpture by youngsters, but older youths and adults take great delight and pride of workmanship in other methods of sculpturing—hacking and carving on a block of snow ice, working with snow slush using armatures, etc. Snow sculpture house decorations and competitions are an important part of winter carnivals.

Sculptures can be painted on a day when the snow has settled but is not too crusty.

Hobbies

The study of snowflakes is a fascinating thing—of the billions of snowflakes that are formed each snowfall, no two are alike. Their only similarity is in the six-sided pattern they all have.

Tracks tell a story. Tracks lead to adventure. Tracking in the snow is a winter hobby many enjoy.

And crafts are not left out in winter—have you made winter decorations and bouquets from natural materials you have collected in the winter woods and fields?

We often think of the summer sky and star gazing, but actually the "winter star show" often is more brilliant than the summer one. The winter positions of constellations give an interesting study in comparison with summer.

In summer everyone seems to have a camera, but winter photography offers new challenges and opportunities.

These are just a few of the many winter hobby opportunities for your community nature-oriented program.

Social Activities

Do not forget the many fine winter social activities. There are the active skiing, skating, sledding, and tobogganing parties. Although sleighs are not as common as when they were used for transportation a generation ago, sleigh riding or converting a hay wagon to runners and using it for a sleigh can be fun, especially on a moonlit night. Hiking in the snow, ending with a picnic or barbecue—yes, even in winter—can be a highlight among social activities when it's cold outside. Climax the evening with a winter campfire. Around the holidays, special "burning of the Christmas tree" celebrations are traditional in many cities. Or where there are sugar maples, what is better than a sugaring-off party? And have you tried snow ice cream parties?

Camping

Both day camping and resident camping can be done on weekends and during holidays, also trip camping. "Camp-ins," especially for enjoyment of winter sports, frequently are held in resident camp facilities by families who camp together in summer.

Carnivals

In summer you have the Fourth of July, in fall, Halloween—
what about winter? Why not have a gala winter carnival with a king
and queen, snow sculpture, contests of all kinds on the ice, and snow
sports?

Snow Games

Snow Angels

Most children like to make patterns in the snow. One of the most
popular is "snow angels." Lie down in the snow, preferably on a
slope, with arms straight out. Now move arms toward the head to
make "angel wings." Get up carefully and you will have an "angel
in the snow."

Fox and Geese

An old-time favorite. Tramp off in the snow a *large* circle in sort
of "follow the leader" fashion, then make two paths across the
center dividing the circle into four parts. If many play, the circle
should be extra large and two concentric circles can be used with six
cross paths. Tramp a "home" in the center about three feet in
diameter. Players must remain in the paths to avoid tramping down
all the snow. One person is "it"—the fox. He chases the others who
are "geese." When the fox tags a goose, the goose becomes the fox
and chases someone else. Players cannot be tagged when standing at
"home." To speed up the game when larger numbers are playing,
more foxes may be used.

Snow Snake

This is an old Indian game which called for highly skilled players
and special "snakes" (sticks). Today children play a variation. They
can make their own "snakes" by taking a branch 3-4' long, 1½-2"
thick, peeling it, and then whittling it down to about 1" thick with an
egg-shaped ball on one end for the snake's tail and some type of
snake's head at the other end. An even stretch of snow is packed
down well with a slight groove in which the "snakes" will travel.
Hold the snake at the head end, with the ball end resting in the
groove in the snow. With the forefinger on the end and the thumb
and other fingers on either side of the stick, the player propels the

snake down the groove in somewhat of a bowling motion. The snake that goes the farthest wins.

Most outdoor games can be modified for snow play—hide and seek, dodge ball, snow football, bombardment, capture the flag, or snowman target.

READING FOR PLEASURE

Many very fine books are available for your reading pleasure. Some are outdoor adventure stories, some point up conservation, others may be read for inspiration, and some are informational. Often when one thinks of nature-oriented activities, the passive, individual activity of reading is overlooked. Every nature-oriented program should have as an integral aspect the encouragement of reading. The local library is always most willing to assist in recommending books for youngsters to read themselves and books which may be read to them. Reading selections for adults should also be stressed.

Included in the reference section For Your Reading Pleasure following this chapter are a few selections for you to begin with. Many more books are published than can be listed in this manual. You can find out about some of them by sharing with friends, by watching magazines and periodicals relating to the out-of-doors, by consulting the book review section of Sunday nexspapers, and by browsing in bookstores and libraries especially for book selections listed by organizations such as the National Wildlife Federation and the National Audubon Society. You can find additional books for reading in the section, Indians, Stories and Legends, in the References for this chapter. Also, some books suitable for children are included in the References, Chapter V, Projects and Hobbies.

REFERENCES

Campfire Programs

Campfire Programs, In-Service Training Series, National Park Service, Washington, D.C. Pamphlet. A helpful guide.

Fun Around the Campfire. Boy Scouts of America, New Brunswick, N.J., 1952.

Thurston, La Rue. *Complete Book of Campfire Programs.* Association Press, New York, 1958.

See also section of Indians—Ceremonials and Dances, Stories and Legends
—and the For Your Reading Pleasure section.

Day Camping

American Camping Association, Bradford Woods, Martinsville, Ind. 46151.
  Minimum standards for day camps.
Bogardus, LaDonna. *The Church Day Camp.* National Council of Churches,
  Chicago, 1955.
Cowle, Irving M. *Day Camping.* Burgess Publishing Company, Min-
  neapolis, 1964. Administration and program.
Larson, Ross H., and Long, Russell M. (editors). *Day Camp Manual: A*
  Practical Guide for Urban Congregations. Fortress Press, Philadelphia,
  1972.
Mitchell, Grace L. *Fundamentals of Day Camping.* Association Press, New
  York, 1961. Administration and program.
Musselman, Virginia W. *The Day Camp Program Book.* Association Press,
  New York, 1963. Administration and program.

Family Camping

Watch the newsstands for magazines on family camping; a good one,
which can be obtained on subscription, is Woodall's *Trailer Travel,* 10
Caravan Ct., Marion, Ohio 43302.

There are a number of good family campground directories issued,
including those of the AAA and state park agencies. Two popular and quite
complete directories available in most bookstores are those published by
Woodall and by Rand McNally.

Bookstores also have a collection of books on family camping. Look for a
book that meets your needs and interests. Basic outdoor living books can
also be helpful.

Indians

Ceremonials and Dances

Buttree, Julia M. *The Rhythm of the Redman.* A. S. Barnes, New York,
  1930.
Jaeger, Ellsworth. *Council Fires.* Macmillan Company, New York, 1954.
Macfarlan, Allan A. *Campfire and Council Ring Programs.* Association
  Press, New York, 1951.
Mason, Bernard S. *Dances and Stories of the American Indians.* A. S.
  Barnes, New York, 1944.

Crafts

Hunt, W. Ben. *The Golden Book of Indian Crafts and Lore.* Simon and
  Schuster, New York, 1945.

Mason, Bernard S. *The Book of Indian Crafts and Costumes.* A. S. Barnes, New York, 1946.
Norbeck, Oscar E. *Book of Indian Life Crafts.* Association Press, New York, 1958.

Games

Macfarlan, Allan A. *Book of American Indian Games.* Association Press, New York, 1958.

Living Skills

Macfarlan, Allan A. *Living Like Indians.* Association Press, New York, 1961.

Stories and Legends

De Angulo, Jaime. *Indian Tales.* Hill and Wang, New York, 1953.
Palmer, William R. *Why the North Star Stands Still and Other Indian Legends.* Prentice-Hall, New York, 1946.
Resslar, Theodore W. *Treasury of American Indian Tales.* Association Press, New York, 1957.

Nighttime Activities

Berrill, Jacquelyn. *Wonders of the Fields and Ponds at Night.* Dodd, Mead and Co., New York, 1962.
———. *Wonders of the Woods and Desert at Night.* Dodd, Mead and Co., New York, 1963.
Brown, Vinson. *Knowing the Outdoors in the Dark.* Stackpole Books, Harrisburg, Pa., 1972.
Pettit, Ted. *Wildlife at Night.* G. P. Putnam's Sons, New York, 1976.
Sterling, Dorothy. *Creatures of the Night.* Doubleday and Co., Inc., Garden City, New York, 1960.

Winter Activities

Adams, Richard. *Nature Through the Seasons.* Simon and Schuster, New York, 1975.
Barker, Will. *Winter-Sleeping Wildlife.* Harper & Row, Publishers, New York, 1958.
Bridge, Raymond. *The Complete Snow Camper's Guide.* Charles Scribner's Sons, New York, 1973.
Buck, Margaret Waring. *Where They Go in Winter.* Abingdon Press, New York, 1968.
Chiappetta, Jerry. *Ice Fishing.* Stackpole Books, Harrisburg, Pa., rev. ed., 1975.
Couchman, J. K., MacBean, J. D., Stecher, A., and Wentworth, D. F. *Snow and Ice, Examining Your Environment.* Holt, Rinehart and Winston of Canada, Limited, Toronto, 1971 (distributed in U.S. by Mine Publications, Inc., Minneapolis).

Information and Research Utilization Center in Physical Education and Research for the Handicapped. *Challenging Opportunities for Special Populations in Aquatics, Outdoor, and Winter Activities.* Unit on Programs for the Handicapped, A.A.H.P.E.R., 1201 Sixteenth St. N.W., Washington, D.C., 1974.

Partridge, J. A. *Natural Science Through the Seasons.* Macmillan Company, Toronto, 1955.

Peterson, Gunnar A., and Edgren, Harry D. *The Book of Outdoor Winter Activities.* Association Press, New York, 1962.

Russell, Helen Ross. *Winter, A Field Trip Guide.* Little, Brown, and Co., Boston, 1972. Children's book.

Russell, Helen Ross. *Winter Search Party.* Thomas Nelson, Inc., Camden, N.J. 1971.

Saskatchewan Provincial Youth Agency. *Winter Fun and Festivals.* Publ. #139. Canadian Parks/Recreation Association, 333 River Road, Vanier, Ottawa K1L 8B9 Canada. Paperback.

Stokes, Donald W. *A Guide to Nature in Winter* (Northeast and North Central North America). Little, Brown and Co., Boston, 1976.

Youngpeter, John M. *Winter Science Activities.* Holiday House, New York, 1966.

Zappler, Georg and Lisbeth. *Science in Winter and Spring.* Doubleday and Co., Inc., Garden City, N.Y., 1974.

For Your Reading Pleasure

Abbott, Winston O. *Come Climb My Hill.* Falmouth Publishing House, Portland, Me., 1949. Seventeen essays, each sharing a mood of nature.

Campbell, Sam. *Nature's Messages.* Rand McNally and Company, New York, 1952. About the Nicolet National Forest in Wisconsin.

Carrighar, Sally. *One Day at Teton Marsh.* Alfred A. Knopf, New York, 1954.

Derleth, August. *Walden West.* Duell, Sloan and Pearce, New York, 1961. Series of studies of the people of Sac Prairie, Wis., interlaced with vignettes of the land in which they live.

Douglas, William O. *My Wilderness: The Pacific West.* Doubleday and Company, Garden City, N.Y., 1960. An intriguing trip through magnificent areas of unspoiled beauty in the great Pacific Northwest. Also, *My Wilderness: East to Katahdin.* 1961. Travels from Arizona to

Maine. Justice Douglas has written additional books related to outdoor adventuring: *America Challenged, North from Malaya, Beyond the High Himalayas.*

Fabre, J. Henri. *The Life of the Ant* (out of print).

Frome, Michael. *Whose Woods These Are.* Doubleday and Company, Garden City, N.Y., 1962. The story of the national forests.

Hamilton, Mary G. *The Call of Algonquin.* Ryerson Press, Toronto, 1958. The story of Camp Tanamakoon, Algonquin Park, in Northern Ontario 1925-1953. A philosophy of camping; paints a picture of camp life and the adventure of life in the Canadian North.

Henry, Thomas R. *The Strangest Things in the World.* Public Affairs Press, Washington, D.C., 1958. A book about extraordinary manifestations of nature.

Jaques, Florence Page. *Canoe Country.* University of Minnesota Press, Minneapolis, 1938. Wife's diary of 3-week trip for the first time into the primeval wilderness. Also, *Snowshoe Country.* 1944. From Gunflint Lake, this husband-and-wife team traveled by snowshoe and dog team into Lake Superior's north shore. Also, *Birds Across the Sky.* Harper, New York, 1942.

Leopold, Aldo. *A Sand County Almanac.* Oxford University Press, New York, 1949. Series of essays in three parts: what Leopold did and saw at his weekend refuge on a Wisconsin Farm; sketches here and there that taught him that few shared concern for preservation of the land; the upshot, a philosophy of conservation.

Madson, John. *Stories From Under the Sky.* Iowa State University Press, Ames, 1961. Thirty-six stories with wildlife portraits. Many with Iowa background. (Out of print.)

Maeterlinck, Maurice. *The Life of the Bee.* New American Library (paper), New York, 1954.

Maxwell, Gavin. *Ring of Bright Water.* E. P. Dutton and Company, New York, 1960. An account of the author's life in a lonely cottage on the northwest coast of Scotland and the animals who shared it with him. Particularly about otters. Also available in a children's edition. Sequel book: *The Rocks Remain.*

Muir, John. *My First Summer in the Sierra* (out of print).

Nute, Grace Lee. *The Voyageur's Highway.* History of Minnesota Lake Country (out of print).

O'Kane, Walter C. *Beyond the Cabin Door.* Richard R. Smith, Rindge, N.H., 1957. A beautiful adventure in seeing, hearing, observing the common things in the realm of nature. Also, *The Cabin.* Wake-Brook House, Sanvornville, N.H., 1955.

Olson, Sigurd F. *Listening Point.* Alfred A. Knopf, New York, 1958. Tells what the author has seen and heard at his "listening point," a bare, glaciated spit of rock in the Quetico-Superior country. Also, *The Lonely Land,* 1961. A true tale of thrilling white-water adventure by canoe down 500 miles of Canada's wild Churchill River, reexploring the same rapids, lakes, portages, ancient campfires, and primitive wilderness haunts of the voyageurs of an earlier time. Also, *The Singing Wilderness,* 1957. Recreates the sights and sounds of the Quetico-Superior country. Also,

Runes of the North, 1963. Legends, yarns, and wilderness reflections from the great northern wildernesses of Canada and Alaska.

Peterson, Roger T., and Fisher, James. *Wild America.* Houghton Mifflin Company, Boston, 1955. Record of a 30,000 mile journey around the continent by a naturalist and his British colleague who was seeing the country for the first time.

Platt, Rutherford. *Wilderness: The Discovery of a Continent of Wonder.* Dodd, Mead and Company, New York, 1961. Also, *This Green World,* 1942. *The River of Life.* Simon and Schuster, 1956. *Adventures in the Wilderness* (with Horace M. Albright). Harper, American Heritage Junior Library, New York, 1963.

Rowlands, John J. *Cache Lake Country.* W. W. Norton and Company, New York, 1959 (wilderness edition). Life in the North Woods with considerable information on the techniques of living in the outdoors.

Ruark, Robert Chester. *The Old Man and the Boy.* Holt, Rinehart, and Winston, New York, 1957.

Russell, Franklin. *Watchers at the Pond.* Alfred A. Knopf, New York, 1961.

Teale, Edwin Way. *Adventures in Nature.* Dodd, Mead and Company, New York, 1959. Thirty-one selections from Teale's earlier writings now out of print. Also, *The Green Treasury,* 1959; *Autumn Across America,* 1956; *Journey Into Summer,* 1960; *North With the Spring,* 1951; *Circle of the Seasons,* 1953; and others.

Terres, John K. (editor). *The Audubon Book of True Nature Stories.* Thomas Y. Crowell Company, New York, 1958. Selected stories from *Audubon* magazine.

Thoreau, Henry David (edited by Brooks Atkinson). *Walden and Other Writings of Henry David Thoreau.* The Modern Library edition, New York, 1950.

Tilden, Freeman. *The State Parks, Their Meaning in American Life.* Alfred A. Knopf, New York, 1962. 80 photographs. Also, *The National Parks, What They Mean to You and Me,* 1954.

Tolman, Newton F. *North of Monadnock.* Atlantic Monthly Press Book, Little, Brown and Company, Boston, 1961. Explores in informal style, with humor and anecdote, north of Monadnock Mountains, New Hampshire.

Webb, Kenneth (editor). *Light From a Thousand Campfires.* Association Press, New York, 1960. Selections from *Camping* magazine.

Webb, Kenneth, and Webb, Susan. *Summer Magic.* Association Press, New York, 1953. What children gain from camp. Interprets for parents the values and benefits their children can receive from camping and what to look for in choosing a camp.

Welker, Robert Henry. *Birds and Men.* Harvard University Press, Cambridge, Mass., 1955.

White, Dale. *Gifford Pinchot.* Julian Messner, Inc., New York, 1957. The story of the father of forestry.

Wiley, Farida A. (editor). *Ernest Thompson Seton's America.* Devin-Adair Company, New York, 1954. Selections from the writings of Seton.

Books Especially for Children

Part I. Books for Children To Read:

Barker, Will. *Winter: Sleeping Wildlife*. Harper and Brothers, New York, 1958. An account of the winter habits of different types of animals. Grades 4-6.

Blough, Glenn O. *Discovering Plants*. McGraw-Hill Book Company, New York, 1966. Grades 1-4.

Burgess, Thornton W. *Burgess Animal Book for Children*. Grosset & Dunlap, New York, 1965.

———. *Burgess Book of Nature Lore*. Little, Brown and Company, Boston, 1965.

Butlenworth, William E. *Wonders of Astronomy*. G. P. Putnam's Sons, New York, 1964.

Conklin, Gladys. *We Like Bugs*. Holiday House, New York, 1962. Presents in an interesting manner and with enthusiasm many bugs which are familiar to children. Grades 1-3.

Cormack, M. B. *The First Book of Trees*. Franklin Watts, Inc., New York, 1951. Good full-page drawings of leaves, flowers, and fruit of fifty-seven of the common American trees with text covering bark, buds, leaves, flowers, seeds, and roots. Grades 3-6. One of a series of books entitled "The First Book of . . ." all of which are suitable for children.

DeFoe, Daniel. *Robinson Crusoe*. The story of a man who is shipwrecked and finds himself as the only survivor on a lonely island. The book contains a good description of how he conquered the obstacles which confronted him and how he was able to live comfortably.

Earle, Olive L. *Birds and Their Nests*. William Morrow and Company, New York, 1952. Text and drawings describe forty-two birds and their nests — the appearance of the bird, where and how the nest is built, the eggs, and feeding of the young. Grades 4-6.

Fiore, Evelyn. *Wonder Wheel of Birds*. Thomas Nelson & Sons, Camden, N.J., 1965. Grades 1-4.

Frisch, Rose. *Plants That Feed the World*. D. Van Nostrand Co., Princeton, N.J., 1966.

Froman, Robert. *Spiders, Snakes, and Other Outcasts*. Lippincott, Philadelphia, 1965. Grades 7-11.

*Gall, Alice, and Crew, Fleming. A series of books on animals: *Wagtail* (frog), 1932; *Ringtail* (raccoon), 1933; *Flat Tail* (beaver), 1935; *Bushy Tail* (chipmunk). Oxford Press, New York, 1941. See footnote p. 250.

George, John, and George, Jean. *Bubo, The Great Horned Owl*. E. P. Dutton and Company, New York, 1954. Beautiful illustrations and sensitive treatment of subject matter give readers a most realistic picture of the life problems of a horned owl. Grades 4-8.

Goudey, Alice E. *Houses From the Sea*. Charles Scribner, New York, 1959. About common shells, their names, how they look, what lives in them, and how they are made. The illustrations by Adrienne Adams make this a notable book. Grades 2-4.

Holling, Holling Clancy. *Minn of the Mississippi.* Houghton Mifflin Company, New York, 1951. Minn is a snapping turtle who was born at the head of the Mississippi River and who travels downstream to the Gulf of Mexico. There is excellent and valuable information about the history of the river, the wildlife in and around it, and the course of it. Many explanations of terms and many diagrams. Grades 4-7. This is one of a series in which Mr. Holling offers children unusual views of their country, concentrating on the wildlife but encompassing geography and history as well. Others include *Pagoo,* panorama of the tidepools along beaches as seen through the eyes of Pagoo, a hermit crab; *Seabird,* a carved ivory gull shares with four generations of the Brown family their ocean and air voyages; *Tree in the Trail,* a cottonwood tree grows with the West and eventually travels the Sante Fe Trail as a yoke for the lead oxen of a caravan; *Paddle-to-the-Sea,* a young boy carves the figure of an Indian as he travels through the Great Lakes, over Niagara Falls, and down the St. Lawrence River to the sea.

Hornblow, Leonora, and Hornblow, Arthur. *Animals Do the Strangest Things.* Random House, New York, 1965. Grades 2-5.

Ipcar, Dahlov. *Wild and Tame Animals.* Doubleday and Company, Garden City, N.Y., 1962. Beginning with "Long, long ago all the animals in the world were wild," the author shows how the tame animals have a different life and importance and all over the world are now working for man. Grades Kindergarten-3.

*Kjelgaard, Jim. *Chip, the Dam Builder.* Holiday, New York, 1950.

Laycock, George. *Never Pet a Porcupine.* W. W. Norton and Company, New York, 1965. Grades 4-6.

Malkus, Alida. *Animals of the High Andes.* Abelard-Schuman, New York, 1965. Grades 5-9.

*Oldrin, John. *Eight Rings on His Tail.* Viking, New York, 1956.

Perry, Phyllis J. *Let's Look at Birds.* Denison Co., Inc., Minneapolis, 1965.

Rey, Lester del. *Rocks and What They Tell Us.* Whitman Publishing Company, Racine, Wisc., 1961. A Whitman "Learn About Book" written under the direction of the Department of Geology, University of Wisconsin, tells how rocks tell the story of the earth, why we find fossils of sea animals on mountaintops, and what rocks tell us about cavemen. Grades 3-7.

*Rush, William Marshall. *Duff, the Story of a Bear.* McKay, New York, 1950.

Selsam, Millicent E. *Animals as Parents.* Morrow, New York, 1965.

———. *Benny's Animals and How He Put Them in Order.* Harper and Brothers, New York, 1966. Grades K-2.

———. *How To Be a Nature Detective.* Harper and Brothers, New York, 1966. Grades 1-4.

* These animal stories for children are particularly of interest to the family camper for they tell of the animals commonly found near the camp site. Recommended by Marjorie Glassco in *Better Camping* 5:1:42, January-February, 1964. "Read Aloud for More Family Fun."

————. *Play With Plants*. William Morrow and Company, New York, 1949. Simply written but good accurate information about how plants grow, use water, and respond to light, with experiments for growing them from roots, stems, leaves, and seeds. Grades 3-7.

Seton, Ernest Thompson. *The Biography of a Grizzly*. Grosset and Dunlap, New York, 1958, and *Wild Animals I Have Known*. Random House, New York, 1959. Seton is one of the noted writers on various experiences he has had while living among his friends in the great outdoors.

*Stearns, David M. *Sniffy, the Story of a Skunk* (out of print).

Sutcliffe, R. C. *Weather and Climate*. W. W. Norton and Company, New York, 1966.

Sutton, Ann, and Sutton, Mywn. *Animals on the Move*. Rand McNally and Company, New York, 1965.

Tyler, A. Edward. *Space Around Us*. Harper and Brothers, New York, 1964. Grades 9-12.

Wilder, Laura I. *On the Banks of Plum Creek* and *Little House in the Big Woods*. Harper and Brothers, New York, 1937. These are two books of a series which tell of the adventures of a little girl and her family as they move west from Wisconsin. On the way they encounter many wild animals, meet Indians, and experience the hardships brought by floods and prairie fires.

Williamson, Margaret. *The First Book of Birds*. Franklin Watts, New York, 1961. Another of the "First Book" series. A very well-written and illustrated informational book either for the young ornithologist or for the interested beginner in the study of the bird world. Grades 3-6.

Zim, Herbert S. *Snakes*. William Morrow and Company, New York, 1949. Confined to North American snakes, this book gives great detail on markings, anatomy, feeding habits, identification, and handling. Grades 4-7.

Zolotow, Charlotte. *The Storm Book*. Harper and Brothers, New York, 1952. A picture book showing a summer storm and its effect on the country, the city, the ocean, and the mountains. Good for nature-study concepts and to help children overcome fear of storms. The illustrations are beautifully done and capture the force and power of the storm without making it something to fear. Grades Kindergarten-4.

Part II. Books To Read Aloud:

Cheley, J. A. *Stories for Talks With Boys and Girls*. Association Press, New York, 1958. A revision of the author's father's classic *Stories for Talks to Boys*. A series of brief stories for special use for campfire meetings and other inspirational gatherings. Not a storybook in the same sense as others.

George, John, and George, Jean. *Dipper of Copper Creek*. E. P. Dutton, New York, 1956. A teenage boy goes to a ghost town to spend the summer with his grandfather. While waiting for the snow to melt he becomes familiar with water ouzels, watches them court, lay their five eggs on the cliff overlooking the waterfall, feed their babies, and dive down to the bottom of swiftly running water.

Grahame, Kenneth. *Wind in the Willows.* Scribner, New York, 1953. Humor and perception are written into an old story in which exquisite descriptions of wood and river bank take on fresh color and meaning when read aloud.

Hylander, Clarence J. *Animals in Fur.* Macmillan, New York, 1956. A scientific book about the animals with fur which will help every reader to find more interest and enjoyment in the world around him. Not a book of identification, but an attempt to bring out the personalities of the more interesting of the native animals of the United States.

Kipling, Rudyard. *Just So Stories.* Doubleday and Company, Garden City, N.Y., 1952. An old classic to read to children.

L'Engle, Madeleine. *The Moon by Night.* Ariel Books, New York, 1963. Story of a family camping trip as the reader follows Vicky who makes many discoveries and has various adventures while camping in National Parks and scenic spots from Connecticut to California.

Macfarlan, Allan A. *Campfire Adventure Stories.* Association Press, New York, 1952. A collection of adventure stories suitable for use around the campfire.

Moe, Virginia, and Winter, Milo. *Animal Inn.* Houghton Mifflin Company, Boston, 1946. A thrilling account of the many kinds of wild animals that visited a feeding station. Good description of animal behavior.

Mukerji, Dhan Gopal. *Gay Neck: The Story of a Pigeon.* E. P. Dutton, New York, 1927. This is a graphic, intimate story of the pet pigeon belonging to a boy in Calcutta. The bravery and skill of the pigeon are keenly portrayed. One becomes personally involved with the misfortune of the pigeon who lost his nerve because of a serious accident.

Mygatt, E. D. (editor). *Trails of Adventure: A Collection of Stories by Members of Western Writers of America.* Dodd, Mead and Company, New York, 1961. Thrilling western tales of Indians, horses, dogs, and breaking of broncos. Very pleasant to read on an outing; each story is complete in itself.

North, Sterling. *Rascal.* E. P. Dutton, New York, 1963. Story of a boy and a raccoon. 1963 Dutton Animal Book Award.

Rawlings, Marjorie. *The Yearling.* Scribner, New York, 1939. In the beautiful backwoods country of Florida the boy Jody learns the bitterness of responsibility when his pet fawn must be killed to save the crops.

Sandburg, Carl. *Rootabaga Stories.* Harcourt Brace, New York, 1922.

Shapiro, Irwin. *Tall Tales of America.* Guild Press, New York, 1958. A collection of the stories of several American legendary heroes—Paul Bunyan, Pecos Bill, etc. Exciting stories that will hold interest and tell a part of American life.

White, E. B. *Charlotte's Web.* Harper Brothers, New York, 1952. A charming perceptive tale of Charlotte's clever rescue of Wilbur the Pig from certain death. A great book to read out loud.

Periodicals

See Chapter 1, References.

Periodicals especially for children:

National Geographic World
Ranger Rick (National Wildlife Federation)